A Legacy of Faith

The Heritage of Menno Simons

A Legacy of Faith

A Sixtieth Anniversary Tribute to Cornelius Krahn

Cornelius J. Dyck, Editor

Faith and Life Press, Newton, Kansas

Mennonite Historical Series

FROM THE STEPPES TO THE PRAIRIES
Cornelius Krahn, Editor

PLOCKHOY FROM ZURIK-ZEE
The Study of a Dutch Reformer
in Puritan England and Colonial America
Leland Harder and Marvin Harder

EXILED BY THE CZAR
Cornelius and the Great Mennonite Migration, 1874
Gustav E. Reimer and G. R. Gaeddert

JAKOB HUTER
Leben, Frömmigkeit, Briefe
HANS FISCHER

A CENTURY OF WITNESS
The General Conference Mennonite Church
Cornelius Krahn and John F. Schmidt, Editors

PRAIRIE PIONEER
The Christian Krehbiel Story
Christian Krehbiel

MENNONITE COUNTRY BOY
The Early Years of C. Henry Smith
C. Henry Smith

A LEGACY OF FAITH
The Heritage of Menno Simons
Cornelius J. Dyck, Editor

Library of Congress Catalogue Card Number: 62-19863

Preface

THE ESSAYS APPEARING in this volume highlight the importance of the Dutch tradition for our understanding of Anabaptism. This study of the Dutch movement should add to our appreciation of Anabaptism, not only in its historical manifestation, but also in its theology, in the practical testing of the force of the original vision.

This is the eighth book in the Mennonite Historical Series published by the Board of Education and Publication and sponsored by its Historical Committee.

Contributors to this volume are the following: Rosella Reimer Duerksen of Ann Arbor, Michigan, choral director, housewife, a long-time student of Anabaptist hymnody. Heinold Fast, pastor and scholar of Emden, Germany, studied under Cornelius Krahn. J. F. G. Goeters, known for his earlier work on Ludwig Haetzer, professor of Church History at the University of Bonn. William Keeney, professor of Bible and Philosophy at Bluffton College, is currently serving in the Netherlands under the Mennonite Central Committee. Frits Kuiper, scholar and churchman, has for many years been pastor of the Mennonite congregation in Amsterdam. Gerhard Lohrenz is professor of Church History at the Canadian Mennonite Bible College and pastor of the Sargent Avenue Mennonite Church

5

of Winnipeg, Manitoba. Hendrik W. Meihuizen is scholar and pastor at The Hague. J. A. Oosterbaan of Haarlem is professor of Theology at the Mennonite seminary and the University of Amsterdam. Henry Poettcker is president of the Canadian Mennonite Bible College, Winnipeg. Horst Quiring is publisher and scholar at Stuttgart, Germany. Nanne van der Zijpp is pastor of the Mennonite congregation in Rotterdam and professor of Church History at the Mennonite seminary, Amsterdam. Cornelius J. Dyck, who also edited this book, is Associate Professor of Historical Theology at the Mennonite Biblical Seminary and director of the Institute of Mennonite Studies, Elkhart, Indiana.

This book is a tribute to Cornelius Krahn, who devoted many years to the promotion of the study of Dutch Anabaptism and related movements, and who has contributed to and succeeded in collecting a significant library of Anabaptist source materials. The book was presented to Cornelius Krahn in connection with his sixtieth anniversary, August 3, 1962.

It is our hope that this historical study will add to our understanding of the Anabaptist movement and its significance for our day.

Willard Claassen, Executive Secretary
Board of Education and Publication
General Conference Mennonite Church

Contents

Cornelius Krahn and the Dutch Mennonites 9
Cornelius J. Dyck

PART ONE

Menno Simons' Concept of the Church 17
Cornelius Krahn

Menno Simons' View of the Bible As Authority 31
Henry Poettcker

The Incarnation, A Central Theological Concept 55
William Keeney

Grace in Dutch Mennonite Theology 69
J. A. Oosterbaan

Sinners and Saints 87
Cornelius J. Dyck

CONTENTS

Dutch Anabaptist Hymnody of the Sixteenth Century 103
Rosella R. Duerksen

Dutch Painters in the Time of Vondel and Rembrandt 119
Hendrik W. Meihuizen

The Dutch Aid the Swiss Mennonites 136
Nanne van der Zijpp

The Discordant Voice of Jan de Liefde 159
Fritz Kuiper

PART TWO

The Mennonites of Russia and the Great Commission 171
Gerhard Lohrenz

Die Danziger Mennoniten: Der Stand der Herkunftsfragen 192
Horst Quiring

Das älteste rheinische Täuferbekenntnis 197
J. F. G. Goeters

Hans Krüsis Büchlein über Glauben und Taufe 213
Heinold Fast

Notes 232

Index 258

CORNELIUS J. DYCK

Cornelius Krahn
and the Dutch Mennonites

THE MENNONITES OF THE NETHERLANDS have constituted a significant segment of the Anabaptist movement from the sixteenth century to the present. During the early years of the movement more martyrs arose from among them than from any other Anabaptist, or Protestant, group. The major martyrologies of Anabaptism were consequently written in the Netherlands as were many other theological treatises and important confessions of faith. Of the many early leaders of Anabaptism, Menno Simons of the Netherlands was the one to give his name permanently to the entire movement. The Dutch were the first among Mennonites to seek meaningful relationships between faith and culture, the first to recover a sense of mission in the nineteenth century. They were the first to stimulate in-group research in the heritage of Anabaptism through the publication of the scholarly *Doopsgezinde Bijdragen* beginning in 1860. They were the first to found a Mennonite seminary, which was in 1735. The historian of Anabaptism does well, therefore, to listen to the Dutch brethren.

Even more significant, however, is another contribution of the Dutch brotherhood—the institutional testing of the essence of Anabaptism in their congregational life. This is true of the first as well as of later generations. Factors of culture and geography, together with the rich source materials available

9

for most periods, make a study of this testing both possible and rewarding. Since toleration came to the Anabaptists first in the Netherlands, the last martyr of the Low Countries dying in 1574, institutional development proceeded rapidly, embodying many of the explicit and implicit emphases of Anabaptism. Nowhere, for example, was the concept of the believers' church worked out as vigorously as among the Dutch congregations. The harsh discipline which followed, together with the subsequent divisions within the group, must be understood and studied as a part of this testing of the Anabaptist vision. The same may be said of the spiritualist motif. The tension between spiritualism and institutionalism within Anabaptism found its sharpest and most persistent expression in the Dutch movement. Thus a study of the Dutch movement adds significantly to our understanding of Anabaptism, not only historically as a regional manifestation, but also theologically in its testing of the force of the original vision.

The essays collected in this volume represent a tribute to the Dutch Anabaptist-Mennonites and are intended to testify to the importance of that movement within Anabaptism. More particularly these chapters are presented in appreciation of the work of Cornelius Krahn, who has given much time for many years to the promotion of the study of Dutch Anabaptism and related movements. The contributors have shown a long-standing interest in the Dutch movement and in the work of their friend and colleague Cornelius Krahn, who reached the sixtieth anniversary of his birth on August 3, 1962.

Cornelius Krahn was born in Chortitza, a village on the banks of the Dnieper River in the Ukraine. This settlement had been established under Catherine II in 1789 by Mennonites from Prussia. It was here that Krahn received his first education. Just before World War I his parents, Kornelius and Maria (Penner) Krahn, moved to the province of Saratov on the Volga River, where the Arkadak Mennonite settlement was established. Krahn has vivid recollections of the end of the Czarist government, the Civil War, the ensuing famine years, the mass executions, and the struggle between the Red and the White Russian armies.

In 1926 Krahn left for Germany to continue his education.

After completing his secondary studies he enrolled successively in the universities of Bonn, Berlin, Amsterdam, and Heidelberg. It was at Heidelberg that he continued his newly aroused interest in Dutch Anabaptism by submitting his doctoral dissertation in 1936 on *Menno Simons (1496-1561): Ein Beitrag zur Geschichte und Theologie der Taufgesinnten* (Karlsruhe, 1936). The first chapters of the second part of this work appear here in free translation as *Menno Simons' Concept of the Church.* The first part of the dissertation is a biography of Menno.

While in Germany Krahn witnessed the rise of National Socialism, the burning of the Reichstag, and the persecution of the Jews. For a time he was a student of both Karl Barth and Dietrich Bonhoeffer. In 1937, after having lived in the Netherlands for a time, Krahn came to America where he taught first at Bethel, then at Tabor College, in Kansas. In 1940 he married Hilda Wiebe. In 1944 he became a citizen of the United States, earned a master's degree in German at the University of Wisconsin, and established himself at Bethel College, North Newton, Kansas, as professor of church history and German. It was here that Krahn was able to pursue his continuing interest in Anabaptism, particularly Dutch Anabaptism.

A historical collection had been initiated by Abraham Warkentin at Bethel College in 1935. A small collection left by C. H. Wedel formed the nucleus for this. Upon coming to Bethel in 1944 Krahn immediately set for himself the task of building this collection into a comprehensive historical library, concentrating particularly on Dutch, Prussian, Russian, and Polish Anabaptist-Mennonite materials. By 1956 the library contained no fewer than 12,000 books and periodicals, to which another 3,000 items have been added during the past five years. Of the 15,000 items, there are 10,000 catalogued books, making it one of the three outstanding Mennonite historical collections in the world, together with the Goshen College Historical Library and the Amsterdam Mennonite Library. The establishing of this vast collection has made possible unlimited research in Anabaptism. Many dissertation writers, including the editor of this work, have relied heavily on the collection at Bethel College.

11

To this collection Krahn is adding a growing bibliography of his own. In 1950 he enlarged and revised C. Henry Smith's *The Story of the Mennonites*, in 1951 C. Wedel's *Bilder aus der Kirchengeschichte für Mennonitische Gemeindeschulen*. In 1949 *From the Steppes to the Prairies (1874-1949)* appeared and in 1959 *A Century of Witness* with Krahn as editor. Pamphlets written by Cornelius Krahn include *Brieven uit Rusland* (1924), *De Mennonietengemeenten onder het Bolsjewisme* (1934), *Menno Simons Lebenswerk* (1951). In 1954 Krahn co-authored a chapter entitled "Altruism in Mennonite Life" for Pitirim Sorokin's *Forms and Techniques of Altruistic and Spiritual Growth: A Symposium*. In 1957 he contributed a chapter on "Anabaptism and the Culture of the Netherlands" to Guy F. Hershberger's *Recovery of the Anabaptist Vision*. As co-editor of the monumental *Mennonite Encyclopedia* Krahn wrote many articles for each of the four volumes. He has likewise contributed an article on Menno Simons to the *Twentieth Century Encyclopedia of Religious Knowledge,* Vol. II (1955) and one on the Mennonites to *Die Religion in Geschichte und Gegenwart*, Vol. III (1957).

In addition to the preceding, Krahn has submitted numerous articles for publication in scholarly journals, particularly the *Mennonite Quarterly Review.* Appearing in the latter are the following: "The Conversion of Menno Simons: A Quadricentennial Tribute" (January 1936), "Some Social Attitudes of the Mennonites of Russia" (October 1935), "Menno Simons' Fundament-Boek of 1539-1540" (October 1939), "Mennonite Community Life in Russia" (July 1942), "The Historiography of the Mennonites in the Netherlands" (October 1944) also in *Church History* (September 1944). "Prolegomena to an Anabaptist Theology" (January 1950), "Some Letters of Bernhard Warkentin Pertaining to the Migration of 1873-1875" (July 1950), "Echo-Verlag Publications" (July 1950), "The Office of Elder in Anabaptist-Mennonite History" (April 1956), "Anabaptism in East Friesland" (October 1956), "The Emden Disputation of 1578" (October 1956), "Mennonite Plattdeutsch" (July 1959). A summary of research on Menno Simons appeared in *Church History* (December 1961).

In addition to his management of the historical collection and his writings just mentioned, Krahn is the first editor of *Mennonite Life,* an illustrated quarterly magazine now in its seventeenth year of publication. Beyond his editorial responsibility he has contributed no less than forty-two articles and as many book reviews to the journal. In connection with this magazine he has sponsored exhibits and, more recently, annual folk festivals on the Bethel College campus.

Further literary activities include the editorship of *Mennonitisches Jahrbuch* during which time Krahn has contributed seven articles to that publication since 1949. He has written three articles for the *Mennonitische Geschichtsblätter* (1936, 1951, 1958), and three for the *American German Review* (February, October, and December 1944). Two articles were published in the *Christlicher Gemeinde-Kalender* (1936, 1937), two in *Proceedings of the Tenth Conference on Mennonite Educational and Cultural Problems* (1955, 1957), two in the *Mennonitische Jugendwarte* (1936, 1937), and two in *Geschriftjes ten behoeve van de Doopsgezinden in de Verstrooing* (No. 59 and 60). Since 1943 Krahn has written no less than 123 separate contributions to the *Mennonite Weekly Review,* the majority of them under the title "Faith of Our Fathers." A number of these articles appeared also in *The Mennonite,* bringing his total contributions to that weekly to eighty-four.

It is clear from this bibliography that Cornelius Krahn is making a significant contribution to Anabaptist-Mennonite historiography, particularly to the study of the Dutch movement. Reference tools are fortunately being prepared to guide the researcher through the vast and growing collections. In addition to the standard two-volume *Inventaris der Archiefstukken* (1883-1884) prepared by J. G. de Hoop Scheffer, and the *Catalogus* (1919) of the Amsterdam Mennonite library, a comprehensive one-volume Anabaptist bibliography has been prepared by the Institute of Mennonite Studies, Elkhart, Indiana (1962). The volume covers the period from 1525 to 1630. A Mennonite bibliography, covering the period from 1630 to the present, is in preparation by the Institute of Mennonite Studies under the direction of Dean Harold S. Bender. A special section on Dutch sources is in preparation in the Netherlands. Irvin B. Horst has published *A Bibliography of Menno Simons, ca. 1496-1561 Dutch Reformer, With a Census of Known Copies* (1962). In view of the fact that most of the sources deposited in the Amsterdam archives are now available to the American student on microfilm, it is to be hoped that research in Dutch Anabaptism will continue unabated both in America and in Europe.

A word of appreciation must be expressed to Henry Poettcker, Irvin B. Horst, and William Keeney for their help in planning this undertaking. William Keeney has also been of particular help in translating and editing several of the Dutch manuscripts. John F. Schmidt of the Bethel College Historical Library, and colleague of Cornelius Krahn, deserves special mention for his careful compilation of the bibliographical material referred to in the preceding pages. The Board of Education and Publication of the General Conference Mennonite Church has made this publication possible. May the following chapters add to the self-understanding of the reader, to a deeper understanding of the nature of the church of Christ, and to the achieving of greater obedience to the call and purposes of the Lord of the church.

Part One

CORNELIUS KRAHN

Menno Simons' Concept of the Church

CHRIST AND THE SCRIPTURES

THE QUESTION HAS been raised whether Menno Simons had a theology. Although Menno was not a theoretical systematic theologian, he nevertheless did have a theology. A careful study of his life and his concerns reveals a core in his theological thinking and his Christian witness from which vantage point his Christian thinking and living can alone be fully understood. It is from this center that we must view his actions and his reactions to other views. This core was his unique concept of the Christian church.

To understand Menno we must first of all, working within the framework of his theology, analyze and describe his concept of the church and then deal with his attempt to realize this concept. Only then can we study the results of this concept within the brotherhood and the attitude of the brotherhood toward the surrounding society. Since Menno's concept of the church was, to a large degree, dependent on his understanding of the Scriptures and his eschatological expectations, we will briefly present them.

*Free translation of the chapters "Das christozentrische Schriftverständnis und die eschatologische Erwartung" and "Der Gemeindebegriff" in my *Menno Simons (1496-1561). Ein Beitrag zur Geschichte und Theologie der Taufgesinnten* (Karlsruhe: H. Schneider, 1936), pp. 103-123.

17

The Scriptures and the Spiritualizers

C. A. Cornelius referred to the early Anabaptists of Switzerland as a "church of radical readers of the Bible."[1] And, indeed, the Anabaptists made a most radical attempt to realize a Christian brotherhood on the basis of the Scriptures. They stood on the extreme left within the Reformation movement in their attitude toward the tradition of the church. Therefore, this movement is spoken of as the "Left Wing" Reformation. The word of God alone was to be the guide in the establishment of the true church or in the attempt to restitute the apostolic church.[2]

This is particularly the case as far as Menno Simons was concerned. His greatest opponent was the Roman Catholic Church, in which the word of God was overshadowed by tradition, the chiliastic speculators, and the spiritualizers, because they neutralized the word of God. He complained that the whole world was building "upon strange foundations such as popes, councils, doctors, doctrines, and commandments of men; upon wrong practices of long standing," and claimed that there is "but one cornerstone laid of God the Almighty Father in the foundation of Zion which is Christ Jesus" and that we should build upon Him alone in conformity to His word.[3]

As Luther denounced the radicals in his Reformation movement, so Menno challenged a similar occurrence within Anabaptism. His first writing, in which he attacked the Münsterite movement—the result of an allegorical interpretation of the Scriptures and chiliastic speculation—was devoted to this struggle. He stated of himself that he was neither Enoch nor Elias and that he was not one who had visions nor a prophet who could "teach and prophesy otherwise than what is written in the Word of God."[4] This was directed against Jan van Leiden of the "kingdom of Münster" and David Joris, the "third David," who was a representative of the allegorical interpretation of the Scriptures.[5]

This mistreatment of the Bible made Menno fearful of a too free approach to the Scriptures and a free interpretation of them. It made him inclined to follow the letter of the word of God rather literally. He denounced the practices of Melchior Hoffman's allegorical interpretation of the Old Testament according to which the Scriptures stand on "two hoofs,"[6] which means that they have a literal and an allegorical meaning. This interpretation was the background for the undisciplined speculations which ushered in the attempt of the establishment of the "kingdom of God" at Münster.[7] Even such co-workers as Dirk Philips and Gillis van Aken were not entirely free of allegorical interpretation. The latter was admonished by Menno Simons to discontinue this kind of interpretation.[8] Menno Simons deserves the credit for having overcome the allegorical interpretation of the Scriptures and the chiliastic speculations within the Anabaptist movement of his territory. Thus, the chiliasm of Melchior Hoffman within the Anabaptist congregations was suppressed and the original scriptural basis of the Swiss brethren re-established.

Consequently, Menno could not fully accept the spiritualism of Hans Denck and Sebastian Franck, although he largely depended on the latter for his historical resources. Dirk Philips, a close co-worker of Menno, wrote against Franck's spiritualism.[9] Menno's writings against David Joris are a good example of his opposition to all claims of special revelations, illuminations, and loose interpretations of the Scriptures. This constant struggle to free the congregations of allegorical scriptural interpretations, false prophecies, and spiritualism led Menno to an emphasis on a more Christ-centered view of the total Scriptures.

A Christ-centered Approach to the Scriptures

Every book and pamphlet written by Menno Simons has as its motto, "For other foundation can no man lay than that is laid, which is Jesus Christ" (1 Cor. 3:11). This concern runs through all of Menno's writings like a red thread. The Christ, who is the Lord, Saviour, and example of his church is both the foundation and the head of the church. The Roman Catholic tradition, with its false concept of the sacraments and unchristian life, had replaced Christ with human institutions. Jan van Leiden also attempted to take the place which rightly belonged to Christ.

That Christ will again be made the Lord of His church and that the latter will be restituted in accordance with the apostolic example was Menno's primary concern. His theology is oriented in a positive way in being founded on the Scriptures with Christ in the center and in a negative way in his attempt to do away with the roadblocks of the tradition of the Roman Catholic Church. Thus, his theology became Christo- and ecclesio-centric. Christ is the focal point of all Scriptures—the Old Testament, the Gospels, and the Epistles. In Christ all prophecies have found fulfillment. Christ is the channel and the criterium of all revelation. The Old Testament precepts, commandments, and traditions which conflict with Christ and His life and work are not binding.

Menno says that "Moses and his successors have served their day with their sword of iron."[10] In opposition to the Münsterite prophets, he did not deal with the eschatological references in the Bible which are hard to understand. Christ became the yardstick for the evaluation of the writings of the Old and New Testaments. Menno's understanding and use of the Scriptures was Christ-centered. He did, however, not completely escape a legalistic application of the Scriptures.[11] This was due to the fact that he abhorred all free and spiritualizing interpretations and that he was radical in his demand that the will of God, as expressed by Christ, be realized in the Christian brotherhood.

Menno Simons insisted that Scriptures must be interpreted by Scriptures when he stated his opposition to those who "mutilate and twist the precious Word of God to suit [themselves]"[12] and again when he said that they "garble and twist them as much as they please, yet this Scripture will remain forever unbroken before them."[13] It is true that Menno Simons was not so much a trained theologian and exegete as a practical applicant of the gospel. Nevertheless, he made full use of all available aids in his effort to understand the meaning of the Scriptures. He made special effort to avail himself of all Bible translations. Menno stated in a writing to J. a Lasco that he did not despise scholarship if it was used for the right purpose. He said, "Learnedness and proficiency in languages I have never disdained, but I have honored and coveted them from my youth; although I have, alas, never attained to them. Praise God, I am not so bereft of my sense that I should disdain and despise the knowledge of languages whereby the precious word of divine grace has come to us."[14] Menno used the Vulgate Bible and translations of Erasmus, Luther, Sebastian Castellio, Christopher Froschauer, J. van Liesveldt, and others, including many commentaries.[15]

Eschatological Expectations

Menno's concept of the church cannot be fully understood unless one realizes how strong his eschatological expectations were. His views pertaining to the second coming of the Lord and the day of judgment were formed through his reading of the Scriptures and the influence of the Anabaptists, of whom Melchior Hoffman was a representative. Nevertheless, he rejected the chiliastic Münsterite movement from the very beginning. In his writings, K. Vos emphasized the significance of the eschatological views of the Dutch Anabaptists. However, his attempt to trace these expectations to the social and political upheavals, as well as the catastrophes of nature, was not sufficient.[16] The sources of the eschatological views which convinced the believing reader that the Lord's coming was at hand were found in the Bible. The events and catastrophes of the day supported this view.[17] Thus, the real source of the eschatological expectations of early Anabaptism was found in the Scriptures, which likewise originated in a similar atmosphere of expectancy.

The strong emphasis on eschatology or the second coming of Christ characterizes the whole Reformation period. Even the spiritualist, Sebastian Franck, expected the Lord to return during his lifetime.[18] It can be expected, however, that the tension and expectancy along these lines would be stronger nowhere than in the "church of radical readers of the Bible." The apocalyptical images and the prophecies of the Scriptures gave nourishment to these expectations. It is true, however, that the early Dutch Anabaptists belonged primarily to the socially and economically deprived class of society which yearned for a change of conditions. The severe persecutions strengthened the longing and the expectation of the Lord, who would end the era of suffering and oppression. It was in this environment and atmosphere that the chiliastic and revolutionary kingdom of Münster was born. It was Menno Simons who helped to bring order and sanity to those who were disillusioned through this

21

experience and prevented many from joining the extremists.

The judgment day played a significant role in the eschatology of Anabaptism. The peaceful and biblical Anabaptists expected nothing but persecution and suffering before the coming of the Lord. Christ himself would be the judge when He came. The chiliastic and revolutionary wing of Anabaptism represented in the Münster revolt was trying to determine the time and place of the second coming of Christ and felt called to help the Lord usher in the day of judgment and revenge. Menno Simons protested against this view when he wrote a pamphlet against Jan van Leiden.[19] Menno expected the return of the Lord with patience and long-suffering.

Menno rejoiced that the light of the gospel was shining again. The proclamation of the gospel constituted the last feast of the year in God's plan of salvation. The angel stated in Revelation that the day of judgment would come after this invitation to the wedding of the lamb.[20] The judgment of God was foreshadowed in the social upheaval, in warfare, and in the catastrophes of nature. However, they were only fulfilling the warnings of the prophets, of Christ, and of the apostles, and calling for repentance before the judgment day comes.[21]

The resurrection will precede the day of judgment. "The children of God who have walked before him in firm faith and patience here on earth shall enter the kingdom of God while those" who rejected the Lord and His word shall be tormented eternally.[22] Menno reminds his persecutors of this day of judgment. He was confident that he was preaching the gospel correctly and that he would, like Paul, be called upon "to judge and sentence not only man, but also angels."[23] Persecution for the sake of the Lord and deprivations because of social injustices would be significant factors in the final judgment day.[24] The government was admonished to heed this warning.[25]

In conclusion we can state that it was Menno's concern to introduce a Christ-centered approach to the Scriptures in the congregations which he served. He was opposed to allegorical interpretation and pseudo-prophetic tendencies. His strong opposition to the Münsterite chiliasm did not prevent him from developing his own eschatological views based on a balanced study of the Bible.

THE CONCEPT OF THE CHURCH

An Ecclesio-centric Theology

It could be stated that all reformers in the days of the Reformation aimed to restitute the true church of Christ and that Menno's attempt was one among many. Let us point out some similarities and some differences in the concept of the church between the other reformers and Menno Simons.

Personally Menno stated that "there is nothing upon earth which my heart loves more than it does the church." In principle he said that "we are begotten by God from His bride, the Holy Church, like unto his image, nature, and being."[26] Luther spoke about the church as the "Gemeine in der Welt, welche ist die Mutter, so einen jeglichen Christen zeugt und trägt durch das Wort Gottes, welches er offenbaret und treibt, die Herzen erleuchtet und anzündet, dass sie es fassen, annehmen, daran hangen und dabei bleiben."[27] Calvin stated, in his *Institutes* in a chapter entitled "Of the True Church," that a Christian is charged with the "duty of cultivating unity with her, as the mother of all the Godly."[28] In the same chapter he speaks of "the visible church" as "her single title of mother" and "how necessary the knowledge of her is, since there is no other means of entering into life unless she conceive us in the womb and give us birth, unless she nourish us . . . in short, keep us under her church and government." He continues by saying that "beyond the pale of the church, no forgiveness of sins, no salvation, can be hoped for."[29] These quotations, only a few of many, are somehow related to the well-known statement by Cyprian, "He can no longer have God for his Father who has not the Church for his mother."[30] However, these statements, although all emphasizing the significance of the Christian church, do not prove that all these representatives had the same church concept. In order to locate the distinguishing features, let us point out what motivated Luther, Calvin, and Menno when they broke away from the Roman Catholic Church.

That the true church is the mother of the believers and that the Roman Catholic Church was neither the true church nor the mother of the believers they all agreed upon. Thus, in their break with Rome they agreed to some extent. In the

23

question of how to establish a true Christian church, however, they disagreed. In his attempt to establish this church, Luther was the first to stop in his break with Rome. In other words, he retained more of the traditions and teachings of the Roman Catholic Church than did Zwingli and Calvin. They went far beyond the stopping point of Luther. Anabaptism was the most radical in its break from Rome and its departure from the Roman tradition. This was in part due to the fact that Anabaptism was in principle more radical and in part due to the fact that Anabaptism was born also as a reaction to the shortcomings of the reformers. If this analysis is right, then the claim by A. Harnack that Anabaptism was "medieval" is wrong.[31]

The question that we should like to raise is this: What was the motivating factor for each to leave the old church? This will give us a clue as to what the basic concerns were when the reformers started new churches. Thus we will find the distinguishing characteristics of their church concepts. The overwhelming experience of Luther was that God justifies man by grace through faith alone. He left the institutionalized Roman Catholic Church, the church of work righteousness, via the road of *sola fide* in order to establish the church of the word. The *sola fide* was the determining factor in the formation of Luther's new church. The center of the new church was the preaching of the word of God in the tenseness of the conflict that developed between "law" and "grace," or "works" and "faith." This was a radical break with the Catholic church, but, beyond this concern, Luther did not radically break with the Roman Catholic tradition.

Calvinism, which went beyond Luther in its break, also stood on the ground of the *sola fide*. In the preaching of the word of God, however, and the emphasis on "faith alone" as a means of salvation and justification, the challenge of obedience to the commandments of God and the fruits of faith were also emphasized. Depravity of man on one side and the grace of God on the other side, as well as obedience to the word of God, were central in the proclamation of the gospel. For both Luther and Calvin this view of the gospel created a new concept of the church.[32] In order to point out the differences between the

24

other reformers and Menno Simons, we could observe that for the other reformers the concept of the church was not the primary reason for the founding of a church independent of Rome. The primary concern was the "new faith" which resulted in a new concept of the church and its realization. For Menno Simons, however, the restitution of the biblical church was the primary reason for the establishment of a church.

We can also formulate the difference as follows. The other reformers preached the *sola fide*. The Anabaptists emphasized repentance, regeneration, and fruits of faith within a church "without spot and wrinkle." This emphasis of the Anabaptists, however, was based on the preaching of the *sola fide* and in a way was also a reaction to a one-sided emphasis on "faith alone."

Luther's statement pertaining to the church in the *Deutsche Messe* of 1526 has been used frequently to point out that he, too, was interested in a "believers' church." In the *Deutsche Messe,* Luther promoted the idea that those who take the word of God seriously and want to be true Christians should meet in private homes for prayer, the study of the word of God, to share in the sacrament, and to practice church discipline in accordance with Matthew 18.[33] The free churches like to point out that Luther abandoned his intentions along these lines; earlier he seemed to have outlined the advantage of cell groups in the *Volkskirche* or the *ecclesiola in ecclesia* of later Pietism and in contemporary Anabaptism. Indeed, the Anabaptist view of the church did not seem to be very different.[34] Nevertheless, we must not overlook the fact that Luther's statements were expressions on the periphery of his theological concern and that they must be viewed in the total context of his theology.[35] For Menno and the Anabaptists, however, the view of the church was basic and central.

A comparison of the Anabaptist view with those of Zwingli and Calvin leads us to different results. First of all, Zwingli in Zürich and Calvin in Strassburg had personal contacts with the Anabaptists. They learned to know them and their views through personal experience. This was particularly the case with Calvin, Capito, Bucer, J. a Lasco, and Martin Micron. Anabaptism was born within the Reformation movement promoted by these leaders. Consequently, there were similarities and dissimilarities. The similarities are particularly noticeable in the matter of discipleship and church discipline. In their practice of church discipline, particularly Calvin in Geneva applied a rigid discipline unknown in the practice of Luther. This points out a similarity between Calvinism and Anabaptism.

At the same time it must be stated that there was a considerable difference in this matter between Calvinism and Anabaptism. Calvin was more Old Testament oriented in his attempt to establish the Christian church. It was a theocratic church that he promoted. For Menno the church was to be established on the basis of the New Testament, patterned after the apostolic church. This is very clearly demonstrated in the application of church discipline. Following the pattern of the Old Testament, Calvin not only tolerated but justified the use of capital punishment as an extreme means of church discipline. Menno stated that the "sword of Moses" was restricted to use in theocratic Israel and that in the church of Christ of the New Testament only Christian means were used in church discipline.[36] In spite of this, Calvin accused the Anabaptists with his statement: "Where the Lord requires mercy, they omit it and give themselves up to immoderate severity."[37] The rigid Calvin found the "Anabaptists of the Sermon on the Mount" too severe. We must remember, however, that Calvin did not speak of the means of church discipline, but of the yardstick which the Anabaptists used to measure the "perfect" church. It is possible that we must evaluate Calvin's statement pertaining to Menno in this context when he said: "You cannot imagine anybody more conceited than this jackass, no one more impudent than this dog."[38]

Ernst Troeltsch, in particular, has pointed out the parallels between the church concept of Anabaptism and Calvinism. That Zwingli, Calvin, Bucer, and Capito had modified Anabaptist views along these lines seems to be accepted without question, although there were differences.[39] In their struggle with Anabaptism, they formulated their own views by accepting some of them in modified form. Capito says about the Anabaptists that they are "dear brethren and strong witnesses of the truth," in spite of the fact that they have "erred in some things." He speaks of them as "marvelous witnesses of the truth and vessels of honor."[40]   It is a fact that the severe criticism of Anabaptism in North Germany and the Netherlands pertaining to the lack of Christian life and discipline within the Reformed churches of these countries challenged the churches and caused improvements along these lines.[41]

In the emphasis on obedience toward God and the Scriptures and in their practice of discipleship, there were some similarities between Calvin and Menno in connection with their concepts of the church.   Nevertheless, there were differences which have already been pointed out.   Others could be named, such as the concepts of God, grace, predestination, and free will.

In summary it can be stated the main differences between Menno's concept of the church and that of the reformers was the fact that for Menno the realization of the true church constituted the center of his theological thinking and concern.   The gathering of regenerated Christians into a brotherhood and the realization or restitution of the apostolic church as a disciplined body of Christ was a primary goal of Menno Simons.

The Catholic and Apostolic Church

The Catholic church and the Scriptures.   In order to fully understand the church concept of Menno Simons it is necessary that we take a look at his relation to the Catholic church after his conversion.   After having started to read the Scriptures as a priest of the church, he soon "discovered that [the people] were deceived" by the church.[42]   This insight was not restricted to the two basic sacraments of the church, namely, baptism and the Mass.   He soon recognized that this deception extended to "all sin and wickedness, all idolatry, and all false worship.[43] Already before he left the Catholic church he was convinced that what "was fulfilled against Babylon, in the country of the Chaldees" would also happen to the "Roman Babylon" which would not "escape the same visitation."[44]

Through the teaching of transubstantiation, the Catholic church had "arrogated to [itself] all power in heaven, upon earth, and in hell.   Therefore, they break the bread into three pieces; with the first they reconcile God, with the second they

27

intercede for the world, and with the third, as they pretend, they pray for the souls in purgatory." Menno continues the accusation, stating that with "this very clever and crafty magic, the Roman Antichrist has gained such respect and authority that even the imperial majesty, the highest sovereignty on earth . . . has to humble himself and kiss his feet."[45] The antichrist has bewitched the whole world with this magic concept of the sacrament, while Christ, the true sacrifice for the atonement of our sins, has been deprived of his throne of majesty.[46] Priests and preachers have "deceitfully mingled the precious fine gold of the divine Word with a dross of human doctrine, and the pure wine of the polluted water of their foolish wisdom."[47] For this reason Menno states that they "are not of God and His Word but of the bottomless pit of the dragon and the beast."[48]

Christ has not commanded a single letter regarding this idolatry. The Scriptures in no wise command us to "obey the Pope and belong to his church, hear Mass, receive the holy water, go on pilgrimages, go to confession at least twice a year, receive papistic absolution, have our children baptized, and keep the holy days and fast days in Lent."[49] No wonder the house of the Lord, or the church, is desolate. "For that which was once a church and kingdom of Christ is now, alas, the church and kingdom of Antichrist," and all this has happened because "they ungratefully reject the word of grace and will not have the ruling Lord Jesus Christ to rule over them with the righteous scepter of His Holy Word and spirit."[50]

Menno was ashamed of every day he spent in "the church of the Antichrist." Now he knew, after having opened the Scriptures, that one can see with "half an eye in the Scriptures" that the Catholic church is an "assembly of the unrighteous, the immoral, the impenitent, the sensual and perverts, yes, of the bloodthirsty wolves, lions, bears, basilisks, serpents, and fiery flying dragons."[51] Looking at these descriptive characteristics of his former church which are repeated constantly, one sees that Menno missed in the Catholic church the authority of the Scriptures and a living faith in Jesus Christ, as well as a disciplined and consecrated life of the believers. The low moral level of the church in which he grew up and which he tried to serve must be seen in the background when we read Menno's reactions.[52]   Now that the Scriptures had opened his eyes, he saw the contrast and gap between the Catholic church and the ideal church referred to in the Scriptures.   This contrast was in his mind as he labored and aimed to restitute the true Christian church.   He constantly emphasized the necessity of an ethical regeneration and a consecrated life of discipleship within the church of believers.

The Apostolic Church.   The decay and the destitute condition of his church was revealed to Menno in the Scriptures. More than that, in the Scriptures he found the guide to a new life in Christ and the example of a true Christian church.   He felt that the New Testament was the only and unshakable ground on which the church should be built.   It was also the guide for the life of the believers.   Menno said that in the "New Testament we are directed to the Spirit, Word, council, admonition, and usage of Christ.   What these allow we are free to do, but what He forbids we are not free to do."[53]

Menno made a most radical break with the Catholic tradition. The only justification and validity of tradition was an "explicit command of Christ and his apostles."   Occasionally he refers to the Nicene Creed[54] with the qualification that it is observed best where "Christ's spirit, word, sacrament, and life are found,"[55] since a mere repetition of a creed is meaningless.

For Menno Simons the "Church of God" did not have its beginning with the coming of Christ but had its origin in God's covenant in the Old Testament.[56]   Menno shared this conviction with the other reformers.[57]   For this reason, "all Scripture, both of the Old and New Testament," must be "rightly explained according to the intent of Christ Jesus and His holy apostles . . . since "there is but one corner stone . . . which is Christ Jesus."[58]

The congregation and the Christian life had to be established on this foundation in conformity to the Scriptures.[59]   For the restitution of the church, "the Scriptures point us to the Spirit, Gospel, example, ordinance and usage of Christ."   Menno said we must "follow Christ's plain Word and command the doctrine and usage of the holy apostles in the first, unfalsified church."[60] It must be pointed out that for Menno the apostolic example in accordance with Christ's command was the sole authority in the realization of the true church.   What this command meant to him and what he accepted from the apostolic example is not presented here. Only a few references will be made at this point.

The true church is a "gathering or congregation of saints, as the Holy Scriptures and the Nicene Creed clearly teach and present, namely, those who through true faith are regenerated by God unto Jesus Christ and are of divine nature, who would gladly regulate their lives according to the Spirit, Word, and example of the Lord."[61] The "Holy Christian Church" has only one doctrine found in the gospel of Christ."[62] Menno was convinced that he had the true understanding of this gospel. For this reason he felt that he and his fellow believers were within "the Apostolic Christian Church" and rejected the accusation that he was a "sectarian."[63] He did not have any noticeable scruples about the fact that he was establishing a new church next to others already in existence. The justification and the inner compulsion were found in the fact that he and his fellow believers found no existing church fully based on the Scriptures.[64]

The following characteristics were named by Menno Simons as prerequisites of the true Christian church: an unadulterated, pure doctrine; a scriptural use of the ordinances; obedience to the word; unfeigned brotherly love; bold confession of God and Christ; and oppression and tribulation for the sake of the Lord's word.[65]

In summary, we must state that for Menno the church was the center of his Christian concern. He broke radically with the tradition of Catholicism and aimed to restitute the church in accordance with the apostolic example. This aim he pursued with great dedication.

HENRY POETTCKER

Menno Simons' View of the Bible As Authority

WHEN MENNO SIMONS wrestled through to a spiritual victory following the doubts which assailed him concerning the Roman Catholic interpretation of the Lord's Supper and baptism, he had found a new authority. The reformational keystone also became his: *sola Scriptura!* The Scriptures now were the source from which came the final answer to his questions. With this source, the message opened up to him through a vital experience with Christ set over against the Catholic church with its teachings (concerning which Menno confessed that they had been betrayed—*bedrogen*), one can readily understand how high would be his estimation of the Bible.

Menno's writings reveal throughout that the Scriptures were both normative and authoritative for him. His question was not, What does this or that source say? but, What do the Scriptures say? No concern of his is more basic in his writings than to prove a point or to set forth a teaching from the Scriptures only. "The Scriptures say," "Scriptures testify abundantly," "prove by the Scriptures," "observe the Scriptures carefully," "if anyone should still be in doubt (impossible to a man of understanding, so clear is the Scripture)"[1]—these are just a few samples from one of his first writings, *Een gantsch duydtlyck ende klaer Bewys, uyt de Heylige Schriftuure,* which indicate that fact.[2]

31

From the very start Menno felt constrained to uphold the authority of the Scriptures. His first writing (the one against Jan van Leyden) was in a sense a polemic against the Münsterites, whose teachings grew out of an allegorical interpretation of Scripture and out of chiliastic prophetism.[3] When challenged to a debate by David Joris, Menno wrote that his preparation and armor were naught else but the word of God, the gospel.[4] Menno had no greater desire than to teach correctly from the word of God. In his *De Oorsake waerom dat ick Menno Symons niet af en late te Leeren ende te Schrijven,* Menno tells his readers about his concern to teach the true love and fear of God, and then says:

Behold, my worthy brethren, against the doctrines, sacraments, and life just considered, imperial decrees, papal bulls, councils of the learned, long standing practices, human philosophy, Origen, Augustine, Luther, Bucer, imprisonment, banishment, or murder mean nothing; for it is the eternal, imperishable Word of God; I repeat, it is the eternal Word of God, and shall so remain forever.[5]

This word of God, which abides forever, Menno seeks to teach. And he is challenged to do so because he knows of a certainty "that His Word is the truth and His commandments life eternal." "Therefore," says Menno, "I am confident and bold to teach it thus."[6]

The Nature of Biblical Authority

It is well to pose the question, What constitutes biblical authority for Menno? Is it that each paragraph is authoritative (or for that matter, each verse), or is it the Bible as a whole? For Luther and for Calvin it was definitely the latter. In Menno's case, the same held true, although a number of qualifications must be made. That the whole Bible was authoritative is seen from the following.

Whenever Menno deals with a problem he is never content to build his case on an isolated passage; e.g., in dealing with Christ as king over all others (contrary to claims such as those made by Jan van Leyden), Menno makes the general statement that the Scriptures testify abundantly to this fact. Then he enumerates specifically David, Paul, Christ himself, Isaiah, Jeremiah, John, and the angel.[7] In another instance, when he accuses one of his opponents, Martin Micron,[8] of teaching contrary to the Scripture in maintaining that Christ Jesus was not the Son of God, Menno seeks to show how Micron has acted contrary to the statements of the Father, of the Son, of Gabriel, of the apostles and of the saints of the New Testament.[9] Similarly, in writing to Gellius Faber[10] Menno enjoins him to "read through the entire Scriptures—Moses and the prophets, Christ and the apostles."[11] Gellius cannot produce "one plain letter from all the Holy Scriptures,"[12] nor can he prove his point "by a single letter of Scripture."[13] Menno argues, "The whole Scriptures, both the Old and the New Testaments on every hand point us to Christ Jesus, that we should hear him,"[14] and again, "All teachings both of the Old and the New Testaments, rightly explained according to the sense or meaning of Christ and His apostles, are profitable. . . ."[15]

Secondly, Menno is intent on maintaining the unity of the Scriptures. In his contention with Martin Micron concerning the nonswearing of oaths, he expresses the concern that this matter be weighed in such a manner that the unity of the Scripture is maintained, which will result in the correct interpretation.[16] This means that one interprets the single passages in terms of the whole. It means further that Scripture cannot be broken. For Menno the unity of the Scriptures is seen in their total thrust, setting forth the redemption in Christ Jesus. Therefore all Scriptures apply, albeit interpreted in keeping with the sense and intent of Christ and His apostles.[17] Christ is the one, the promised prophet, to whom all the Scriptures point.[18] In the discussion of true Christian faith, Menno begins:

We teach and believe, and this is the assertion of the whole Scripture, that the whole Christ is from head to foot, inside and outside, visible and invisible, God's first-born and only begotten Son; the incomprehensible, eternal Word, by whom all things were created . . . He taught us the will and good pleasure of His Father, went before us in a blameless example, and freely offered Himself upon the cross for our sins. He was a sweet-smelling sacrifice to the Father, the one through whom all we that sincerely believe have received the pardon for our sins; and grace, favor, mercy, freedom, peace, life eternal, a reconciled Father and free access to God in the Spirit.[19]

It is to be observed that the reference here is not only to Christ, but to Christ as an example. While for Luther the

redemptive aspect was uppermost, for Menno the strong insistence on a fruitful life led him to point to the exemplary life
of Christ. This is not to say that he discounted the redemption
through Christ. The weakness of Luther's position was the fact
that he saw the forgiveness of sins and justification as the whole
of Christ's work. This raises the question, Is the new life an
incidental outcome or is it the very goal for which Christ died?
Both Calvin and Menno would say that Christ died for us that
we might live. With the Brethren of the Common Life the
Imitatio Christi tended toward a sheer moralism. Menno's view
was much deeper, and this view relating to the new life was a
lasting feature of his ever since his conversion experience. Therefore, to interpret any one passage in contradiction to this
central place of Christ would be a practice ruled out of court.

A third observation that would speak for the whole Bible
as being authoritative is Menno's position that Scripture interprets Scripture. Here again it is evident that there was a difference between Luther and Menno. Luther contended that
Scripture is *sui ipsius interpres,* not in the sense that a clear
passage may be used to interpret an unclear one through a type
of logical theological deduction, but rather in the sense that
the clear passages captivate the interpreter and work such faith
in Christ in him that this faith now enables him also to understand the unclear passages.[20] Menno's idea was that the obscure passages should be interpreted by the clear ones. One
notices this in the accumulation of a large number of references
which are to enlarge upon or bring out more clearly the meaning of a given passage.[21] This also reveals an interesting principle on which Menno based his polemics and which has its
value in hermeneutics: The more Scripture passages that can
be collected for a particular point or interpretation, the stronger
the case will be. At the same time this drawing upon any
section of the Bible for support is a practice which indicates
the unity the Scriptures had in the eyes of Menno.

Menno's use of the Bible seems to indicate that it is a collection of infallible statements. Anything in the book is authoritative. But this raises the question, What allows Menno to
differentiate in Holy Scripture? In the first place, it is apparent
that there is a marked difference between the Old and New

Testaments. The Old Testament has only provisional authority. (Notwithstanding, in the area of supplying examples of faith the Old Testament can offer illustrations just as does the New Testament.) In the second place, Menno sees a difference between those things referring to outward facts only and those having spiritual significance. Similarly, there is a difference between clear-cut commands and practical applications—some are more readily applied than others. Further, Menno was quite clear on the fact that one ought to act only on specific injunctions rather than to institute practices which can be substantiated only by logical deductions, e.g., infant baptism. To the question, Why did Menno interpret passages as he did? the answer is that in large measure he was governed by an attitude (obedience to all that Christ had commanded) and by an approach that would substantiate his religious experience. There must be evidence of the new life in Christ. This practical test was constantly applied, no matter what topic was being discussed.

The strong emphasis on Christ's being central is a further support of the view that Scripture interprets Scripture. Menno insists that an interpretation must always be in keeping with this central place of Christ. An example may be cited from the polemic against Jan van Leyden. Menno argues that the only weapon which the Christian may use is the word of God. On what does he base this? He argues as follows: The Scriptures say that Christ is to have a sword (Psalm 45:3), but this sword cannot be construed as being a carnal sword. It is the word of His mouth.

If Christ fights against His enemies with the sword of His mouth, and if He smites the earth with the staff of His mouth and slays the ungodly with the breath of His lips; and if we are to be conformed to His image, how can we then oppose our enemies with any other sword?[22]

Then a reference is brought in from Peter, admonishing the reader to follow in Christ's steps. Similarly John and Christ himself support the use of a spiritual sword only.

Menno followed the current practice of the reformers, viz., seeing Christ almost everywhere in the Old Testament, particularly in the Psalms, although also in many other sections. Luther insisted that in their original sense the Scriptures constantly

35

speak of Christ, "the goal and center of all, to whom everything points."[23] Schwenckfeld set as one of the guides for the study of the Scriptures: Seek Christ everywhere, judging all things according to His Spirit. Menno did something very similar. He also had Christ speaking in the Old Testament, and like Calvin he was often unconcerned about the historical setting.

There is a fourth reason why it may be concluded that Menno considered the whole Bible as authoritative. This is the distinction that he makes between the different commands in Scripture. As strongly in favor as he was of enforcing the ban, he nevertheless insisted that one must distinguish carefully between this commandment and others. One cannot consider all commandments as equally weighty.[24] When situations arise where the question of shunning must be decided, it is necessary to compare Scripture with Scripture. To illustrate, if one should understand by shunning that it is imperative that such a person be avoided, even to the point of not talking to him, this would be to reject Paul's counsel in his letter to the Thessalonians: "Consider him not as an enemy, but admonish him as a brother." Besides, it would reflect very unfavorably (*genen goeden roem maecken*) on the gospel of Christ.[25]

But if it is true in a general way that the entire Bible is authoritative for Menno, there is still a distinction between the authority ascribed to it by the reformers on the one hand and by Menno on the other. It is obvious that the reformed theologians start from the authority of the book, whereas Menno turned to the events. Calvin often appears to have a view of Scripture that is quite mechanical.[26] Similarly, Luther makes statements which would lead one to conclude that he too held a mechanical view.[27] What does a careful study of Menno's writings reveal?

It is apparent that Menno frequently refers to the Scriptures as the word of God. But this phrase may have several different meanings. To see these different meanings it is in order to make several observations on the relationship of *Word of God* and *Scriptures*.

It is clear that wherever the word *Scripture(s)* is used (coupled as it may be with a variety of adjectives, e.g., holy, sacred, etc.), there the Bible is meant.

Often a number of different terms are used as synonyms for the word *Scripture*. Examples are Word (*Woord*, fol. 139a), Holy Word (*Heyligen Woord*, fol. 143b), Word of the Lord (*Heeren Woordt*, fol. 145b), God's Word or Word of God (*Godts Woordt*, fol. 146b), living Word of the Gospel (*levendige Woordt des Heyligen Euangeliums*, fol. 137a)—this term could also refer to Christ—Jesus Christ and His Word (*Christum Jesum en sijn Woord*, fol. 146b), etc.[28]

Apart from the fact that Menno uses the above terms in a general way to refer to the Scriptures, he also gives them a more specific meaning.

1. This term may refer to the message which God commanded someone to speak, *e.g.*, Jeremiah was to proclaim the word of the Lord (*Heeren Woordt*, fol. 142a); Stephen spoke the word of the Lord (*Woordt des Heeren*, fol. 143a).

2. It may mean the living Christ, e.g., the Almighty Word (*dat Almachtige Woordt*, fol. 144b), Word of God (*sijnen naem is Gods Woordt*, fol. 10b), Word of the Lord and His people (*des Heeren woordt ende volck*, fol. 17a), God's Word (*Godts Woordt*, fol. 147b). There are times when a definite distinction is made between Christ, as the eternal Word, and the spoken and written word.

This [the eternal Word] does not refer to a spoken word, for it is divine and spiritual, and not carnal and literal. A spoken word is a passing breeze, grasped in the letter, beginning and ceasing. If thus understood, Christ Jesus before the incarnation must have been a literal word. O no, rather He is the eternal, wise, Almighty, holy, true, living and incomprehensible Word. . . .[29]

In a similar way, when Menno says that he resisted the Lord's precious word and His holy will in former times, he may have been referring to the Scriptures, but it may also be that he was thinking of Christ's working in his heart.[30]

3. The term may mean Scripture, but Scripture interpreted correctly. When Menno told his opponents that he was sure that he had the Word of God (want ik weet gewisse dat ik Godts Woordt hebbe), he meant more than just the Scriptures, for the others also had the written text.[31]

4. When Menno says that God sent His beloved Son who preached His word (*u Woord*), he is undoubtedly thinking of

God's purpose with Christ, and the message which Christ was in himself, God's speech to men.[32]

5. A further indication that Menno differentiated between Scriptures and other terms is seen at places where they occur together. When he says: "We will nevertheless, by the grace of God, abide by the Word of the Lord and comfort ourselves with the Scripture which says . . ." he may have been using the two terms *woort* and *Schrift* synonymously, but it is more likely that the first term does not refer to the written Scriptures.[33]

The above observations lead to the conclusion that although Menno often equated various terms with the Scriptures, it does not follow that these terms always mean the Scriptures. Often more specific designations are intended. Further, it is evident that the freedom with which Menno does interchange the terms, speaking of the Bible so very often as the word of God, indicates the high regard that he has for the written word, the Bible. For him there is no question that it, the written word of God, is authoritative for the believer and for the church. Therefore it was not what men might think proper, but what was commanded by the Scriptures that was to be the norm for action.[34] Even the opponents referred to the high regard which Menno had for the authority of Scripture, a most revealing statement even though it was made in a slighting and negative way.[35]

The reference to this statement on authority calls for a further comment. Menno is arguing with a Lasco that his rebukes and his teaching are based on the authority of God's Spirit and word. If a Lasco accuses Menno of slander because of this, then it must be true that Isaiah, Jeremiah, all the prophets, and Christ and His apostles are guilty of slander. One notices here how Menno invariably resorts to the teachings and practices of those about whom the Scriptures speak for the substantiation of his arguments. He laments the fact that "philosophy, rationalization and glosses" abound, "but very little of the power of Scripture, its basis and truth." Menno is quite clear on the fact that there is a necessity for having teachers in the church as over against the natural knowledge of God. But he considers the canonical writings as the true teacher. God has spoken in the Holy Scriptures once revealed. For him the word is a spiritual reality, for it is the word that engenders seed and creates the church—the communion of saints.[36]   Therefore Menno is interested in the Bible as a record of what God accomplishes in men.   And that is why in the New Testament it is the example of Christ and the apostles (as they taught and lived) that is so relevant.   The institution, the way in which these things are expressed, is of a secondary character.   What Menno is particularly interested in is how God engenders spiritual life and how that expresses itself in the personal life.   In that respect the Old Testament is as authoritative as the New.   Menno makes a distinction between the two covenants, as his practice makes clear; but, while the subject matter differs, the attitude on the part of individuals is the same, and there are Old Testament examples of men of faith.   In this respect Menno is closer to the reformers than Marpeck was.   Because Marpeck made such a radical break between the two covenants, he did not see so clearly that the unity of purpose with God implies the oneness of faith.[37]   For Menno, forms were different, to be sure, but institutions which people create are considered as being human and only indications of what is going on.   Thus the sacrifices of the Old Testament, for example, have primarily historical significance.   It is the redemptive relationship that is essential.   For that reason, with the newness of Christ the Old Covenant is to be considered as a preparation of the new one and from this perspective the principle is to be explained that only what is commanded may be tolerated in the church. Therefore Christ's injunctions are to be taken seriously.   People have no right to institute other forms (such as infant baptism) of the God-man relationship apart from those given by Christ himself.   As far as obedience expresses itself by faith, the Old Testament is on a par with the New Testament, but this does not permit men to transfer circumcision to the New Testament. Menno says that since obviously the command of Christ referred to believers' baptism, we have no right to find justification for infant baptism by way of implication.   Exegetically this, of course, becomes a very important point, for the reformers held that logical conclusions drawn from the Bible had equal authority with the Bible itself.   To this Menno said no.   This was the philosophizing and rationalizing with which he could not agree.

The parallel drawn earlier, therefore, may be repeated here: While the reformed theologians start from the authority of the book, Menno turns to the events.

Menno's constant desire to remain true to God's revealed word caused him to express the wish on more than one occasion that he might not say or write anything which was contrary to what God had spoken. Furthermore, he never ceased calling in Moses, the prophets, the evangelists, and other apostolic writings as witnesses to what he taught. For him the Scriptures were not just a record of past events or of divine speech. Through them God was speaking to men in that day. He was calling them to respond to the glorious gospel. Repeatedly Menno applies the term *word of God* to the Scriptures, and in his comments he points to the writers of Scripture or characters in Scripture, speaking God's word.

O apostate children, consider how grievously you slander the holy Moses, who teaches you out of the mouth of God saying, I will raise up a prophet for them from among their brethren, like unto you, and will put my Word in his mouth. He shall speak all that I shall command him, and whoever will not hear my words, those which he shall speak in my Name, I will require it of him.

How do you do away with all the great prophets of God, such as David, Isaiah, Jeremiah and Ezekiel, who through the inspiration of the Holy Spirit, so often and with such clear words, point us to Christ and His Kindom? Truly, they must speak falsely, or your prophets must be deceivers and false teachers.[38]

That God is seen to be speaking here is further indicated in Menno's deep concern about those who neglect to obey the Scriptures. He sees human reason as having become so perverse and haughty that it "dares to alter, bend, break, gainsay, judge and dominate the Word of the Lord God." In fact, Menno sees such disobedience as a definite affront to the living Word, Jesus Christ. He, Menno, would do naught else but abide by the holy Word and commandment "as the mouth of Truth has commanded me and all true Christians."[39] He counsels all children of God to observe that "the true teacher and finisher of the New Testament, the eternally blessed One, Jesus Christ, has clearly commanded and taught with His guileless mouth." Is this not what the Scriptures teach us to do? Menno can only counsel and teach with the sure word of the holy gospel

40

and "with the authority of the divine Word." It cannot be otherwise: In and through the Scriptures God speaks to people.

The above has shown that the terms *word of God* and *Scriptures* are very close together for Menno, at least more so than with either Luther or Schwenckfeld. Luther differentiated logically between *word of God* and *Holy Scriptures*. The word of God is primarily something that is inner, abiding in God. It is that which God speaks with himself, which remains with Him and which is God. This Word is the second person of the Trinity, the Son, and it can come from God (out of God) only through an incarnation. Then it becomes external and visible. This is the historical appearance of Jesus Christ, who is at the same time the content of the Holy Scriptures—the entire Scriptures. Luther can say that the whole Scriptures are contained in the four Gospels, and vice versa, the Gospels are contained in the whole Scriptures. In their original meaning the Scriptures speak of Christ constantly. To be sure, the truth of Christ is not the same in all parts of the Scripture; there are different levels. But how high the Psalter stood in Luther's estimation is seen in his common practice of placing the words of the Psalms into the very mouth of Christ. The great men of the Old Testament are said to have the full Christian knowledge.[40]

Schwenckfeld also differentiated between the Scriptures and the word of God. To get the Scriptures' meaning Scripture must be compared with Scripture; God's will is learned exclusively from the Scriptures. Schwenckfeld could accept nothing, regardless of its origin, which was contrary to the truth as he recognized it through the revelation and testimony of Holy Writ and of Christ in the Holy Spirit. When his opponents objected that the Scriptures were obscure and the sayings in them dark and contradictory, and when they desired a judge who had authority to decide the meaning, his answer was: "The Scriptures and the Word of God are wholly a bright light which brings its own clarity with it to the believing heart. . . . Christ is of course the true light. . . . Therefore it is not the fault of the Scriptures if we do not understand them, but our own darkened hearts are to blame. . . ."[41] He went on to say that only the word of God should be his judge. Only God could not err in His divine word.

41

Marpeck differed from both Luther and Schwenckfeld and in some respects was very close to Menno. He refused to differentiate between the oral and the written word of God because the Holy Spirit wrote the Gospels and other New Testament writings through the evangelists and apostles. For Marpeck it is not the ink and paper or the "perishable, creaturely parts of books, or human speech that is God's word"; rather the sense, the idea, is the important thing. "It is faith that makes the written word become spirit and life in the heart of the recipient."[42] Bergsten has evaluated Marpeck's position and maintains that he does not show the orthodox verbal inspiration position, but what he would term *eine Kombination der Real- und Personalinspirationstheorie.*[43] For Menno the Word of God is God's revelation to men. The eternal Word became flesh and fulfilled what the Old Testament prophets had spoken concerning Him. He taught His disciples and they in turn taught others. Menno was not concerned about spelling out how the writings of the New Testament arose. He was convinced, however, that through them God was speaking and that therefore they needed to be obeyed. Along with the majority of the biblical Anabaptists of the sixteenth century Menno could and did use "Word of God" synonymously with the self-proclamation of God through Christ Jesus, with the Scriptures, with their message, and also with the witness of the Spirit in his heart.[44]

Law and Gospel

A further matter that touches the problem of authority and reveals how far for Menno the New Testament took precedence over the Old is his understanding of law and gospel. What has been said of the Anabaptists in general, that they were legalists because of their strong emphasis on obedience to the biblical injunctions, has also been an epithet hurled at Menno in his day and at his followers in later times. That the issue was a live one for Menno is evidenced by the fact that one of his writings, *Rechte Christen geloove,* was written in part as an apology to counteract the charges of legalism made against him. In this selection Menno sets forth the true Christian faith as he understands it. Drawing attention to God's incomprehensible grace in Christ, which men have been able to find through God's Spirit, Menno goes on to show how men now have the possibility of receiving the true knowledge of the kingdom of God and the true regenerating knowledge of His holy gospel. With the key of His word and Spirit God opened the saving truth and has redeemed men from the power of darkness, leading them into the kingdom of His dear Son—all for the purpose that they may be kings and priests, loving and serving Him by publishing abroad His glorious redemption.

What does all this mean? It means that those anointed with the oil of the Holy Ghost and the blood of Christ and clad in the garment of righteousness will henceforth transcend the Old Covenant practices. No longer will they slay sacrificially victims on an altar as Moses commanded under the law.

But you will slay human beings all your life with the knife of the Holy Word (spiritually understood) together with your own contrary flesh and blood. That is, you are to teach and reprove them and yourselves with the Spirit and Word of the Lord, that you may die to your unrighteousness and evil lusts, destroy them, and thus offer in the spiritual tabernacle or temple, not made with hands, upon the only and eternal altar of reconciliation, Christ Jesus.[45]

Because of this grace of God and because of what it brings with it, Menno is intent on showing all lovers of the eternal truth, from the word of God, the true faith *"dat voor Godt gelt/ ende in de Scrift belofte heeft: Namelijck/ dat nadruck/kracht/ werck ende vrucht heeft/ Christus Euangelio ende der Aposteln Leere gelijckformigh."*

With the use of a number of illustrations from Scripture Menno sets forth the biblical faith as it is revealed in the life of the righteous, concluding with a clear call to repentance and true faith. Outstanding is the emphasis that to take this up in the soul means an obedient walk, a fruitful life.

At first sight the presentation seems to bypass an encounter with the charge of legalism. But this is not the case. The charge is answered, indirectly to be sure, but very effectively nevertheless. Certainly it would be difficult to charge Menno with legalism on the basis of this writing. It fairly glows with the spontaneity of the fruits of a life of faith. But what about the many New Testament commandments to which attention is drawn? It may rightly be asked whether these do not merely take us out of an Old Testament legalism into a New Testament one? They who speak thus have not understood faith.

Further I say, if you really believed and rightly understood that by or in Adam's disobedience you become children of the devil, of wrath, and of eternal death; become subject to the righteous judgment and curse of God; and that now all your faults and sins are taken away and reconciled through the stainless blood of Christ, so that you are called from wrath unto grace, from cursings unto blessings and out of death to life, not to mention the gracious benefits which are shown you daily; then your hearts would blossom forth as the sweet-scented blooming violet, full of pure love. Yes, they would leap forth as a living fountain, yielding the sweet and pleasant waters of righteousness, and with the holy Paul you would say from the depth of your soul, Who shall separate us from the love of God? It can never be, if I am in the bonds of perfectness with Him and love Him with a pure heart, a good conscience and unfeigned faith, that anything could turn me away or separate me from Him. For it is my only desire and highest joy to hear and to speak His Word and in my weakness to walk as He has commanded and taught through His Son; let it cost money or goods, flesh or blood, as it pleases Him.[46]

Obedience to these commandments is the loving response of the believer who has recognized God's Son as Redeemer and as Lord of his life. God's love is born in the believer through faith and this enables him to love in return. Because faith knows the unsearchable riches of grace from the testimony of Scripture and through the understanding of the Spirit, love is the inevitable result. This spontaneous love must be seen in every situation. And despite the strong emphasis which Menno places on the cross and suffering, he insists that even this is of no avail if love is not there.[47]

Logically legalism is therefore ruled out by the very nature of the gospel and the faith which it produces in the hearts and lives of men. But there remain for consideration several passages where the statements have been interpreted as incriminating Menno on the charge of legalism. On occasion Gelius Faber accused Menno and his followers of stipulating that those who partake of the Lord's Supper are to be well grounded in the law and principally in the holy gospel. The issue has to do with permitting those flagrantly living in sin to participate in the Lord's Supper, something which Menno and his group would not tolerate. Menno answered:

Wherever the Law is rightly preached and taken to heart so that it reveals its true nature and power, there one finds a broken spirit, a penitent, humble heart and a conscience which trembles before the Word of its God—the true fear of God which checks and drives out sin as Sirach says.

For this is the real function and end of law: to picture God's will to us, to open (discover) sin unto us, to threaten with the wrath and punishment of the Lord, to proclaim death and to point us from it to Christ, in order that we, crushed in spirit, may before God die to sin and seek and find the only and eternal medicine and remedy for our souls, Christ Jesus.[48]

Coupled with this brief statement of the purpose of the law is one that speaks also to the nature of the gospel.

So also where the Gospel is preached in true zeal, according to God's pleasure and unblameably in the power of the Spirit, so that it penetrates the hearts of the listeners, there one finds a converted, changed and new mind, which joyfully and gratefully gives praises to God for His inexpressibly great love toward us miserable sinners, shown in Christ Jesus. Thus it enters into the new life willingly and voluntarily, by the power of a true faith and a new birth.

Like Marpeck Menno also followed in the footsteps of Luther in maintaining that one should note the function of the law as bringing the knowledge and conviction of sin. For Luther the law was the vestibule to the gospel,[49] while Marpeck insisted that no one could come to the gospel without first recognizing his sin through the law. "How can a man come to the Gospel unless he is first convicted by the law?"[50] Menno seems to take the very same position in seeing the law as threatening with the wrath and punishment of God, and to point to Christ, so that the prepared individual may find the remedy for his soul, viz., Jesus Christ.

With the close relationship which Menno saw between the law and the gospel, he could go one step further to speak of the law book of Christ.[51] Josiah found the Book of the Law, heard its message and turned to the Lord with his whole being. But Menno must confess that in his day the lives of the people in the church are such that *Christum en sijn Waerheydt/ Sacramenten/Geest en Leven* are not known to them. And Menno laments, *Dat Wet-boeck Christi is gantsch ende geheel by u verloren!* The association is clear. Josiah found the Book of the Law, repented, and brought forth fruits accordingly.

45

But the New Testament, God's revelation in Christ, could impossibly be known to Menno's readers, for if it were, it should certainly bring forth fruits as the Book of the Law did centuries earlier.

But this raises the very point at issue. Are the Scriptures then not a law book for Menno? To this question the following may be said. In some ways Menno did give the Scriptures—even the New Testament—the connotation of law. There is a continual emphasis on the commandments of Christ and the apostles. Menno would have his readers observe that not a letter of the law of Moses could be changed until the new Moses, Christ Jesus, came. If now the word of the literal law was so strong, effective, and firm and its time unchangeable, even though given only through a servant and sealed by perishable blood, "how much more powerful, effectual, firm and unchangeable is the free law of the Spirit, given by the Son Himself and confirmed by the blood of the eternal covenant!"[52] If the literal law of Moses could not be changed by princes, then how does anyone dare to operate or teach contrary to the "doctrine, sacraments, obedience, and life of Jesus Christ?" It is from this standpoint that Menno's strong insistence on obedience to the commands of Christ must be seen.[53] Men may not change these commands, e.g., arguing for infant baptism, when it is obvious that Christ referred to believers being baptized.

One notices here how Menno makes a distinction between the Old and the New, although he is not so explicit as was Marpeck in delineating what he (Marpeck) called God's order. However, in the emphasis on the sequence of baptism following upon faith, they were very similar. Marpeck insisted that when the Scriptures say that Christians are first to make disciples, then baptize, then teach—this order must be observed with scrupulous care. Much of the trouble in the church had resulted from ignoring this order.[54] That Luther continued with infant baptism and the Mass was considered outside the realm of God's word and this, too, Menno claimed.

There is then no denying the fact that Menno placed a strong emphasis on the keeping of the scriptural demands. Commands were given to be obeyed. Menno says that without the command of the holy Scripture nothing righteous can be done and nothing pleasing to God can be practiced. Furthermore, the commands of Christ were even more important than the commands given under the Old Covenant. This emphasis certainly tends toward a legalistic strain, something that is evident particularly when Menno is aroused by his opponents. Then he is quick to say that he can operate only by the "express and literal command of Christ."[55]

In Menno's defense it must be added that in the majority of instances the Spirit was to guide and the "intent of Christ" was to motivate both the interpretation as also the acting upon such commands. Menno could speak of the New Testament being a ministry not of the letter but of the Spirit,[56] and on occasion he said that the archenemy of our souls knows well how to "clothe his cause with the letter of the Scriptures."[57] One cannot evaluate Menno's legalism without being aware of the "gospel air" which surrounds the commands to which he draws the reader's attention. Menno belonged to the larger group of Anabaptists who understood justification by faith in the Protestant sense of coming through grace alone.[58] But they did insist that faith without works is dead. With the Reformers Menno believed God to be sovereign, but the final word on what this Sovereign demands of His children is not spoken by those under the Old Testament, but by Christ, the eternal Son of God. He brought to completion what was in process in the Old Testament. Menno refers repeatedly to the letter to the Hebrews with its message that the old had passed away. But because the old was gone, those under the New Covenant were thereby not given the privilege of ignoring the commands of Christ. An expression of one's love to God necessitated also the pledge to obedience.

Following from this obedience a further word is necessary on the relationship of the literal and spiritual law. The former had its place and was certainly important. But when compared with the spiritual law, the free law of the Spirit, it is classed as inferior. Menno laments that Jesus Christ, the fulfiller of the law, was killed by those who taught the literal law.[59] As long as the literal law was not yet fulfilled, people were to keep it; even Christ directed His disciples to it. But now something new has been realized through Christ and therefore we are now directed to those preachers who sit in Christ's seat (as the scribes and Pharisees sat in Moses' seat) and teach His doctrine unblamably. Menno says that Christ fulfilled the spiritual law, by which he apparently means that Christ kept the law completely, something which no human being could do, and thereby made it possible that sinful men could become righteous. If, therefore, one might not be disobedient to what the Old Testament teachers gave by way of instruction, much less can he be disobedient to the instruction given by Christ. For Menno the spiritual law is not a freedom from stipulations, but a completion of that to which the Old Testament law pointed. Since the completion was in Christ, what He said and what He instructed His disciples to say becomes paramount in the believer's life.[60]

The Canon and Inspiration

Menno's understanding of the canon and of inspiration has a further bearing on his view of biblical authority. His Bible, as all the Bibles in his day, contained the Apocrypha. For him these books along with those of the Old and New Testaments constituted the biblical canon. He did not hesitate to quote from any of these books as he had occasion.[61] A careful analysis of the Scripture references or citations which Menno gave in five of his writings showed that from the Old Testament he omitted eight books, while from the New Testament he omitted two books.[62] Several other meaningful observations may be made from the analysis. In the New Testament there is a fairly even distribution between the Gospels and Paul's letters. The Gospels are used a bit more often, although if one adds Hebrews (which Menno held to have been written by Paul) to the Pauline letters, one gets a higher number for Paul than for the Gospels. Matthew is the most frequently used of the Gospels, with John next in line. Matthew is used four times as often as Mark and more than twice as often as Luke. Unlike Marpeck, who used Johannine writings most,[63] Menno used the Synoptics most, with both agreeing in the prominence given to Paul when citing from the epistles.

In the Old Testament the Pentateuch and the Prophets are used about the same number of times (417 and 440 respectively), with Genesis being highest of those in the Pentateuch (157 references) and Isaiah highest of the prophetic books (168 references). Menno cites or alludes to at least eight apocryphal books, with a total of 100 references in the five books counted. This would certainly not indicate that Menno considered the apocryphal books as less significant than other Old Testament books, nor does he make any comments that he considers them less canonical than the other books.

By far the majority of quotations or citations are given from the New Testament. When compared with the number taken from the Old Testament the ratio is about 3:1. This prominence of the New Testament one would expect since the New Testament was seen as the fulfillment of the Old—it depicted the life of the one in whom the Old Testament prophecies found their fulfillment. Even in the selection, *Meditation on the 25th Psalm,* there are more references from the New Testament than from the Old. This emphasis indicates a similar position to that of the reformers and Marpeck, viz., that the Old Covenant cannot be understood without the New.

There is one passage which might be taken to mean that for Menno the biblical canon is closed. He argues that anyone, past or present, who teaches anything contrary to the word of Moses or contrary to the Spirit, word, commands, prohibitions, ordinations, and example of Christ is false. "But that they persuade you that the apostles' doctrine was only in part and that now they teach that which is perfect, this is a deception above all deceptions."[64] This statement, contained in a section against the corrupt sects, indicates that one of the problems with which Menno had to deal was that of Scripture losing its authority. This was undoubtedly one of the reasons why he so often came back to the emphasis on the text, particularly that of the New Testament. For the Batenburgers and the Davidians the biblical text could not be binding, for the Spirit was giving them further "enlightenment." This Menno could not grant, for Münster was too real for him—he knew to what excesses such stress on the Spirit could lead.

Unlike Luther, Menno did not discuss the validity of the books within the canon.[65] He did, however, take Luther to task for holding that James was a "strawy epistle." "O bold

49

folly! If the teaching is straw, then the faithful servant and witness of Christ, the chosen apostle who has written this and taught it, must be a strawy man."[66] This of course, could not be. Nor could he go along with Luther in the freedom with which the latter used the biblical text. To be sure, Luther was quite clear in his emphasis on 2 Peter 1:21. "Holy men of God spoke. . . ." Prophets were so moved by the Spirit that they had to pass on what they had received. But the emphasis on the words never became a principle for Luther. He could say, *Es ist dem heiligen Geist ein schlecht Ding um ein Wort.* Koehler observes that for Luther there was no sacred text: *Gottes Wort hing nicht am Buchstaben, sondern lag im Sinn.* While he made continual use of the original languages, i.e., the Hebrew and the Greek, in the Old Testament particularly he continued to use the Latin Vulgate, and in his revision of the Latin text he made use not so much of the originals as of his own German translation. Nor did Luther hesitate to engage in textual criticism where he felt it necessary.[67]

Menno also held to the statement that the holy men of God spoke as they were moved by the Spirit. The Scriptures were inspired of God because God speaks through them. God uses human agents, but these are His mouthpieces. The holy Moses teaches and speaks *uyt Godts mondt.* Disobedience to what God speaks is a serious thing. "How do you dispose of the great prophets of God, such as David, Isaiah, Jeremiah, Ezekiel, etc., who through the inspiration of the Holy Spirit have with such clear words in so many places, pointed to Christ and His Kingdom?"[68] This same inspiration is claimed for the apostles. They have presented the actions and doctrines of Christ *door den Heyligen Geest geschreven.* Or Menno asks his readers, "Tell me, dear friends, what do you do with the revealed and infallible Word and testimony of the Almighty Father, which He Himself testified of His Son, saying, This is my beloved Son, in whom I am well pleased; hear ye Him"?[69] And at this point Menno inserts the reference from Matthew 17:5. It cannot be otherwise; the Scriptures are the inspired word of God.

The earlier discussion has already revealed that Menno often refers to the letter of the Scriptures. But it is interesting to observe that in the majority of instances this comes in the context of polemics. Menno maintains that for their arguments or for their position the opponents cannot show *een eenigh woort uyt der gantscher Schrift,* cannot bring forth *een duydt-lijcke Letter uyt der gantscher Heylige Schrift,* cannot prove *met een eenigh letterken uyt der Schrift,* and Menno wants the opponent to show *een Letter uyt dat gantsche Nieuwe Testament,* that the magistrates are to be called upon to protect the church.[70] Menno also varies the statement to say that Christ has not with one letter in the whole New Testament taught or commanded that which the opponents practice, nor is there *een tittelken* that children are to be baptized.[71]

Another observation is in order at this point. Many of the references of this nature are used in the discussion of infant baptism. Statements such as the above indicate not only how strongly Menno felt about the issue, but they also show that he resorted to extreme expressions in the heat of controversy.[72] It is necessary to bear this in mind in the delineation of the view of inspiration which Menno held. Unfortunately, he did not define or spell out what he meant by inspiration. The above statements, spoken as they were primarily from the negative standpoint, do not give the whole picture. As they stand they tend to give the impression that Menno had a mechanical view of inspiration. There are a number of things, however, which temper this impression considerably. In the first place, there are other negative statements which do not restrict themselves to the letter, e.g., when Menno speaks of the unbiblical prac-tices of his time he says negatively that they are such that they cannot be supported *niet een stipken noch met Letter noch met Geest/ in de gantsche Schrift.* But secondly, on the positive side, Menno goes on to insist that the Scriptures support, testify, sustain, command, direct us, urge us, teach us, etc., yet never does he make a statement where "a single word" or "letter" is called in to witness to a doctrine or practice.

But there are yet stronger arguments which mitigate against the conclusion that Menno held a mechanical view of inspira-tion. These have to do with the approach he took to the Scrip-tures. In his polemic against Martin Micron, Menno gives a brief summary of the discussion which he and Micron had several years earlier. He mentions that it is impossible for him to describe the meeting exactly as it transpired. But the description of what happened is not the most important thing. The correct *interpretation* must be given, something which Micron had not done. He says:

I think it impossible to describe word for word those parts of the discussion which Micron has purposely omitted or misinterpreted, just as the conversation unfolded. Nor have the holy Apostles and Evangelists who described the doctrine and work of Christ through the inspiration of the Holy Spirit done so. For the one describes the same occurrence one way, and the other in another way. They deemed it sufficient to give the basis of truth; it is the same with me.

Menno did not care to wrangle over words.

My purpose is not to wrangle over words; I wish only to show the reader that the crucified Christ Jesus is God's first-born and only-begotten true Son, and to show that Micron has given an untrue account of the discussion and that he has deceived his readers with open falsehood.[73]

This would indicate that Menno certainly was not a slavish literalist, a fact that is seen also in the following statement:

My brethren, I tell you the truth and lie not. I am no Enoch, I am no Elias, I am no seer nor Prophet who can teach other than what is written in the Word of God and understood in the Spirit. All those who seek to teach differently will soon stray from the right track and be deceived. I do not doubt that the merciful Father will keep me in His Word so that I will not write or say anything except that which I can powerfully support with Moses, or with the Prophets, or with the evangelists or other apostolic writings and doctrines, *rightly interpreted according to the sense, Spirit, and intent of Christ.* Judge you who are spiritually minded.[74]

This passage draws attention to a combination of terms which needs a further comment. On the one hand Menno refers to the *uytgedruckte letterlijke beschreven Godts Woordt,* while on the other he speaks of it *in den Geest recht gevaet.* Whenever either of these are seen alone only a partial picture is presented. It is true that Menno's interpreters in the past have sought to place him into either of two camps. On the one side he has been seen as being too literalistic in his approach to Scripture. The numerous expressions cited above bear this out. Luther was undoubtedly thinking of such "literal" interpretations when he accused the Anabaptists of leaning "too far to the right when they teach miserable stuff like this: that it is wrong to own private property, to swear, to hold office as a ruler or judge, to protect or defend oneself, to stay with wife and children."[75] Others made similar charges.

Then on the other side Menno is said to be too "free" with his interpretation. The quotations from the polemic against Micron showed that it was the "foundation of truth," not the "wrangling about a word" which Micron sought. Menno himself could take others to task for being too literal. "For he [the antichrist] knows how to clothe his cause with the letter of the Scriptures beautifully."[76] In the section on excommunication he says:

O men! arm yourselves, for Paul's word is true, that the ministry of the New Testament is not one of the letter but of the Spirit. Therefore it cannot be performed to the glory of God by the proud, the arrogant, the ambitious or the self-willed who wish to do everything after their own mind, notion and inclination. These always pull down more than they build up, they harm more than they help. This is inevitable since according to the doctrine of Paul it is not depth of the intellect, nor human eloquence, nor a dead letter of which they have plenty, but God, Spirit, truth, power and life of which they are destitute that matters. Oh, take heed![77]

Menno's concern is that the ministry of the New Testament is not one of the letter but of the Spirit. Here Luther can be quoted on the other side.

Our Anabaptist schismatics seduce many people by yelling that the Gospel we have is not the right one, since they claim that it does not produce any fruit and that the people remain wicked, proud and greedy. Or they say that you have to have something more than the mere Word and letter; you have to have the Spirit working, and an honest resolution to improve your life. If what we have really were the Word of God, it would certainly produce fruit.[78]

Menno's emphasis on the Spirit has led some to accuse him of a similar spiritualization to that which marked the writings of Franck and Schwenckfeld. But this is certainly not the case. When accused of giving his own pronouncements, Menno was first in his denial. "I am no prophet who can teach and prophesy otherwise than what is written in the Word of God and understood by the Spirit." He says further:

Again, I have no visions or angelic inspirations. Nor do I desire them, lest I be deceived. The Word of Christ alone is sufficient for me. If I do not follow His testimony, then truly all that I do is useless, and even if I had such visions and inspirations, which is not the case, they would have to conform to the Word and Spirit of Christ, or else they would be mere imagination, deceit and temptations of Satan.[79]

A further comparison may be made at this point with the reformers and their view of authority. As Calvin developed his position, he came to the point where not the Bible as such, but the church built on the Bible as the word of God constituted supreme authority. Luther's view of the connection between the Bible and the church was not so narrow. He never permitted the authority of the church to become supreme. Rather he saw himself as a mouthpiece of God—God himself was speaking through the word of the preacher.[80] Menno's position was still different. He saw it as the preacher's task to turn the audience to the Bible, and thus the Bible which gave the enlightenment that sinful man needed became the supreme authority. How the role of the Spirit comes in at the point of revealing the truth cannot be fully discussed here, but it may be mentioned that for both Calvin and Menno the Spirit gives the subjective confirmation of the truth. Unlike Luther, Menno denied a creative activity of the Spirit, at least insofar as he insisted that the Spirit cannot speak apart from the Bible.[81] While this view leaves something to be desired, it may be said from the positive standpoint that when the Bible and the Spirit are coupled, the Spirit shows the significance of outward events for man's inner life. Menno never ceased insisting that the two, Scripture and Spirit, must be held together.[82]

While Menno endeavored to avoid extremes when it came to the use of the text of Scripture and the role of the Spirit, it is clear that he did not succeed so well as did Marpeck in avoiding a biblicism marked by an unhealthy adherence to the letter of the Scriptures (particularly the New Testament). Although he recognized the human elements of the biblical text, he did not follow either Luther or Calvin in their scholarly pursuit of the biblical text.[83] For him it was sufficient that these books were the inspired word of God and as such completely authoritative for him. To live by them and to teach them, to interpret them only by the Spirit of Christ—this was his deepest desire.

WILLIAM KEENEY

The Incarnation,
A Central Theological Concept

A CENTRAL POINT of controversy between the Dutch Anabaptists and their Lutheran or Calvinist reformers in the sixteenth century was the issue of the Incarnation. It was even a point of contention with the South German and Swiss Anabaptists, as is readily seen in the conference held in Strasbourg in 1555.[1] The South German and Swiss Anabaptists were not ready to reject the position of Dutch and North Germans summarily, but they were no doubt concerned about removing the odium associated with Melchior Hoffman, and to a lesser degree Caspar Schwenckfeld, who held similar views on the issue. Indeed, the conference of 1555 tried to take a position that might be a mild rebuke, but could also be ambiguous enough to afford grounds for a conciliatory position. They said, "For just as the Scripture in many places lets it appear as if Christ brought His flesh from heaven . . . in similar fashion the Scripture also lets it appear as if Christ has received and assumed His flesh from Mary. . . . And from now on we desist from speaking outside of the clear Scripture, over how far or near, high or low Christ has become flesh. . . ."[2]

Despite the opposition from several sides, the Dutch and north German Mennonites continued to hold the position of Menno Simons and Dirk Philips for some years to come. This is evidenced by the inclusion of the question of the Incarnation

55

in the debates at Emden in 1578 and even later at Leeuwaarden in 1596. The question must arise as to why the Dutch and north German Mennonites held so tenaciously to the doctrine and the peculiar explanation of Menno Simons. It can scarcely be maintained over such a period out of stubbornness if it is in radical error.

A deeper, more central issue must be at stake. This appears to have been true. Despite some difficulties, if not outright error on the part of Menno in the formulation of how the event occurred, the Incarnation with its theological implications was a central organizing concept for much of Menno and Dirk's theology when they attempted to express it systematically.

An attempt will be made here to show the central importance of the particular formulation of the Incarnation with regard to their position on (1) Soteriology, (2) The Sacraments, and (3) Ethics. It would be more difficult to demonstrate directly the integral relationship between this position and the doctrine of the church or the Scriptures, but this could be done also.

The Doctrine of the Incarnation

Before these relationships are examined, it is necessary first to state clearly what the position on the Incarnation was. There is much misunderstanding of what to Menno and Dirk was a very clear and precise formulation of the doctrine.

Menno and Dirk repeatedly said that Jesus Christ was conceived in Mary from God through the Holy Spirit, and was born *out of* but not *from* Mary. Careful attention must be paid to the use of prepositions, for they are used so as to distinguish precisely the origin, and therefore the nature of Jesus Christ.[3]

By this careful formulation of the manner of the Incarnation, Menno and Dirk attempted to solve several theological problems. First of all it must be said that they were not Valentinian or Docetic in their views. Melchior Hoffman, from whom they no doubt received their original material for their position, may have been closer to the position since he used expressions that are definitely Valentinian in nature.[4] Menno and Dirk were careful to point out that their view denied neither the deity nor the humanity of Jesus Christ. That they did not deny the deity scarcely needs to be argued. That charge was never made even by their most extreme and least informed opponents.

That Menno and Dirk denied the humanity of Jesus or so construed it that only logical inconsistency could permit them to assert their belief in it is more frequently charged against them. The attempt to explain the Incarnation in such a manner as to obviate the necessity for Jesus to partake of His human nature from Mary was considered necessary by them in order to resolve the Anselmic problem. How can a man who partakes of Adamic sin be a savior for other men? By postulating the Incarnation in such a manner as to eliminate the origin of Jesus' humanity from another human being Menno and Dirk would relieve Him of the taint of Adamic sin. Dirk Philips says:

> If Christ did not receive His flesh and blood *from* Mary, how then could He suffer and die? In reply we ask: If the flesh of Christ is of the earth and earthly, from Adam and his seed (that was of a sinful nature and was subjected to the curse) how then was the Word of God made flesh? How could Christ make an everlasting atonement for our sins and pay for them?[5] Menno attempted to explain the Incarnation by a physiology which would not be accepted today as accurate. He maintained that the woman's seed was not active, only passive, and therefore did not grant its substance to the child. Thus, Jesus could be a normal child in so far as nourishment and birth *out of* Mary would be concerned, but would not thereby receive His human nature *from* her.[6]

In Menno's defense it might be pointed out that this physiological view was common in the medieval period and was accepted also by Thomas Aquinas, though the latter did not draw the same conclusions as Menno did with regard to the Incarnation.[7] Dirk Philips did not use the same physiological arguments as Menno, but nevertheless would agree on the theological explanations of how Jesus would be fully human without partaking of His human nature from Mary.

Both Menno and Dirk further argued that the humanity of Jesus was of the same origin and nature as Adam prior to the fall. Thus Jesus could be fully and perfectly human without participating in the guilt of Adamic sin. If God created Adamic nature guiltless, there is no logical difficulty in His repeating the act through the activity of the Holy Spirit, and thereby providing Jesus with a true human nature, but of a prelapsarian purity. Thus Jesus Christ could be truly God and truly man.

Menno and Dirk never attempted to explain how the two natures were united in one person, but they were explicit in their rejection of Nestorianism. Menno rejected the explanation that the unity of the two natures in Jesus Christ is a consequence of the communication of names (*communication oft gemeynsaemheyt der Namen*) an obvious parallel to the *communicatio idiomatum*. He maintained that this was a uniting of two persons and two sons into one person and son.[8] The unity of the two natures is a miraculous creation of God and requires no further logical or rational explanation. It is accepted on faith.[9]

The Incarnation and Soteriology

The problem for man is that he has received by inheritance from Adam a fallen nature. As evidently implied in the above statement of Menno and Dirk's concept of the Incarnation, they viewed the Adamic nature of man as a consequence of physical transmission. Man is doomed to act in disobedience to God because of the nature he has received by inheritance. Since it is a matter of his substantial nature and man has no power to transform his substance, salvation cannot be a matter of will power or effort. No legalism or merit could be efficacious in changing a nature that was fundamentally at fault.

Nevertheless, true human nature in God's original intention and His original creative act was not of this kind. Human nature was originally created in the divine image, in God's "own image and likeness, as the Holy Scripture testifies in many places, namely, that in the beginning God had created man into eternal life, in the image and likeness of His only begotten son Jesus Christ. . . ."[10] The fall resulted in a nature transmitted through the impure seed, presumably made impure when Eve was bitten by the serpent.[11] One might observe parenthetically that this should have been impossible, according to Menno's understanding of the woman's seed as passive. If the nature of man is transmitted only through the male seed, then the bite of the serpent should have no effect on the transmission of the nature of man. This problem does not seem to occur to Menno.

Despite man's disobedience in Adam with the subsequent fall and the disobedience of each man of Adam's progeny after reaching the age of understanding and thus becoming personally responsible for his disobedience, God has provided for the restoration of the divine image in man. It is with regard to the restoration of the divine image or the partaking of the divine nature by man that the Incarnation becomes of central importance. Man even with a fallen nature has an understanding of right and wrong. This was not obliterated by the fall. The will to be obedient to the right was the basic loss, along with immortality. Man may still recognize his wrongdoing and may respond to the promptings of the Holy Spirit by the act of repentance. This is the "Anknüpfungspunkt," the point of contact remaining in man even prior to redemption.

By the moral act of response to wrong with repentance, man is enabled to receive the grace of God and to be justified by faith. This justification results in the granting again of the divine nature by the act of the Holy Spirit. Man now becomes "bone of his bone and flesh of his flesh," a Pauline phrase which both Menno and Dirk repeat again and again.[12]

Salvation becomes the reverse process of the Incarnation. God became man. The divine nature by the creative act of the Holy Spirit assumed true human nature. Thus the Incarnation demonstrates the compatibility of the two natures and the spiritual basis for both. In salvation man becomes a new creature in Christ. Man becomes God in a restricted sense. Dirk Phillips says:

In order to understand this more fundamentally, everyone thus notes the similarity and fellowship of God and Christ with all the believers, to wit, that all believers are partakers of the divine nature, yea, are and shall be called children of the Most High, and are in the world just as Christ has been in the world, and shall be in His future the same as He. If now men become partakers of the divine nature, yea, gods and children of the Most High, in like manner as Christ on earth and in heaven, then they are still not of the identical essence and person that God and Christ are. Oh no, the creature never becomes the Creator, and that flesh and word never become the eternal spirit itself, which God is, for that is impossible. But the believers become gods and children of the

Most High by the rebirth, sharing and fellowship of the divine nature. . . . But men are there and remain as creatures, and God as the Creator and Ruler, nevertheless they be one, and God all in all.[13]

Human nature becomes a partaker of the divine nature. Since this latter point of view was not as directly under attack as was their concept of the Incarnation, Menno and Dirk were not as careful in their formulation of the reverse of the Incarnation in salvation.

While Menno and Dirk maintained that men could become gods in a restricted sense, they were careful to point out the limitations which prevented them from falling into pantheism. They found justification for the view that men could become gods in a certain sense in Psalm 82:6, which says, "I say, 'You are gods, sons of the Most High, all of you'" (RSV). But the origin of a substance determines in a real sense its nature. Jesus Christ has His nature from God. His human nature is from God and out of man. In the reverse fashion, man's human nature is from Adam, but he is born anew out of God. His divine nature is a conferred nature and so can never become identical to God's, or to the divine nature in Jesus Christ. There is never a mystical, pantheistic absorption of man into the divine nature.

The transformation into the new creature in Christ also provided the basis for hope in eternal life. A presupposition of Menno's was that all substances tend ultimately toward their sources.[14] Adamic nature is of the earth, earthly. Therefore it is subject to decay, corruption, and death. It tends back to its source in the earth. The divine nature is of another source. It is divine, spiritual, heavenly. Therefore it is nonmaterial, incorruptible, and eternal. The partakers of the divine nature tend toward their source, and in this is found the hope of eternal life. Indeed, the divine nature is only finally freed of the imperfections and weaknesses of the Adamic nature when it is separated from the earthly with the death of the flesh.

The Incarnation and the Sacraments

To understand the relationship between the Incarnation and the sacraments in the view of Menno and Dirk, it is necessary to understand some of their presuppositions concerning the way in which men come into contact with and to knowledge of the spiritual reality. Man does not grasp spiritual reality directly. It has been communicated in the Old Testament period through institutions, ceremonies, laws, persons, and historical events.[15] These gave man some understanding of the spiritual reality, but it could only be a dim or "shadowy" image since it was only mediated knowledge. The correspondence between the "shadowy" image and the spiritual reality could never be absolute though it might be more or less direct. It took faith to know the spiritual reality mediated through the various means which God used to disclose himself to man.

In the Incarnation the Word became flesh. The true being became man as well as God. In Jesus Christ the true being, the reality of the spirit, was immediately present. The means and the reality were not only in direct correspondence, but there was an absolute identity. Through Jesus Christ the shadowy image revealed in the Old Testament was now illuminated and fully disclosed. One could now have a standard by which to judge the means used in the Old Testament and could determine to what extent they were adequate or inadequate, how direct the correspondence was between that which the means sought to convey and the reality itself.

The primary capacity which man has to discover the spiritual reality is faith. Faith was understood by Menno and Dirk to be largely a moral response of trust and obedience. Faith was not mainly an intellectual grasp of certain ideas or propositions, though faith did have its intellectual content. Faith was above all a response of the will to the reality which is unseen, immaterial, but nevertheless the truth, as revealed in the person of Jesus Christ.

Regeneration, the birth of the new creature in Christ and the death of the old nature, is also a spiritual reality, the consequence of the response of man to the spiritual reality in repentance with the subsequent gift of faith. Such regeneration has not only personal significance, it results in incorporation into a new society, the fellowship of believers, the church. The church as it exists on earth as a spiritual reality must be revealed by some means. A part of the function of the sacraments is to reveal to other Christians the fact that a person has been incorporated into the body of Christ, the church.

Baptism is the outward symbol of the inward reality of the new birth. Through it the Christian discloses the beginning of the new reality with himself, and so the church may be gathered out of the world.[16] Baptism becomes the necessary means of communicating to others who have experienced the reality of the new birth the fact which makes possible the establishing of the visible reality which must be in as direct correspondence as humanly possible to the invisible, spiritual reality. Thus the sacrament of baptism has a function similar to the Incarnation. It is to communicate the spiritual reality to men who can only perceive it in mediated fashion.

This all implies, of course, the baptism of believers who have reached the "age of understanding" so that they are able to respond personally and freely by the act of will and can exercise the gift of faith in trust and obedience, once the gift has been granted by the act of the Holy Spirit.[17] Those within the church, having already been granted the gift of faith which enables them to know the true being of Jesus Christ, are those who are enabled to recognize in others the existence of the spiritual reality which binds them into a unity in Christ.

The close relationship between the sacrament of the Lord's Supper and the Incarnation is even easier to demonstrate. Great emphasis was placed upon the significance of John 6 for understanding the full meaning of the Lord's Supper. Menno and Dirk understood John 6 to be Jesus' own interpretation of what it means to eat His flesh and drink His blood. To eat His flesh and drink His blood signifies the acts of trust and obedience which are the spiritual equivalents to carnal eating and drinking (John 6:51ff.).

The life of the new creature was dynamic. Salvation was not merely an event; it was also a process as long as man remained in the flesh. The new creature in Christ had a birth analogous to the birth of a child; it had also a growth analogous to the growth of the physical body. To grow the physical must be nurtured with food and drink. In analogous fashion, the new spiritual reality must be nourished for growth by the spiritual equivalents of feeding and drinking. The believer must be nourished by the Word which had become flesh. By believing, trusting, and obeying the new reality of the spirit might be nourished and would grow.

The partaking of the Word was therefore not only symbolic, not only a memorial, though the sacrament of the Lord's Supper has this significance. It has further the real experience of partaking of the same being of Christ, but not in a physical sense. It is a spiritual reality, and in this sense Jesus Christ is really present in the Lord's Supper. Dirk Philips says:

Therefore whoever believes in the Lord Jesus Christ, the Son of the Living God, who was crucified and died for us, and trusts in Him, those receive Jesus Christ, the Word of the Father; those are fed with the heavenly Manna, yea, those eat the flesh and drink the blood of Jesus, but spiritually, with the mouth of the soul and not carnally with the mouth of the body. For spiritual food (as the flesh and blood of Christ are) must be received spiritually.[18]

Just as in the Incarnation Menno and Dirk would never admit to any dichotomy between the human and divine nature of Jesus Christ in the Word become flesh, they were also quick to point out that there should be no divorce between the spiritual concern of the believers and the concern for the physical needs of the brethren. The Lord's Supper always had within it the mystery of the manner in which the physical acts of feeding and drinking could facilitate in the believer the spiritual realities of trusting and obeying. Nevertheless, it did occur. Therefore, there was a special responsibility which the believer carried for others who were incorporated into the body of Christ in the same experience. Menno says:

Just as natural bread is made of many grains, pulverized by the mill, kneaded with water, and baked by the heat of the fire, so is the church of Christ made up of true believers, broken in their hearts with the mill of the divine Word, baptized with the water of the Holy Ghost, and with the fire of pure, unfeigned love made into one body. . . . But in all things, one toward another, long-suffering, friendly, peaceable, ever ready in true Christian love to serve one's neighbor in all things possible: by exhortation, by reproof, by comforting, by assisting, by counseling, with deed and with possessions, yes, with bitter and hard labor, with body and life, ready to forgive one another as Christ forgives and serves us with His Word, life, and death.[19]

Here again one sees not only the rather mystical experience of union with Christ and the fellow believer by partaking of the divine nature, but also the practical moral and social consequences of the Incarnation. They both flowed from a consciousness of a spiritual reality that was the dominant reality, giving meaning to all others, and governing every relationship for the Christian.

The Incarnation and Ethics

It is not the intention here to give a survey of the ethical teachings of Menno and Dirk. It is only to show the fundamental significance of the Incarnation for their approach to ethical action. It should already be clear that ethical consequences were always a strong consideration for them.

The Incarnation by providing the revelation of the highest possible, the perfect manifestation of man as he should have been except for the fall, gives a standard for measuring righteousness in man. The ethical judgments of the Dutch Anabaptists who followed Menno and Dirk always intended to be Christocentric. Jesus Christ is the plumbline or the touchstone. Thus again the Old Testament standards are to be understood and interpreted in the light of the true being. Jesus Christ is not to be understood in terms of the Old Testament ethical teachings, but the Old Testament is to be interpreted in terms of the full revelation given in Him.

But the standard of the Word is not simply an impossible ideal, a counsel of despair for imperfect man. It is the function of the law to bring man to an understanding of his own inability to achieve goodness, to render obedience to the divine demands out of his own strength. The Incarnation through the new creature in Christ offers the ontological basis for real obedience. The nature of a being must express itself in accordance with that nature. If the regeneration of man results in the partaking of the divine nature, this divine nature must manifest itself in ethical acts that are in accord with it. The new creature in Christ does not exist unless the Christian gives positive evidence by obedience to the clear and positive commands of Jesus Christ as given in the New Testament.

The positive commands of Jesus Christ are no new legalism, no new moralism of self-effort. It is possible to be obedient to them because a dynamic for righteousness and holiness is granted by the Holy Spirit. Obedience is not the result of self-will, but of the transformation of the will that must express itself in loving obedience. It is not a cheap "imitation of Jesus" found in sentimental attempts to mimic His acts, a kind of moralism that can be individually pietistic but ignores the larger social injustices. Rather it is the dynamic encounter of evil with goodness because one's very nature is repulsed by evil and moves even as Christ did to overcome it with suffering love wherever it is discovered.

But Menno and Dirk were also no perfectionists, as has been charged against them.[20] The human nature, while defeated and no longer the ruling principle in the Christian life, is still present and active until death. As a consequence the Christian may still stumble and fall because of error, weakness, or ignorance. Nevertheless, the Christian will not persist in willful opposition to the will of God when he knows the right. The possibilities of improvement are always open and so the Christian needs constantly to study the word of God, to be a part of an admonishing and disciplining fellowship, and to bear responsibilities for others in an attitude of repentant obedience.

The persistent nonresistance of the early Dutch Anabaptists in the face of persecution and martyrdom is grounded ultimately in their understanding of the relationship of the Incarnation to ethics. They understood themselves to be new creatures in Christ. This gave them both the possibility of obedience and the gift of eternal life. Obedience required that they manifest only the love and forgiveness of Jesus Christ as revealed supremely in His own death on the cross. It did not ask if such testimony was going to be successful in "stopping the Spaniards," or whether it was a "politically responsible" act. They asked only if it were obedient to the will of God. They assumed without question that He could use both their obedience and their testimony to accomplish His purposes in His own time.

Because eternal life was given along with obedience, they had the hope which could overcome the drive for self-preservation. In the firm hope in the fulfillment of that which they had already tasted in part by the partaking of the divine nature, martyrdom could be a victory. Death of the body would release one from that old nature which must then return to dust, and full participation in the perfection of the divine nature could be realized.

Thus the Anabaptists had the pessimism about human nature that characterized Lutherans and Calvinists, but they combined with it an optimism about the possibilities of ethical achievement which at times appears and is judged to be identical to that of modern liberalism. They overcame the defeatist attitude of Lutherans with regard to works because of their understanding of the Incarnation. The evangelical reliance on the power of the Holy Spirit prevented them from falling into the shallow optimism of the liberal "do-gooders" who expect to transform society by their moral efforts. Even less are the deeds of the Christian a kind of "works righteousness" by which to accomplish salvation. Their holy acts were lived in everyday life not to gain salvation, but as a manifestation of the salvation already received. Nevertheless, the believing and trusting entailed in such acts enables the Christian to partake further of the divine nature by communion with Christ and through the power of the Holy Spirit. Goodness is not an "impossible possibility" even if it cannot of itself produce a good world unless the transformation of man is accomplished by the redeeming activity of God in Jesus Christ. The fulfillment of such hope is eschatological.

Conclusion

Menno and Dirk's doctrine of the Incarnation arose directly out of their own experience of salvation through a personal encounter with Jesus Christ. They experienced this as a central fact of their own religious experience. It gave them a new spiritual reality. It resulted not simply from a change of mind or an act of the will. It was a gift of grace. The gift resulted not simply in a change in their status before God by the removal of guilt or the acceptance by God in the midst of guilt. It resulted in a transformed nature, a new reality in which they became partakers of the divine nature. Though still possessing weakness, they discovered a new power which had to manifest itself in a new ethical life of obedience. The sacraments were symbols of the realities both of the new birth effected by the Holy Spirit and the continual growth in Christ whereby through trust and obedience they were enabled to partake more and more of the divine nature.

The reality of the Incarnation and its consequence for salvation provided Menno Simons and Dirk Philips with a ground for a dynamic concept of the Christian life. Salvation could not be by human effort, a change of mind, a new status or an arbitrary divine decree. The reality of the Incarnation also provided a ground for holy living, not as a consequence of unaided human endeavor, but as the fruit of the gracious act of God in Christ through the Holy Spirit. For these reasons they were unwilling to abandon their view of the Incarnation in the face of attacks from Roman Catholics, whose view of salvation they understood to be based on merit; or from Lutherans, whose views of salvation they understood to be a change of status, a forensic act; or from Zwinglians and Calvinists, whose view of salvation they understood to be an arbitrary divine decree that would cut the nerve of moral response. Even the criticisms of brethren from Switzerland and South Germany who offered no positive alternative answer to the difficulties but shared a similar, more intuitional or experiential view of salvation would not shake so basic a conviction.

While we may not agree with certain aspects of the particular formulation of the doctrine of Incarnation, such as the physiology of transmission of human nature, the experience of the reality of the divine nature and the possibility of the transformation of man by the power of the Holy Spirit so that he may become a partaker of the divine nature which results in ethical activity would offset the pessimism and futility that can arise from a concentration on the failures of human nature. The life of discipleship can be grounded in a new reality. The possibilities of growth may be infinite, but this does not deny some real possibilities of obedient response to the grace of God, even unto martyrdom if this is demanded in the conflict with the powers of evil. The Christian does not transform society by his own moral goodness, or by persuading others to adopt certain policies that are Christian, or by pragmatic effectiveness in stopping evildoers from carrying out their evil intentions. The establishment of the perfect society is to be seen eschatologically and the implications of the Incarnation should make this abundantly clear.

With so much at stake soteriologically, sacramentally, and ethically, it is understandable that Menno, Dirk, and their followers for decades afterward were slow to relinquish their views of the Incarnation. As with Jonah and the whale, it is regrettable that controversy over the particular way in which an event happened becomes the focal point of argument which obscures the significant theological truth established by the event. Even with what would be considered a false physiology on the part of Menno, the central importance of the Incarnation protected him and others from errors more basic, which others with more accurate physiology have committed.

J . A . O O S T E R B A A N

Grace in Dutch Mennonite Theology

THE DISTINCTIONS AND CONTRASTS among the various forms
that theology has assumed in the course of its development
come into being through a complex of shifts in the significance
of the most important theological terms.   In such shifts in significance two things always occur.   In the first place there is
a change in the material sense, such as can be described in a
definition, and in the second place there is a change in the position and rank which the concept occupies in the total theology.
For the word *significance* ("Bedeutung") unites in itself these
two meanings: first of all a designation of a certain content
(it signifies *something*) and secondly a designation of a certain rank (we also speak of "a man of significance").   The material richness of a concept signifies a certain weight and through
it a certain power of the concept in the whole structure of a
science.   The subsumption or subordination of concepts is influenced by one's concept of the material significance, but on the
other hand it is often true that the intention to establish and
maintain a definite order of concepts leads or seduces one to
make the material significance of the concepts conform to the
desired order.   In theology the latter happens as often as the
former.

It is clear that the question of the truth of a theology has
to deal directly with this relation between the content and the
rank of concepts.   The concept *truth* has significance in theology in the double sense of the word: both as to its implicit

meaning and as to its rank.   Therefore, a theology can only
be predicated as *true* whenever it has accepted the signifiance
of the concept *truth* to be above all other concepts, that is to
say, whenever it has not subsumed truth under any other concepts.   We can also say it in different ways.   True theology
must deal primarily with the truth; or, truth must be above
every other consideration; or, truth must be the most comprehensive concept.   There is thus no higher concept; there is
only the name of Him who is the truth.   Where this is not
the case, where the concept *truth* is limited and restricted by
other concepts, there by definition a moment of untruth has
crept into theology.   Wherever, for example, a church will not
let itself be directed by the truth, but instead wants to be the
authority over truth, and thus places the concept of the church
higher in rank than the concept of truth, there the concepts
theology and truth do not coincide, and theology degenerates
to a limited form of ecclesiastical dogmatics, which in a strained
fashion attempts to maintain itself as a confessional dogmatism
and, since it has to do it without the power of the truth, often
calls upon other kinds of power.

Of the same significance and importance as the concept of
truth in theology is the concept of grace.   Grace and truth
are both primary concepts that must not be restricted and limited by any others, but which on the contrary restrict all other
concepts and indicate their theological position.   Exactly as
it is in the case of the concept *truth,* a theology stands or falls
to the extent that it does or does not recognize the significance
of grace as a primary theological concept.   Therefore the concepts of grace and truth are so very closely related to each
other in theology that they cannot be understood separately.
Theologically, truth is always the truth of grace, or gracious
truth; grace is always the grace of truth, or grace revealing itself, grace giving itself openly.   Both grace and truth are primary perfections and characteristics of the essence of God, as
He lets himself be known by us in the fullness of His trinitarian
life.   Both concepts are terms for the primary forms in which
the light of God's being breaks up in the prism of our own
finite human spirit.   Therefore, they flow into each other as
theological thought seeks to search deeper into their distinc-

tion. They are, after all, a unity in their foundation, in God's being. Nowhere is this relationship more clearly and openly established than in the prologue to the Gospel according to John, where the glory of the incarnate Word is described as "a glory as of the only begotten of the Father, full of grace and truth," and is still further stated, "and of his fulness have all we received, and grace for grace; for the law was given by Moses, but grace and truth came by Jesus Christ." Therefore the *kerygma* can be abbreviated as the "gospel of the grace of God" (Acts 20:24) or "the word of His grace" (Acts 14:3; 20:32) and in still other places "the word of truth" (2 Cor. 6:7; Eph. 1:13; Col. 1:5; 2 Tim. 2:15; James 1:18).

Because of the close relationship between these concepts, it is scarcely possible to have a shift in significance of the one without also causing a shift in the significance of the other, which can effect a total reformation of the theology. Thus Luther's reformation had its origin in his vision of the significance of the Pauline concept of grace as found in the letters to the Romans and to the Galatians. Here is the answer to his desperate lament, "How shall I find a gracious God?" Through his new concept of grace, he came to a new hermeneutic, a new method of exegesis of the Scriptures, and he came to a more christological understanding of the Old and New Testaments. On this account the whole structure of Roman Catholic theology came to be upset; and, because of the changed insight concerning ecclesiology, the division in the church had to be consummated.

It is not possible to fully understand the Anabaptist movement in the Reformation without an insight into the shift in significance that took place in the concept of grace held by the pioneers of this movement. Within the scope of this chapter we, of course, cannot give an extended history of the development and change of significance concerning the concept of grace, but we will attempt to indicate some main points. In order to compare the Roman Catholic, Lutheran-Calvinistic, and Mennonite views about grace we will give an exposition of the thoughts of Thomas Aquinas, Melanchthon, and Menno Simons about this subject.

71

J . A . O O S T E R B A A N

Grace in Thomistic Theology

Certainly the concept of grace played an important role in Roman Catholic theology, but it cannot be said that it was actually considered as a primary concept from which their thinking proceeded, and that it was definitive for the whole of Roman Catholic theology, both for the content and the rank of the remaining concepts. On the contrary, in Roman Catholic theology the concept of grace is restricted and bounded by other concepts that are granted a higher rank. One could even posit the thesis that the shift in significance of the concept of grace already in the first century has been the actual fall of Christendom. For as a consequence of this change in concept whereby the significance of the biblical concept came to be lost, the church eventually made itself to be the master of grace in the literal sense of the word; and, as the church became Roman Catholic, it developed into the power structure which it has remained since then. Grace came to be viewed as a "thing," an entity, and as a quality of the soul.[1] The soul is therefore the subject "wherein" grace is; which, according to Thomas, can only be said to the extent that the soul is of an intellectual and rational nature (*natura*).[2] Because of its rational nature the human soul is in a certain sense the image of God and therefore in a position to possess grace; for grace is a kind of participation in the divine nature *secundum quandum similitudinem* (according to a certain similarity).[3] But it is also essential for this Thomistic theology that the "possession" of this grace does not altogether coincide with the original being or nature of man. The creation of man does not signify the same thing as the receiving of grace; the created nature is not the same as that resulting from grace. Grace is infused into man after creation and added to his created nature as a supernatural gift (the *donum supernaturale gratiae*).[4] Thus creation and grace, the natural and supernatural, are separated from each other. As preparation for this division Thomas had first of all made a distinction between the concepts *image* and *similarity*. Similarity (*similitudo*) is a perfection of the image (*imago*) and therefore must follow later.[5] In the same manner grace is secondary with regard to nature and makes it more complete.

72

Gratia non tollit sed perficit naturam is the well-known saying (Grace does not abolish but perfects nature). The righteousness which flows forth from grace is thus a mere accident of the original nature of man, not of man as an individual, but of man as a species. Therefore, this righteousness would also have been transferred to the children, if the first man had not sinned; but since he did sin, the opposite of righteousness, original sin (*peccatum originalis*) is transferred.[6] The original righteousness that was a supernatural gift of grace existed in the subjection of the will of man to the will of God; the original sin existed in the opposite of it, the lack of this subjection. That is the formal side of sin. Materially, according to Thomas, and here he followed Augustine, sin consisted of desire or concupiscence (*concupescentia*).[7] In the fall only the supernatural gift of grace, righteousness, was lost; the originally created nature retained its good essence. Only the accident was lost. Thomas meant three things when he spoke of the good nature of man: first, he says, it is the substance from which man's nature is constituted, that out of which his nature is composed with all of its characteristics (*ipsa principia naturae, ex quibus natura constituitur, et proprietates ex his causatae*); secondly, the good nature is the inclination to virtue (*inclinatio ad virtutem*); thirdly, it can be understood as the gift of the original justice (*donum originalis iustitiae*). Only this last-named accidental property now disappears because of the fall. The second property—the inclination to virtue—is only diminished; but the original substance and basis of the good nature of man are neither taken away nor diminished.[8] Thus, even without the grace of God man has a good nature by his creation.

According to Thomas, the special work of grace, when it is infused into man, is to restore the supernatural gift of righteousness and so to remove the effects of original sin in man. So on one side grace can be called a thing; on the other, a quality in the soul.[9] The further subtle distinctions which Thomas made concerning the concept of grace we will leave unmentioned here.

Important, however, are the problems which are raised by his view of the significance of the concept of grace. After he had established in I. IIae Q. 112, a. 1 that God alone can be the cause of grace in man, because grace as a certain participation in the divine nature could never be caused by something out of created nature (for, after all, the cause is always more than it causes), he poses the question, Can there be a certain disposition or preparation from the side of man for the reception of grace? Here Thomas has to give an ambiguous answer. For the concept of grace does imply on one side that it depends entirely on the giver, but on the other side everything that receives something must be in such a position as to be able to receive it. A note is inserted along with this statement: *Aliqua preparatio ad gratiam exigitur tantum in adultis, non in pueris* (Some preparation for grace is only required in adults, not in children). This exception needs to be made in order to justify infant baptism and the sacramental grace attached to it.

The second point that follows from Thomas' definition of grace is the matter of the justification of the sinner through the forgiveness of sins. Thomas understands by the justification of the sinner (*iustificatio impii*) a change in the condition of man whereby he goes from a state of sin to a state of righteousness by the forgiveness of sins.[10] The remission of sins, which effects justification, changes the condition of the one whose sins are forgiven and is not only a disposition of the one who forgives, but according to Rome this change in condition concerns only the quality of man and not his substance. Therefore, according to Thomas this forgiveness of sins is not conceivable without an infusion of grace (*infusio gratiae*) which, as a thing, grants a new quality to man. The thought that the grace of God should only be His favor on which account he grants to us the righteousness of Jesus Christ without any merit or worth of our own has no place whatsoever in Thomas' thinking. Grace is the effect of God's love whereby man becomes worthy (*dignus*) of eternal life.[11] At the Council of Trent this doctrine of the necessity of the infusion of grace as a thing that clings to the believer was established.[12] Therefore, whenever he who would be baptized is responsible for his own will, he must come of his own accord to be baptized, while it is assumed that in infants the will is present. Therefore, in the Roman Catholic baptismal rite the godfather is asked: "Will you be baptized?" and he answers in the name of the child, "I will."

We now come to the point concerning the relationship of grace to the sacraments according to Thomas. Grace is the first and most important effect of the sacraments (*effectus principalis*). The sacraments are the cause of grace, as the instrument is the cause of that which it effects. God has made the sacraments suitable to serve as instruments for the infusion of grace.[13] Therefore, the sacraments are to be called at the same time a sign and a cause, so that at the same time they effect what they symbolize figuratively.[14] The "thing" of grace must be effected by the "thing" of the sacramental means. Therefore, the sacraments are necessary to receive grace.

The Roman Catholic Church, because she proceeds from the view that the sacraments may be administered only by those who have been ordained, has in this manner the pretense that she possesses the disposition of and authority over grace. For, in this theology, grace and salvation are not given in the word and in the faith answering it, but in the sacramental action, which can only be administered by the priests. Therefore, the assurance that one has received God's grace is not a certainty that is immediately given with faith, which man obtains in himself by faith, but an assurance that is mixed with uncertainty because it depends on the work of man and external sacramental means. The believer can come no further than to assume that he possesses grace on the basis of certain signs (*cognoscitur aliquid coniecturaliter per aliqua signa*).[15] Since the believer can go no further than to an assumption, to a certain uncertainty regarding the reception of grace, he must constantly continue to enjoy the means of grace and, naturally, the sacrament of the eucharist in particular. Herein according to this theology he partakes of Christ himself in a substantial manner, while in the other sacraments he gets only a certain part of Christ's power.[16]

From this survey of Thomistic doctrine regarding grace, it readily appears how this interpretation of the concept of grace, by means of Aristotelian concepts and theological arguments, has been of very fundamental significance for the whole organism of this theology and for the whole structure of the body of the Roman Catholic Church. The subsuming of grace under the concept of a thing or quality, this objectifying (*Verding-lichung*) of an essential perfection of God (out of which only the self arises through the word), is the first reason for the Roman Catholic deviation from the biblical truth, but perhaps it must also be seen as the first result of this deviation. It is also scarcely possible that a revision of the significance of the concept of grace should lead anywhere else than to a reformation of the church. It is understandable that this revision, this correction of the Roman doctrine of grace, in itself a reaction, should in its first form degenerate into an opposing, one-sided position; that for this reason a second phase of the Reformation had to come which in a new form of Protestantism would signify a correction of the correction and would abolish the one-sidedness is also understandable.

Melanchthon and the Doctrine of Grace

We will first see how the doctrine of grace in the Lutheran Reformation has received a classic form in the *Loci Communes* of Melanchthon. We can summarize this position briefly.

Already in the first notes which Melanchthon made for his *Loci* and did not publish but which were only published later in the *Corpus Reformatorum*, it appears that he was conscious of where the principal fault in Roman theology lay. In his notes under the title *De Gratia* he wrote that the word *grace* in its proper sense signifies favor, and immediately he followed it with the warning: "Be careful that you do not imagine in Thomistic fashion that it signifies this or that quality in the soul."[17] Therefore, this grace, which thus is only in God as His good will inclined toward men, was sharply distinguished from the gift, *the donum*, that is joined to it. The words of Paul in Romans 5:15 wherein he speaks about grace and the gift of grace, were explained by Melanchthon as follows: The gift in grace, that is, the gift through grace, that is, the gift that the favorable God imparts. (*Donum in gratia, i.e. donum per gratiam id est, Donum quod favens deus impertit*).[18] "Thus the word *grace* signifies something in God, not in man, as the good will which Curio enjoys, is in Julius and not in Curio. At the same time, however, God who is gracious to man is with

76

him and at work in him. The works, however, or the consequences of grace in man are faith, hope, and love."

In the later expansion of the *Loci* this significance of the concept of grace and the distinction from the gift of grace was maintained.[19]   But the content naturally came to be more specific, especially through the use of grace as a specifically soteriological term.   While in Roman Catholic theology the point is the contrast between nature and grace, in the Lutheran-Calvinistic reformation it is the contrast between sin and grace. "So on this account let the definition of grace be: Grace is the forgiving of sins, or the mercy which is promised for Christ's sake, or the acceptance gratis, which must of necessity be accompanied by the gift of the Holy Spirit."[20]   The gift of the Holy Spirit was described as "the new and eternal righteousness and the life that is begun here and completed in the hereafter."[21]   Melanchthon with great emphasis pointed out that in the Pauline concept of grace (*gratia*) the concept *gratis,* for nothing, is implied; through this excluding word every single merit or worth is excluded and justification is due to Christ alone.   He continues by giving four reasons why it is so highly important that this "for nothing" that excludes all of one's own merit and virtue must above all be understood as essential and proper to the concept of grace.   First, he says, in order to pay the due respect to Christ.   Second, so that the conscience receives a sure and firm solace, and the pestilent error of those who recommend that one must doubt about it might be rejected.   Third, so that men can pray in the true manner. Fourth, so that men might plainly see the distinction between law and gospel.

We must make a few observations about these points.   In the first place, all basis for our justification is thus dissociated from our own merit and worth.   Only Christ has merit.   The Lutheran as well as the Calvanistic dogmatics held firmly to the concept of Christ's merit.[22]   It is God's grace that He has let Christ earn the justifying grace for us.   By this stress on the concept of merit in the work of Christ the juridical character of their doctrine of grace was accentuated; through it the concept of substitution also took a more external and abstract significance.

77

Melanchthon's second point about the certainty of the belief in grace and the expulsion of doubt is also important. Our righteousness is in the work of Christ alone (*Solo Christo*), and we partake of it by faith alone (*sola fide*), and we come to faith by the hearing of the gospel out of the Scriptures alone (*sola scriptura*). In this triple repetition of *alone,* in these *Solisms* or *exclusivae particulae,* lies the basis for the certainty of our justification; through this all doubt in that respect is excluded. For doubt is a form of unbelief which is excluded by faith. This anchoring of certainty with regard to grace in faith alone (which also remained a central point in Anabaptist reformation) is a rejection in principle of all other means to mediate grace. All official or priestly actions can at best only have illustrative or proclamatory functions, but absolutely no causal significance for either bringing faith into existence or for the reception of grace and the promise of justification. When all essential merit resides in Christ alone, He is the only mediator and one can no longer speak of a special means of grace, not even under the cover of the concept of an instrumental mediation. By the Anabaptists this consequence was developed more radically than in the Lutheran-Calvinistic churches.

The last point listed by Melanchthon concerned the contrast between law and gospel. It is clear that a narrowing of the concept of grace by placing it in polarity with the concept of sin and identifying it with the forgiving and remission of guilt brought with it the danger that the positive significance of the law would be neglected and the negative would be overstressed. Grace comes to be dissociated from the law, that is, the law becomes a graceless law, that serves as a disciplinarian (*paedagogus*), and lets us see that we are transgressors and thus sinners. The accent on the contrast, which was always made between law and gospel—above all, in Lutheran theology and is also not alien to Calvinism—is the effect of this narrowing of the concept of grace.

Although the Lutheran-Calvinistic reformation rightly rejected and corrected the Roman Catholic doctrine of grace, it did not itself escape another onesidedness. In its eagerness to reject the objectivation (*Verdinglichung*) of grace and to see it only in the well disposed favor of God toward the sinner, it has isolated grace from the other deeds of God so that creation and the giving of the law appear no longer to have anything to do with grace directly. It was otherwise in Anabaptist theology.

There always has been much misunderstanding of the theology of the earlier and the later Anabaptists in the churches of the Reformation. This was in part the fault of the critics themselves. In their resistance to the very clear and just arguments of the Anabaptists, such as on the issue of baptism, they took a very defensive attitude and so were inclined to discover all sorts of heresies in their opponents. It was also partly the fault of the Anabaptists themselves. In general, under the pressure of persecution they never got around to writing extensive theological works and did not have the opportunity after basic training to set forth their doctrinal system. In addition they mistrusted academic education and scholarship. That will not, however, in any way imply that no systematic thought, no principle of unity of form and content (which gave the whole an inner consistency and a fixed theological form) ever came to be expressed in Anabaptist theology. The discovery of the basic thoughts and principles is, however, a requirement in order to see this inner consistency. To discover these principles, it appears good as a general point of departure to accept that the Anabaptist movement is a secondary movement within the Reformation, that is, a reaction called forth by the action of the great reformers. As a necessary countermovement within the stream of the Reformation, it was a correction of a correction, a negation of a negation. As such the Anabaptist movement signified the completion and conclusion of the whole Reformation. Therefore, the Anabaptist theology was in many respects more radically anti-Roman Catholic than the Lutheran-Calvinistic theology, but at the same time less sharp and onesidedly defensive with respect to some aspects of Roman theology that the first reformers rejected because of their position of protest.

The Council of Trent is an abstract negation of the Reformation, while the Anabaptist current must be seen as a concrete negation that wanted to correct and eliminate certain extremes and all that was still unscriptural and thereby to complete the Reformation. The Council of Trent has expressed some thoughts which, although they proceeded from other reasons, manifest a certain agreement with the thoughts of the early Anabaptists. Thus Trent has, for example, made a distinction between the merits that our works can have and the boasting on the ground of these works. They did so in order to retain the relationship between faith and meritorious works. Although a work is good and meritorious, we may not boast about it, for it is God's gift that enables us to do good works. "Far be it from the Christian to trust or glory in himself and not in the Lord whose goodness is so great toward all men that He wants His own gifts to be their merit."[23] This distinction between merit and boast, whereby Trent intended to maintain *sola fide* and at the same time would unite to it the doctrine of meritorious works was the Roman reaction to an extreme Lutheran rejection of the concept of merit except where it related to the merit of Christ. A similar reasoning, however, even if arising out of other basic motives, one can already find much earlier than Trent in the correction which was introduced from the Anabaptist side against a too abstract Lutheran doctrine of grace. Thus Hans Denck wrote in his *Vom Gesetz Gottes*: "You say, 'If the law shall accomplish so much, then Christ is in vain. There merit is erected and grace rejected.' Answer: No one may satisfy the law who does not truly know Christ and love Him. Whoever fulfills the law through Him, he certainly has merit, but no glory before God, for all glory belongs to God through whose grace a way is given, which was impossible for the whole world. Therefore merit belongs not to man but to Christ through whom everything that man has has been given from God. But whoever seeks to boast in his merit as if it comes from himself, the same destroys the grace through Christ."[24] But, I repeat, such agreements proceed from entirely different grounds.

Grace in the Theology of Menno Simons

In order to get a clear picture of the significance which the concept of grace had in the Anabaptist theology, we may consult the writings of Menno Simons, because it seems to me that no other of the Anabaptists has been so conscious as he of the method and unity of his thinking.[25]   But we shall only be able to get an insight into Menno's view about grace by comparing and combining various places in his writings, for he has never devoted a special writing to this subject.   And yet we may call Menno's theology a real theology of grace, because even more than for Rome and more than for Luther and Calvin his concept of grace received a significance which determined the whole of his thinking and effected the unity and consistency of his faith and thought.   While for Rome the too narrowly defined concept of grace effected a division between nature and the supernatural, and while for Luther and Calvin the purely soteriologically defined concept of grace effected a division between law and gospel, the comprehensive significance of grace for Menno was exactly the space needed for the dialectical tension so that the theological concepts could find their basis and unity.

In order to make clear the broad significance which the concept of grace had for Menno, I must give an extended citation from his *Opera Omnia*.[26]

Notice, my dear reader, that we do not believe nor teach that we are to be saved by our merits and works as the envious assert without truth. We are to be saved solely by grace through Christ Jesus, as has been said before.

By grace the human race was created through Jesus Christ when as yet it was not.

By grace it was again accepted through Christ when it was lost.

By grace Christ was sent to us of the Father. John 3:34.

By grace He has sought the lost sheep, taught repentance and remission of sins, and died for us when we were yet ungodly and enemies.

By grace it is given us to believe.

By grace the Holy Ghost was given us in the name of Jesus. John 14:16.

In short, by grace eternal life is given us through Christ Jesus.

Above all, the emphasis with which Menno in this "Basic Confession about Justification" defends the doctrine of justification by faith and out of grace alone is striking.   But it is not because of this agreement with the other reformers that I give just this citation.   The most important thing is that Menno does not let the work of God's grace begin at the reconciliation and the forgiveness of sins, but at creation.   The human race is created *ex nihilo* by Jesus Christ "out of grace," as he says.

81

The broad range of Menno's concept of grace appears here. Every work of God is a work out of grace. For God's essence *is* grace, just as His essence *is* truth. "All who from their heart believe that God is, also believe that he is true . . . for He is the God of truth" and still further "all who believe that God is, they also believe that He is gracious and merciful."[27] Grace is not a disposition of God that came after the creation and fall, but is His essential perfection out of which He does everything. Just as He has created Adam and Eve out of grace, so He also out of grace gave Abraham his son Isaac. Therefore Menno writes that Abraham praised God for His grace, "for he well knew that the same God who had by His word created the heaven and earth with its fullness . . . also no doubt had the power to make the body of a no longer fruitful wife once more fruitful, if He but so desired." And this same grace, through which God created the human race *ex nihilo* and through which out of nothing He also created His covenant people from the bodily death, is also active, says Menno, whenever He creates the new man in us. "For if we believe with our whole heart this promised word of grace which is the gospel of peace through which was proclaimed to us the remission of our sins through the blood of the Lord, then our dead conscience becomes fruitful and living, it receives the new and spiritual Isaac, Christ Jesus the eternally blessed."[28] This parallel between the three works of God which He has done out of grace better than anything else makes clear what grace signifies in this theology. Grace is not, as for Rome, a thing that is poured out by God and gives as a mere accident to the soul of a man a certain quality. Grace is also not, as in Lutheran-Calvinistic theology, a specific soteriological term which points to the favor and readiness of God to forgive. No, for Menno, and I believe on this point he is representative of a great part of his Anabaptist contemporaries, grace signifies nothing less than the creating love itself, which is the essence of God. Therefore, Menno can say that God has created the human race out of grace and that He also has the power to recreate man out of the same grace. Wherever God works out of His grace, there He calls into existence that which previously was not. Grace, therefore, is not only given for nothing, but also calls into existence out of nothing. Grace is not a strength that is poured into nature, as for Rome, but is God's creating love through which nature itself is created and, when it has degenerated, is recreated. And it is also the creating love which reveals itself as the essence of God himself and thereby appears as the truth of God to all those who believe in Him. Therefore, Menno also writes, "Out of grace Christ was sent to us from the Father; it is out of grace that we believe this."[29] Because grace is creative in the fullest sense of the word, no point of contact (*Anknüpfungspunkt*) is needed for God's grace. No disposition or worthiness is needed; no conditions or means are needed to mediate grace or its gifts. In the beginning it created entirely out of nothing; just as easily it recreates the new man out of the nothingness of his lost manhood.

It is necessary to recognize this typical Anabaptist concept of grace in order to be able to understand the different specific forms of Anabaptist theology and to be able to acknowledge their biblical character of truth. I here want to point out briefly the fundamental significance of this view of grace for several doctrinal points of faith.

For the Anabaptists of the same conviction as Menno Simons the doctrine of the Incarnation was central. The thought that Jesus had not "taken" human flesh by means of Mary (who, after all, had a part in original sin) but that He himself "became" flesh, without human means, is only to be understood if one thinks of God's will to create in Christ as implicit in grace. The principal argument of the opponents of this Anabaptist doctrine of Incarnation was that in one manner or another Jesus' flesh must be the same as our flesh and therefore must have come of human flesh, for otherwise we would not be able to participate in any way in the justfication which Christ gained by the cross. This rebuttal misunderstood the creating power of God's grace, which has the power to give Jesus true human nature on earth without using man, and also has the power to recreate us in the totality of our being, both body and soul, as new creatures who are flesh of Jesus' flesh and bone of His bone. The text from Ephesians 5:25f. is very important for Menno's concept of the Incarnation.

The rejection of infant baptism and in general of any sacramental interpretation of baptism and the Lord's Supper as means of grace is a consequence of the Anabaptist view of grace. All through his works Menno speaks about the exclusiveness of the mediation of grace through Jesus Christ.[30]

There is no other means by which to take part in grace than faith in Jesus Christ alone. He is the only sign of grace. Therefore the fact that infants are not baptized does not mean that they fall outside of grace. For grace is the ground of man's being, even if he does not know it, at least as long as he has not consciously put himself outside of it. Because grace is prior to sin, grace is also granted to infants before they come of age. "For Jesus' sake no sin is reckoned to innocent children before they reach the age of responsibility, but life is promised them, not through any ceremonies, but out of pure grace which is provided by the blood of the Lord, as He said, 'Let the children come to me and prevent them not, for to such belongs the kingdom of Heaven.' But about baptism he has not said a word."[31] The grace of God in Christ has no need of human aid or external means; for He is sovereign and free in the demonstration of His creating love. Baptism and the Lord's Supper, however, must be celebrated out of obedience to Christ.

That grace may not be made dependent on external means, ecclesiastical offices, institutions, or actions, but must be acknowledged as the free creating love of God also appears out of the fact that the church of God is much older than the present churches. According to Menno the church has been there "from the beginning," though there have been other forms and "ordinances" from time to time. For Abel there was the sacrifice alone; from Abraham on also circumcision; from Moses on also the law; and at last Christ has come. But all, whether they have believed and hoped in Christ before the law, or under the law, or after the law, have been "one church and one body. They shall so remain eternally for they have all been saved by Christ, accepted by God, and endowed with the spirit of His grace."[32]

Thus this view of grace as the term for God's free and sovereign, creative love is an internal foundation for all sorts of typical Anabaptist views of faith which even yet pervade the whole life of faith of Doopsgezinden and Mennonites to a greater or lesser degree. The freedom of grace is reflected in the doctrine of the free Christian congregation; the creating power of grace is reflected in true repentance and the new life. Thus Menno endeavored to build his congregation, and as long as the other churches will not agree, there can be no unity. "For we desire never in all eternity to enter your churches and become one body with you until the time when true repentance and penitence will be found in you, a free Christian doctrine that is neither hired nor sold, but only compelled by the Holy Spirit through true brotherly love."[33]

The Doopsgezinde and Mennonite congregations and brotherhoods have existed now for 400 years since Menno as an independent form of Christian living. Whether they have always been justified in this independence through the retaining and developing of their fathers' great faith is a question for their conscience. We sometimes see in modern Protestant theology outside our brotherhood a notable approach to the Anabaptist view of faith. Whoever is familiar with the theology of Karl Barth, for example, knows that much has been said by him that can be seen as a correction of classic Lutheran-Calvinistic theology, and that as such can often be considered as a broad, scholarly working out of what Menno Simons, Dirk Philips, and other Anabaptists already said in the sixteenth century. This is also valid for their view of grace. One of Menno's principal works, *The Foundation Book,* begins with a chapter that bears the title, "Concerning the Time of Grace," and starting from this proclamation of grace proceeds to discuss the different aspects of faith. So one may say concerning this Anabaptist theology that it bore the character of a theology of grace.

CORNELIUS J. DYCK

Sinners and Saints

IT MAY BE SAID that most Anabaptists denied the doctrine of original sin as Augustine had defined it. Because of this the classical reformers considered them Pelagian, pointing to their rejection of sacramentalism and their emphasis on morality. This classification did not do justice to the seriousness with which Anabaptists regarded the biblical doctrines of the fall and redemption. Luther's radical rejection of the semi-Pelagianism of Roman Catholicism, however, with its corollary, the penitential system, explains his fear of any work-righteousness. Anabaptism taught a strong doctrine of grace, as the works of Alvin J. Beachy and John C. Wenger have also shown.[1] It must be admitted, however, that in their definition of grace the Anabaptists differed from the classical reformers even as Pelagius differed from Augustine.

To affirm the centrality of grace while denying the reality of original sin did not seem paradoxical to the Anabaptists. Without exception they affirmed the historical reality of original sin, but most Anabaptists denied its existential power. In the Netherlands this understandably became a primary point of discussion with their Calvinist neighbors, e.g., at Emden 1578, and Leeuwarden 1596. In these and other confrontations the Anabaptists consistently refused to discuss anthropology apart from Christology (first and second Adam). Among themselves,

87

however, they seldom mentioned original sin.[2] In his *Chronica* Sebastian Franck had anticipated much of what the Anabaptists were later to teach, though his emphasis lacked something of the Christological dimension given to the doctrine by the Anabaptists.[3] The term *original sin,* in any case, was not found in the Bible and, therefore, was unnecessary. A notable exception to this, albeit a man of the second generation, was Hans de Ries (1553-1638). The doctrine is given specific treatment in his confessions and other writings. It is significant, furthermore, that de Ries not only rejected the Augustinian view of original sin, but followed Pelagius closely in asserting the possibility of moral and ethical perfection, an infrequent emphasis among the Anabaptist-Mennonites.[4]

The first extant discussion of original sin by de Ries is contained in a letter written in 1576 to a friend, Hendrik van Berg, of Cologne.[5] De Ries had just left the Reformed Church at this time. After restating the biblical narrative of the temptation of Eve and Adam in the garden, describing this as the fall, de Ries continues:

All men, therefore, stand by nature in the place of Adam . . . [but] this Fall does not mean that man is no longer a creature of God. Rather there remained something of the nature and mark of God in man even after the Fall. . . . This lies in man, and is visible only to God who judges justly. Man knows his Creator by nature. Does not Paul speak of the fact that the heathen have no excuse? Some knowledge clearly remains in their heart though they too are under the Fall. They do have a knowledge of God's will and law. This does not mean that they are not also sinners, as Paul clearly states, but that they have a knowledge of God, of good and evil. This all men have by creation.[6]

There was definite physical corruption because of the fall. The natural goodness was marred and weakened. The penalty of death was received and continues to be the legacy for all men. The image of God, however, has not been totally lost. "The origin of the nature of man is the nature of God." To say that there "is no more light in fallen man than in a stone," as his friend did, is to confess "that the nature of God is dark and as a stone."[7] God is the Father of light! How can man, His creation, be totally dark? God is not the author of evil but of good.

How do the heathen, de Ries continued to ask, know the

law of God? Not through the spoken or written word of which they do not have access, but through this light which remained after the other gifts of God to man had been lost in the fall.[8] "Paul clearly points out that the heathen, though they do not know the written law, nevertheless have been inwardly addressed through the Spirit so that they know the law of God in their hearts (Rom. 2:14, 15)." The same could be said of the patriarchs. "The Fathers before Moses, Abel, Enoch were thus instructed of God through the inner word . . . all these believed, and were addressed, and finally saved through the witness of the unwritten Word within." Not that they were saved by the inner light, but rather that this light provided the necessary point of contact for the Holy Spirit. "Why were the people before the flood so guilty that God destroyed them? Because they knew the will of God and did not obey. How did they know it? Through the inner witness of the Spirit of God, the Word, and through the work of his hands, his creation."[9]

Through this light as channel for the Spirit, man is able to achieve virtue, reject sin, and can "by faithful obedience receive more light through the grace of God."[10] This light is the conscience of man. The conscience is dependable, even to knowing the perfect will of God; it is "God's free agent given to man to judge evil and to guide him in the good."[11] It is a tool of God. If this light were not in man he would be like the devil, said de Ries, but in giving the conscience to man God has lighted up the darkness and made His will known.[12] So much is this so that the punishment of the conscience is really the punishment of God in man (cf: the hell of the existentialist). The conscience is the image of God in his highest creation.

Thus it is clear to begin with that de Ries did not consider the fall to have radically changed the very nature of man. Original sin is not part of the essence of man. In this he stood with Roman Catholicism. For Aquinas the fall robbed man of the special gift, the *donum superadditum*, which God had bestowed on man. The loss of this *extra* limited the potential of man, but it could be restored, said Aquinas, by sacramental grace.[13] For de Ries the alternative to sacramental grace was

89

the finished work of Christ. He distinguished between the consequences of the fall and personal guilt. All people suffer death as the judgment of God on the disobedience of the human race.[14] Even children die. But they do not die because of their own sinfulness.[15] This on two counts. First, Christ, the second Adam, has restored every believer to a position similar to that before the fall with the exception of death as judgment. Second, faith so purifies that the children of Christian parents are born clean.[16] Therefore child baptism is unnecessary. It cannot be proved from the Scriptures either, he believed. Children do not need to be born again for they are the natural children of God, they have never fallen into dis-grace. God does not create little children only to prepare them for hell.[17]

It was very clear to de Ries that Christ, through His obedience and death, had freed all humanity from the stain of original sin. To deny this would be tantamount to saying that the *sin of the first Adam was stronger than the grace of the second Adam*. While in prison in 1578 de Ries wrote:

Concerning original sin or our inheritance, the seed from which sin proceeds [I have taught] that it is in all people through the relationship to Adam, but that the power of original sin, which apart from Christ leads to death, has been completely removed through the perfect obedience of our Saviour Jesus Christ. Therefore I believe and have taught that young, innocent children who are born of unbelieving parents and then die in their youth, are saved by the shed blood of Christ. They will find a merciful God and judge since original sin cannot condemn them, unless they wilfully turn against the law.[18]

This was essentially the same position as agreed on the previous year at Alkmaar, where de Ries and four other brethren had confessed that:

We confess and believe concerning original sin that Christ has freed the entire human race from the power of it, which is death. Therefore we know that no innocent children are condemned before the time when man of his own inner decision will go his own way. Therefore we confess man's rehabilitation [through Christ] to equal the Fall.[19]

We have noticed, therefore, that de Ries appeals to natural law and to the second Adam in his refutation of the power of original sin. The rational knowledge of God can move man in the right direction. Before Christ this knowledge was sufficient for salvation to those who were obedient. Since the Incarnation, however, the legacy of the first Adam can be removed only by faith in the second Adam, except with those who have not had opportunity to hear the word of God. These, he says, "are innocent and not subject to damnation."[20] Christ is able to restore fallen man to the position he held before the fall. For this to take place man must know Christ not only "according to historical knowledge"; he must "rise higher and confess Christ also according to the Spirit," receiving this new knowledge "with a believing heart."[21] The case is rested heavily on Romans 5. As in Adam all died, so in Christ all have been given the potential for life. There is no *decretum horrible*. The only requirement is faith.

A further argument by de Ries in support of the innocence of children implies a social-environmental theory of sin but is actually a literal application of the words of Jesus (Matt. 7) that a tree can be known by its fruit. Children of Christian parents are sinless because their parents are pure, said de Ries. Original sin is not physical, it is spiritual pride, and this cannot be biologically transmitted.[22] If the flesh were sinful Christ, being of the lineage of David, would also have been sinful. (In this connection de Ries refused to accept the heavenly flesh doctrine of Menno as a way out.) "Paul," he said, "nowhere speaks of physical guilt. He speaks of sin and death, not sinfulness of the soul."[23] The new birth makes all things new. The tree is no longer corrupt; how can good trees bear bad fruit?

In his further discussion de Ries spent considerable time analyzing the sinfulness of the psalmist David. What did the psalmist mean when he said, "In sin was I born, and in sin did my mother conceive me"? The answer is startling; these words reflect a low moral character on the part of King David's mother. "There is a big difference between her who conceives and that which is conceived and born." If, for example, she had been blind he could also have written truthfully that he was conceived and born in blindness. But this would not have meant that he himself was born blind.[24] Granted for a moment, however, that David's sinfulness can be proved from this passage, does this prove others' and our sin? In no way, de Ries concluded:

If a son is conceived and born of a born-again, holy, virtuous, and pure mother one can say in truth: in virtue, holiness, and purity I was conceived and born. If the child of a sinful mother is a sinner then it must also be true that the child of a Christian, virtuous mother is not a sinner but virtuous and Christian.[25]

He believed that the Scriptures nowhere taught that man is born sinful of soul, but that they do say that pure and holy people are born primarily to believing parents who have themselves been purified by Christ (1 Cor. 7).[26] The soul is the real seat of life. The body is no more than a home, the tabernacle of the soul. Therefore the soul determines whether the body shall be sinful or perfect, not vice versa. If sin in David was by birth, why did he continually ask for forgiveness?[27]

Thus de Ries concludes that (1) there is a natural knowledge of God which at one time was sufficient for salvation and even after Christ is sufficient for those who have no other knowledge of the will of God. Predestination seemed to him a complete denial of the work of Christ. (2) The loss suffered in the fall of Adam has been recovered by Christ and becomes potentially available to all, faith being the requirement. (3) Children of unbelieving parents are "saved by the shed blood of Christ" until they are old enough to sin willfully. (4) Children of believing parents are born pure and holy. At the heart of his understanding is the work of Christ and the new birth by which it is appropriated:

The new birth is an act of God worked in the soul of the truly repentant, a restoring of the image of God in man, a renewing of the mind and heart, an enlightening of reason through an acknowledgment of the truth. This new birth brings with it a transformation of the will, of carnal desires and lust, a sincere putting to death of all evil within. . . . At the same time the new birth brings an awakening of new life in God . . . it is worked in us by the Holy Spirit with his fire and power, not by any creaturely means. . . . Hereby we become children of God, spiritual-minded, righteous and holy. We believe and teach that this new birth is necessary for salvation according to the words of Christ [John 3].[28]

The possibility of a radical transformation grew out of de Ries's belief in the power of the new birth and out of his total dualistic understanding of life. A persistent dichotomy runs through his thought after the manner of Tauler and other mystics. There is an external world and an internal world, a spiritual world and a material world, an external word and an internal word, an external sacrament and an internal sacrament,

an external (historical) Christ, and an internal (spiritual) Christ.
It is clear that Dirck V. Coornhert, and particularly Caspar
Schwenckfeld, are his tutors here. It led logically, as we shall
see presently, to the assertion of the possibility of sinlessness, with
a complete rejection of the Lutheran *simul justus et peccator*.

This central emphasis on the work of Christ notwithstanding,
de Ries believed firmly in freedom of the will. To sin from
necessity is not to sin at all. Sin, he believed, is the deliberate
choice of evil where good was also present as a live option. Sin
is succumbing of the spirit to the flesh; it arises out of a perverse
will, rather than out of solidarity with Adam. "Sin is not that in
which we are born but that which we do, commit . . . *we are
children of wrath because of what we do, not because of our
parents.*"[29] It was clear to de Ries that sin was primarily action,
though there are sins of omission. Children do not sin and so
cannot be called sinners. Sin is moral, not ontological. Children
are not under the law but under grace, and where there is no
law there is no sin. De Ries continues:

All men are born with good seed and bad seed in them. Both grow
together until they make a decision. According to this decision man
then becomes a good man or a bad man. It depends upon his own
choice. . . . In Romans 7 Paul says that man strives towards the good.
Thus it appears that there can be a tendency towards good in man
without his being totally good.[30]

Sin, being moral, depends on the will of man. Though de Ries
denies the notion of depravity, he is not a resounding optimist
concerning man. The tendency may be toward the good, but
evil seeds are there, nevertheless, waiting their moment to come
forth. Whereas Augustine believed that man's will was free but
not to choose the good, and Calvin, while asserting freedom as
the basis of responsibility still held the fall to have worked a
basic defect in the will, de Ries retained the dynamic power of
the will for good or ill. But this freedom is asserted more in relation to accepting or rejecting the grace of God than in relation
to ethical choice. Those who reject the grace of God are not
free to do good consistently:

Because man was created good he had in himself the ability to hear,
accept, or reject the wrong with which he was tempted by the spirit of
evil. Thus when man fell he still had the ability, though standing in

93

this evil, to hear, accept, or reject the good which the Lord himself placed before him. Even as he was able to hear and accept the evil before the Fall, so also he is able to hear and accept the good that is before him after the Fall. This ability to accept or reject the grace of God has remained with the posterity of the first man as a gift of grace.[31]

The *justitia originalis* included that which has again been restored by Christ, the ability to hear and respond to the word of God. More recently Emil Brunner has spoken of this in terms of addressability—*Ansprechbarkeit*—as the presupposition for moral responsibility.[32] For de Ries this endowment, both before and after the fall, was not a natural endowment, but a gift of God to all men. Thus every man in his own life faces both the glory and the potential tragedy of the first Adam. "The cause of man's tragedy and damnation," wrote de Ries, "is man's free choice of darkness, of sin, and his decision to live in it."[33]

Coupled with this emphasis was de Ries's central concern for the place of the Holy Spirit. Freedom of the will is not so much antinomianism, nor simply individualism, he implies, but a freedom to let the Holy Spirit have His way. The new man in Christ, said de Ries, "lives by the love which the Holy Spirit has poured into his heart, with joy in all good works, keeping the law and virtues which God has given him through Christ." The person thus freed is as a tree planted by God himself, living for the good of all and waiting for the reward which God, in His infinite mercy, has promised.[34] This is, obviously, much more than simple humanism or naturalism.

In contrast to Pelagius, de Ries believed that Adam had not been born to die. The judgment of death which all men suffer, however, is the inevitable *consequence* of man's humanity, not a continuing *punishment* of guilt. Nevertheless, he believed the life in the Spirit more than compensated for the experience of physical death. He also differed from Pelagius in his dualism. Sin is not simply the result of natural desires, but the fruit of a scheming and enticing evil power, seeking to bring men to destruction. "Not the good God but evil man, through his free choice of sin, together with the spirit of evil within him, is the author, source, and worker of sin and evil."[35] For this reason the unrighteous shall be sent into eternal fire prepared "for the devil and his angels."[36] Nevertheless, the Pauline dualism of flesh and spirit (e.g., Rom. 7:13ff.) is largely lacking. De Ries does not seem to have tasted the depths of despair over human nature. Was he able to fathom the height of mercy and grace without this disparity?

We have seen that de Ries believed God to be offering grace equally to all without favor. One may speak of predestination only in accordance with the foreknowledge of God.[37] From time to time the ethical emphasis of de Ries seems to imply an understanding of grace as new knowledge and teaching, new insight. "Within his life and teaching he [Christ] pointed out the *law* of Christ, the *rule* of life, and the *path* to eternal life."[38] The context for all of these statements, however, is the ministry of Christ. As priest Christ "teaches, comforts, strengthens, and baptizes us with the Holy Spirit and with fire, bringing us heavenly gifts. He celebrates his spiritual Supper with believing souls. . . . In these sacraments alone is the fruit, power, and worth of his work upon the cross appropriated."[39] In the capacity of his royal office Christ rules over the hearts of the believers. He "takes them into his care, covers them with the shadow of his wings, arms them with spiritual weapons. . . ."[40] In his prophetic office Christ "preached to us the good news."[41] Revelation in the form of new knowledge is not rejected. Neither is the law of Moses. The primary focus, however, is Christ himself, supplying the fullness of the meaning of grace for de Ries. "All those who now receive this grace of God in Christ . . . are and remain the elect of God."[42] God bestows his gifts bountifully to all who by faith have come into a new relationship with him through Christ:

All the spiritual gifts and mercies which Jesus Christ won for the salvation of sinners through his own merit, we enjoy by grace through a living faith active in love. This faith is a certain heart-felt assurance or inner knowledge of God, of Christ, and other heavenly things received by grace out of the Word of God. This knowledge, together with the love of God, a hearty trust in the one, only gracious, heavenly Father who provides all our physical and spiritual needs for Christ's sake, is necessary for salvation.[43]

Men do not become righteous by merit but by grace through faith. Grace is operative in forgiveness and the new birth, strengthening the good desires in man without removing the possibility of evil choice; grace bestows the gifts of the Spirit: comfort, power, communion with God, protection, spiritual weapons; grace brings the good news to mankind. De Ries was much more optimistic about the grace of God than he was about the ability of man.

The Call to Perfection

At no point does de Ries give more emphasis to the primacy of grace than in his teaching of the doctrine of perfection, a doctrine seldom found among the Anabaptist-Mennonites. He did not arrive at this emphasis unaided. During his years of ministry he had developed a deep friendship with Dirck V. Coornhert (d. 1590), the "Sebastian Franck of the Netherlands." Coornhert's undogmatic piety and ethical sensitivity had made a profound impression upon de Ries. Consequently the latter became indebted to him at many points in his theological development. This was particularly true of his understanding of the nature of the holy life.

Following discussions on this subject between the two, Coornhert dedicated a treatise to de Ries to "supplement their mutual understanding of this truth."[44] De Ries's ready response to this doctrine led to various charges against Coornhert from Mennonite ministers. To these de Ries replied, "I will let God judge. Your judgment is hard and heavy. Do not judge before the time, said Paul. Since you are neither God nor an angel it is daring of you to judge another man as a devil."[45] De Ries's debt to Schwenckfeld at this point, though less obvious, is also implicit. Schwenckfeld was not a spirit-mystic in the same sense as de Ries, nor did he share the latter's view on original sin, but his emphasis on the newness of a man in Christ and the requirement of love find their parallels in de Ries in relation to his teaching of perfection.

The practice of church discipline has frequently earned for the Anabaptist-Mennonites the charge that they held to a justification by works doctrine. Yet few of them were actual perfectionists. It was precisely because of the constant presence of sin that discipline became, in the words of Menno, the "jewel of the church." The fact that de Ries could teach perfection while rejecting the rigorous church discipline of his contemporaries indicates that his faith was not in man, nor in any neo-Roman reliance upon merit. Though he did not share the pessimism of the classical reformers concerning the nature of man he may have been closer to Luther's emphasis on fulfilling all the law by keeping the first commandment than seems possible at first reading. Justification, the new birth, is the basis of righteousness before God in the thought of both Luther and de Ries. We know of Luther's love for the mystics, especially the *Theologia Deutsch* and Tauler. The freedom of which he speaks in his treatise on Christian liberty and the service to which this freedom leads (becoming a "little Christ" to one's neighbor) is not unrelated to the freedom and obedience emphasis we find in de Ries.

The primary sources for de Ries's thoughts on perfection are his letter to Simon Jacobs and a treatise of twenty articles written in 1583.[46] "This continues our earlier discussion," he writes to Jacobs, "as to whether a born-again person cannot fully keep the command of God, not of himself, but in the power of God and his Saviour Jesus Christ. To this you answered no, I answered yes." He then continues:

You say no one can be saved without Christ; therefore the law does not save. I answer that no man is strong enough by nature to keep the law of God. Many live against the law, in sin (Deut. 27). All have sinned against the law. Therefore none can be justified by it (Gal. 2:17). But in the new birth all receive power to live the godly life, power to keep his commandments. Thus none receive salvation because of what they do, for all have sinned (Rom. 3:9). Since even after the new birth they can never do more than the day requires (Luke 17:10), they can never store up enough to atone for past sins. These previous sins, therefore, are forgiven alone through Jesus Christ (Acts 13:39).[47]

Thus de Ries begins by clarifyng his understanding of the potential in man. Perfection could never be the work of man. The Christian who is grafted into Christ the vine, grows as a branch in all things, but "they must stay close to Christ if they would be perfect."[48] The charge against those who rejected this doctrine of perfection was not so much pessimism concerning man but that they lacked an adequate doctrine of the majesty and power of God. In this he differed from Pelagius. For the latter, though frequent appeal is made to the Scriptures, the emphasis is on man, and on the example rather than the work of Christ. Those are truly Christian who can say "I have injured no one, I have lived righteously with all."[49] This level of life comes about through strenuous effort and continual vigilance, de Ries believed.

The central argument, taken directly from Coornhert, is closely related to Kant's "I ought, therefore I can." God does not demand the impossible of his children. Man cannot be held responsible for the keeping of a law of God if he lacks the capacity to do so. Either God wants His commandments kept, and has given the ability to do this, or He does not want them kept.

God either desires that those who believe in him keep his commandments or he desires that they do not keep them. . . . If you say, as some do, that God gave his commandments in order that man may become aware of his sinfulness, you confess thereby that God does not want his commandments kept perfectly. . . . If then God wills that we do not keep his commandments perfectly but imperfectly then he who keeps them imperfectly does not sin. Or one might even say it would be sin to keep them if it is not his will that they be kept.[50]

Thus he concludes that if it is true that they were given to be kept it must also be true that this is possible. In asserting this he did not take seriously enough the demonic dimensions of all existence. "If a father should command his children or servants to do things which are actually impossible, would not everyone say that this command was useless, vain and unprofitable?"[51] To accept the impossibility of keeping these commands leads only to frustration and futility. Why should the believer, he asked, attempt the impossible? If sin is from choice, it can be avoided; if from necessity, it is not sin.

Is there anyone, de Ries asks, who has achieved perfection in this world? Yes, the Saviour himself has achieved it, not in heaven but on earth as man. Therefore, those who are completely obedient to Him become one with Him and participate in His perfection. This is what Paul meant when he said "not I, but Christ lives in me."[52] His presence provides the enabling grace. Christ is, in fact, not only in the heart of the believer by imputation, but actually present. The soul becomes His temple. Surely Christ, who on earth cleansed the temple in which He did not dwell, would not live in an impure temple of the heart.[53] Furthermore, to deny that Christ is fully able to grant complete victory over sin is to refuse His power. He is, after all, the victorious lion of the tribe of Juda; He has destroyed the kingdom of the devil. "Did Christ not overcome all his enemies?" de Ries asks. "Therefore, I confess that he is fully able to drive all evil out of the lives of those who love him and follow him, and to perfect them."[54]

This is not a form of naturalism. Little credit is given to man. Nevertheless, the prevalence of sin among all peoples, the propensity of man to choose from the point of self-interest, and the actual if not definitional bondage to which the will of man is subjected prevent us from asserting as optimistic a picture, Christo-centrism and new birth notwithstanding. This does not mean that de Ries neglected the dimension of grace as indicated in the preceding. He was closer to monergism than to synergism. He never claimed that he himself was perfect. The stress is on the power of God and the response of love. Anticipating, as it were, John Wesley of a century later, perfect love leads to, actually is, perfection.[55] "When the love of God is perfect, they [we] are able also perfectly to keep commandments, 1 John."[56] Grace, love, and obedience become the three strands in his understanding of the doctrine of perfection.

It is helpful for our understanding of de Ries to remember the spirit-mystic dimensions of all his thoughts. As a practical mystic he stands in the tradition of the Brethren of the Common Life, of Thomas a Kempis, and later of William Law.[57] With them he emphasized purity of motive (intention) and the desire to become perfectly conformed to Christ in the spirit of the *Imitation of Christ* of a Kempis. He was not content, however, as Law seems to have been, to hold perfection simply as an ideal.[58] The union between God and the believer is perfect because the perfect God initiated it and sustains the union. This perfection was to be more than a perfection of faith; it was perfect love, and so brought forth perfect obedience. In contrast to Wesley's position later that the believer is not sinless, but does not sin willfully or knowingly because of the depth of his love, an emphasis few Protestants would disagree with, de Ries asserted actual sinlessness.

Note now that the Apostle John says those who are born of God do not commit sin. He does not say that he sins but that he does not, cannot sin. John means that the new creatures keep the commandments of God in all points. You say that this means they are weak in Christ

99

and that, though they fall, Christ will not give them up (2 Cor. 3:2, 1 Peter 2:2). Is it true that there are many weak Christians who may even, and do sin. But does it follow from this that there cannot be strong Christians, youths and old people who through the power of Christ are able to do his will and keep his law? . . . Is he not strong who, through Christ, can do all things (Phil. 4:13)? Are they not strong who have fought the good fight and kept the faith . . . (2 Tim. 4:7, Rom. 8:35). Did not Paul tell us to follow him even as he followed Christ? . . . Must we assume that even the best vine brings forth thistles? No, God himself has pruned and purified it so that it bears good fruit.[59]

De Ries agrees that there are Christians who sin, but they need not if they grow up in Christ. "Children fall, but not when they have reached the [spiritual] maturity of manhood."[60] Thus he grounds the holy life in the experience of justification and sees its continuation until it reaches its fullness in the perfectly loving Christ. The person and work of Christ are held together, de Ries taking seriously not only the death of Christ but also His earthly life. The cross has set the pattern, the shape of the new life to be lived in Christ. Both the life and the resurrection of the Lord constitute the good news of salvation, the latter validating and reaffirming the witness of the former.

This does not mean that de Ries is asserting the deification of man, but rather that the Incarnation made possible already on earth the fullness of eternal life with Christ. Man does not become God but participates in the divine nature as a son and heir. This sonship is first a gift of grace, i.e., God providing both the potential and the ability to achieve this potential, in the new birth. Obedient imitation of Christ then constitutes the fulfillment of this potential. Lest we charge de Ries with simple moralism, however, it must be remembered that he was in some sense a Christ-mystic, experiencing the inner presence of Christ so keenly that this awareness became the new reality for him to the exclusion of the evil inherent in externals.

Did de Ries overstate the spiritual capacity arising out of conversion? Is not the belief that man can achieve sinlessness the very epitome of spiritual pride? Did his error lie in taking the promises of God too literally? From the standpoint of western theology de Ries did not take seriously enough the demonic legacy of the fall; he was too logical in drawing conclusions from the requirements of the law of God. His dualism prevented him from seeing the necessity of a *both/and* position (i.e., to be a sinner and to be justified both together) and led him to a categorical *either/or*. Salvation for de Ries, nevertheless, was not a forensic *paper* transaction, but a dying with Christ in order to live with Him in daily intimate discipleship. That forgiveness is not a daily requirement, as he implies, is difficult to reconcile with Pauline Christianity, but de Ries would have found ample support for this in the church of the third century. As a spirit-mystic he was not aware, as modern man is, of the dimension of anxiety and sin in existence itself. That his emphasis upon perfection also arose, in part, as a reaction against the Calvinistic pessimism concerning man is clear from his writings. His early training in that tradition and the dominance of Calvinism in the Netherlands prodded him to emphasize the other dimension of the relationship between God and man.

De Ries's indebtedness to Johannine theology has become obvious. He does quote from the Gospel and Epistles of John frequently. He does not, however, use the classic passages of 1 John 1:8, 10 and 1 John 2:4 excessively as proof texts. The references to Paul exceed those to John: the power of love (Romans and Corinthians), the victory of Christ (Romans, Ephesians, Philippians, Timothy), the cleansing, forgiving power of Christ (1 Corinthians). Hebrews, the Psalms, and the Synoptics are also used. The Book of Judith is referred to once parenthetically and Esdras is rejected as evidence against perfection as his friend had sought to make it. De Ries is not aware of a conflict between the Apostle Paul and the writer of the fourth Gospel and the Epistles. The message is basically one.

The seriousness with which de Ries gave himself to this doctrine of perfection is seen in his own life. Irenic beyond anything the Mennonites had thus far witnessed in a leader, he had few enemies. Even Nittert Obbesz was won eventually. De Ries drew his sanction for the doctrine of perfection out of his own experience with the living Christ. His concern for unity through love grew out of this image of the potential Christ held for the corporate life of the believers. His was a tremendous vision for the church, but love rather than discipline by coercion was to be the instrument of God.

It is understandable also that he had no desire for debates. Though the great debates of Emden, 1578, and Leeuwarden, 1596, were held near his own home, he did not attend them. A friend who did confirmed de Ries's feelings when he wrote, "No fruit will come from these discussions."[61] His humility and patience in the face of division and strife is heart-warming. He had desired to lead a quiet life of seclusion, but was inevitably drawn into the midst of the problems of the church. Thus he did not seek perfection through withdrawal (monasticism). He believed that life becomes holy as it is lived in union with Christ, becoming perfect in love and obedience by the grace of God. For man to benefit from the Incarnation and the Atonement he must become one with Christ through the operation of the Holy Spirit.

ROSELLA REIMER DUERKSEN

Dutch Anabaptist Hymnody
of the Sixteenth Century

ONE OF THE MOST significant pillars of the sixteenth century
Reformation movement was the simple, tuneful hymn. Luther
had taken the position that, after the word of God, "only
music deserves to be praised as the mistress and governess of
emotions of the human heart . . . [and] out of consideration
for this power of music the Fathers and Prophets willed . . .
that nothing be more closely bound up with the Word of God
than music."[1] Second only to its spiritual significance, Luther
had placed the didactic value of the hymn. By teaching the
people to sing the truths of the Christian faith in an easily remembered form, he had reasoned, both the understanding and
the retention would be deeply enhanced. Thus Luther and
his co-workers had set about to provide a body of material for
use within the new, rapidly growing movement.

Anabaptist reformers, at first reluctant to allow or endorse
the use of the hymn in the service, were, nevertheless, soon
caught up in the momentum of the influence of the popular religious song. Thus there exists today a considerable body of
both German and Dutch Anabaptist hymnody of great significance in the evaluation of this movement.

103

ROSELLA R. DUERKSEN

The Earliest Hymnbook Publications of the Dutch Anabaptists

While German chorales produced by the followers of Luther and the metrical Psalm versions produced by the followers of Calvin spread rapidly to all parts of the continent, the German hymns of the Anabaptists appear to have remained largely unknown to their contemporaries. Sixteenth century German Anabaptist hymnbooks available today verify that very few hymns of Anabaptist authorship found their way into non-Anabaptist hymnbooks. Among the Dutch, however, there is significant evidence of the intermingling of Anabaptist and non-Anabaptist hymnody, and distinct lines are not always evident between Anabaptist and non-Anabaptist publications. This problem exists because many early Dutch hymnbooks, devoted mainly to the printing of martyr hymns, embraced hymns eulogizing members of a variety of sects. It exists also because the allegiance of many folk changed with the tide of the Reformation. The majority of Dutch martyrs before 1530, for example, belonged to the Sacramentarians, a group which had arisen under the influence of Johan Wessel Gansfort, Hoen, Zwingli, and others, and was distinguished by the rejection of the sacraments of the Roman Catholic Church in favor of Hoen's symbolic conception of the Eucharist. After 1531 the influence of the Anabaptists superseded the former, and they, in turn, suffered more extreme persecution and martyrdom.

A study of Dutch Anabaptist hymnody thus requires a consideration of at least one non-Anabaptist source. This is a book with the title *Veelderhande Liedekes gemaeckt wt den ouden ende nieuwen Testamente nv derdewerf gecorrigeert en meer ander doer by gheset en op den A B C by den andern gheuoecht* (Many hymns based on the Old and New Testaments, now printed for the third time, corrected, enlarged, and alphabetically arranged), printed by Magnus van den Merberghe van Osterhout in 1556. The date of publication appeared on the title page. The book contained 216 songs. Since the title of this book specifically suggested that this was the third edition of this particular work, F. C. Wieder, who has prepared an extensive bibliography of Protestant Dutch hymnbooks containing hymns written before 1566, suggests that the first two editions of this book probably appeared in 1554 and 1555 respectively.[2] This book, believed to have been of Sacramentarian origin, nevertheless incorporated a large number of hymns identified today as Anabaptist. Non-Anabaptist publications with a similar title and similar contents appeared also in 1558 and 1563.

In 1566 there appeared another book with a similar title: *Veelderhande Liedekens gemaect wt den Ouden ende Nieuwen Testamente die voortijts in druck zijn wtgegaen: Waer toe noch veel Liedekens ghestelt zijn die noyt in druck geweest en hebben ende zijn in ordininge van den A. B. C. by den andern gevoecht* (. . . which have been previously printed: Added to these are many hymns not previously printed, arranged alphabetically with the former). According to Wieder, this book, published by Nicolasen Biestkens, is the oldest extant publication of the *Veelderhande Liedekens* by the Dutch Anabaptists.[3] Of its 289 hymns, many appear to have been taken directly from the *Veelderhande Liedekes* of 1556. The preface, too, is identical with that of the previous publication. There is also strong evidence that this Dutch Anabaptist publication had two previous editions: the first on May 28, 1560, and second on February 19, 1562.[4] Neither of the earlier books is now extant, but if these books actually existed, they would indicate that the Dutch were the first among the Anabaptists to publish their hymnody.

The continued use and popularity of the *Veelderhande Liedekens* is evidenced by the fact that there were many subsequent editions in the sixteenth century. A fourth edition, probably also by Biestkens, appears to have been published in 1566. Later editions, sometimes with minor changes, appeared in 1569, 1575, 1577, 1579 (two editions), 1580, and 1582 (three editions). It is likely that seven editions (including the first two no longer extant) were printed by Biestkens. On three title pages there occurs the suggestion that the publication is based on one by Biestkens. Among the hymns in this collection is one attributed to Menno Simons, *Mijn God waer sal ic henen gaen*. Although the author is not mentioned in the publication, Menno is elsewhere credited with writing the hymn, perhaps in 1540.[5]

As suggested in the title, the hymns of this book were arranged not by subject matter, but alphabetically by the first word. Many are martyr songs. A large number are didactic pieces admonishing the brethren to be true and courageous in their belief. Some are pleas and warnings to the non-Christian. A great many are devotional, praising God and praying for His continued guidance and strength. Others are paraphrased directly from Old and New Testament passages.

Evidence for the wide use of these hymns among both Dutch and other Anabaptist groups lies not only in the surprising number of editions, but also in the fact that translations of eight hymns were printed in the German Anabaptist book *Ein schön Gesangbüchlein Geistlicher Lieder* (beautiful hymnbook of spiritual songs). The preface of the Dutch book, exhorting the singer that the hymn must come from the heart and not from the mouth alone, was further directly translated and printed in the German book.

A second collection of hymns of major importance to the study of Dutch Anabaptist hymnody is one which first appeared in 1562 with the title *Een nieu Liedenboeck van alle nieuwe ghedichte Liedekens die noyt in druck en zijn ghe weest ghemaect wt den Ouden ende Nieuwen Testamente nv eerst by den anderen vergadert ende nieus in Druck ghebracht* (A new hymnbook of all newly composed hymns from the Old and New Testaments, not previously printed, together with others, now first collected and printed in a new volume). Because this collection had no hymns in common with the above-mentioned *Veelderhande Liedekens* of 1566, and because the preface specifically stated that the publication of this book was in preparation while an earlier book went through two editions in 1560 and 1562, it is reasonable to assume that the present book was intended as the second of a two-volume series of which the *Veelderhande Liedekens* served as the first. The hymns of this book were reprinted in 1582 under the title *Het tweede Liedeboeck va vele diuersche Liedekens ghemaect wt den ouden ende nieuwen Testamente Waer of sommighe eertryts in Druck zijn wtghegan ende sommige noyt in Druck gheweest hebbende daer by gheuoecht.* (The second hymnbook of many varied hymns composed from the Old and New Testaments, some of which are already in print and some of which have not previously appeared in print), the second of a series in which the 1582 publication of *Veelderhande Liedekens* was apparently the first. The hymns of both *Een nieu Liedenboeck* and *Het tweede Liedeboeck* also appeared in a publication of 1569 entitled *Veelderhande liedekens ghemaeckt wt den Ouden ende Nieuwen Testament wtgelsen en vergadert wt verschegden copien Oock zijn hier by geuoecht veel niewe Liedekens va verscheyde Historien des oude testaments met veel andre die noyte in druc en zijn geweest en zijn in ordeninge vande A. B. C. gestelt.* (Many hymns based on the Old and New Testaments edited and gathered from various sources; also added here are many new hymns based on various stories of the Old Testament, as well as many others which have not appeared in print—all are listed in alphabetical order.)

In general the hymns of this second major collection remain anonymous; the writers or individuals eulogized are in some cases identified when the hymns appear in other sources (see below, p. 108). Most of the hymns are occasional, lamenting the persecutions which the children of God are undergoing. Consolation is sought in the Scripture; complete faith in God is expressed again and again. But in at least two respects the hymns differ greatly from those of the German and Swiss Anabaptists: (1) They are less concerned with purely Anabaptist doctrine; and (2) they are not joyful songs, but *Klagelieder* (lamentations). The book is filled with outbursts of protests against the unrelenting persecutions; there is no evidence of a desire for physical retaliation, however. Several times passages from the Psalms are paraphrased; three times the Lord's Prayer serves as the basis of a hymn. Many times there occur admonitions to fellow Christians not to lose the faith in spite of persecutions and martyrdoms; sometimes there occur admonitions to the persecutors not to spill innocent blood, for God will surely try them in turn. Running through all the hymns is the belief that those who renounce the way of the world will enjoy the blessing of the cross. Persecution and martyrdom are not too great a price to pay for an eternal fellowship with God.

The emphasis on the martyr hymn reached its height among the Dutch Anabaptists in an interesting hymnbook which appeared as the second part of *Het Offer des Heeren*, first published in 1562-63, also by Biestkens. This second part had the following title: *Een Lietboecxke tracterende van den Offer des Heeren int welche oude en nieuwe Liedekens wt verscheyde Copien vergadert zijn, om by het Offerboeck gheuoecht to worden, want het van eender materien roert, also van verraden, vanghen ende dooden, aengaende der Slachtschaepkens Christi, die de stemme haers Herders Jesu Christi getrouwelijck gehoorsaem zijn gheweest tot der doodt toe* (A songbook concerned with sacrifice to the Lord, for which old and new songs have been collected out of the various sources in order to be added to the *Offerboeck*, relating the stories of the betrayal, capture, and martyrdom of the lambs of Christ, who have been loyally obedient to the voice of their Shepherd Jesus until their death). With the exception of the first, all twenty-five hymns in this collection tell the stories of martyrdoms occurring in the Netherlands from 1546 to 1561. The first hymn is apparently intended as an introduction to the Anabaptist martyrology, for it tells the story of the crucifixion of Christ, placing Christ at the head of all Anabaptist martyrs. As the title of the book indicates, the hymns were collected from various sources and were perhaps, in the opinion of the editor, the most significant of the circulating martyr ballads. Eleven of these twenty-five hymns were printed also in *Een nieu Liedenboeck* of 1562; five appear also in the *Veelderhande Liedekens* of 1566 (and presumably also in its 1560 and 1562 editions); for the remainder this is its earliest known source. One appeared later in a German translation in the *Ausbund*. *Een Lietboecxken*, as part of the complete *Het Offer des Heeren*, enjoyed many subsequent editions: in 1566, 1567, 1570, 1578 (two editions), 1580, 1590, 1591, 1595, and 1611. A number of the hymns appeared also in a variety of other hymnbooks, some non-Anabaptist. In the seventeenth century, however, the popularity of the martyr hymn waned, and these hymns were gradually dropped from new publications.

In its 1570 edition, the first part of *Het Offer des Heeren* was greatly enlarged with the addition of twenty-nine hymns correlated with the letters and confessions of Anabaptist martyrs it had previously contained. Thirty-one martyrs were repre-

108

sented in the first part; thus, with two exceptions, there was a hymn based on the story of each martyr. In two instances, the hymns combined two martyr accounts. Ten of these hymns appeared also in the first section of the *Ausbund,* and were probably printed there in a German translation at approximately the same time as their printing in the original Dutch. Later editions of *Het Offer des Heeren* added several more hymns.

Although none of the original manuscripts of this long list of martyr hymns has been preserved, it seems logical to conjecture that most of those in *Een Lietboecxken* were written very soon after the time of the martyrdom with which they are concerned. Perhaps the martyr hymn was used in the funeral or memorial service of the victim. This would indicate that the hymn was written within a day or two after the martyr's death. The major part of some of the martyr hymns may have been composed by the victim himself while still in prison. On his execution, a friend may have added the concluding stanzas depicting his death.

Two other books appear to have been printed for use among the Dutch Anabaptists during the latter part of the sixteenth century. The first of these, edited by Hans de Ries and first printed in Rotterdam in 1582 was entitled, *Lietboeck, inhoudende Schriftuerlijcke Vermaen Liederen, Claech Liederen, Gebeden, Danck Liederen, Lofsanghen, Psalmen ende ander stichtelijcke Liederen, de welcke gheoeffent ende ghesongen worden onder de medeleden der Ghemeenten Christi* (Hymnbook, consisting of hymns of scriptural exhortation, lamentation, prayer, thanksgiving, praise, Psalms, and other miscellaneous hymns, some of which have been introduced and sung by the fellowship of the Church of Christ). The second, edited by German-born Lenaert Klock, appeared in 1593 with the title *Veelderhande Schriftuerlijdke Nieuwe Liedekens, Vermaningen Leeringen gebeden, ende Lofsangen, Die sommighe eertijts by partijen in Druck wt gegaen, ende nu wederom t'samen by een vergadert, met noch vele die noyt gedruct en waren, nu op die Lettern vanden A. B. C. ende in een ordentlich Register by malcanderen vergadert* (Many new hymns based on the Holy Scripture, including exhortation, teaching, prayer, and praise, the majority of which have been printed separately earlier, together with many not previously printed, now collected and arranged alphabetically and furnished with an index).

The Hans de Ries *Lietboek* enjoyed subsequent editions in 1604 and 1618. That these books were not intended to include only hymns of Anabaptist origin is evidenced by the fact that the 1618 edition contained many metrical Psalms of Peter Dathenus. The hymnbook edited by Klock seems to have been widely used in the seventeenth century in spite of the fact that Klock became separated from the Dutch Anabaptists as the result of a difference of opinion regarding the enforcement of the ban. A greatly enlarged edition of his hymnbook appeared in 1625 and was known as *Het groote Liedboeck* (The large hymnbook). Ten years later Klock also edited *Het Klein Liedboeck* (The small hymnbook).

Dutch Anabaptist Hymn Tunes

A study of melodies adopted by Dutch Anabaptists for their hymnody shows a close parallel to the process in which other Reformation bodies assimilated melodic material for use within the church. It was not practical or possible, for example, for Luther and his co-workers to use original melodies with all of the vernacular hymns being used in the service. Instead, it was considered desirable to use many tunes already familiar to the congregations. These came from three major sources: (1) the liturgical hymns of the Roman Catholic Church, (2) the pre-Reformation German sacred songs, and (3) the secular folk-songs. To these were added some original tunes.

Early Anabaptist hymnody made use of all the above tune sources, leaning most heavily on the secular folk-song tunes, and adding a further source—the original or borrowed tunes already popularized within the Lutheran and Calvinistic movements. Unfortunately, however, none of the Anabaptist hymnbooks contained the printed tunes to which their texts were sung. All hymns merely carried headnotes designating the first line of a tune, or tunes (many carried alternate suggestions), to which the text might be sung. While this fact makes it impossible to determine the exact nature in which the tunes were adapted to the text, it does, however, give us a basic insight into the melodic material which served as common property among the majority of the folk of this era.

A representative view of melodies used within Dutch Anabaptism may be obtained by observing the tunes suggested for
use with hymns appearing in *Het Offer des Herren,* both of
Een Lietboecxken, containing songs from various earlier sources,
and of the twenty-nine songs added to the first part of the
book in 1570. For the twenty-five hymns of *Een Lietboecxken,*
there are twenty-one different tune indications; twelve of these
fall into the general classification of earlier Reformation hymns,
nine into the category of the secular song. The first extant
sources for many of the earlier Reformation hymn titles are
either the *Veelderhande Liedekes* of 1556 or *Een nieu Liedenboeck,* first printed in 1562. Very likely these hymns circulated
in manuscript form long before they appeared in published
form, and both the texts and the tunes became widely known.

Each of the secular tunes can be identified as one popular
in the Netherlands during the sixteenth century, some originated centuries earlier. In many cases the Anabaptists were
not the first to adapt them for sacred usage; a large number,
for instance, had appeared in the Antwerp hymnal of 1540
bearing the title *Souter Liedekens Ghemaect ter eeren Gods op
alle de Psalmen va David.* One hundred fifty-eight monophonic
Psalm tunes, taken mainly from contemporary folk melodies,
had been printed in this book. With each melody had been
indicated the original secular text.

Dutch folk tunes, and through them Dutch hymn tunes,
shared many characteristics popularized by the German *Minne-
singer* and *Meistersinger* movements: among these the most
prominent were the use of the AAB (German Bar) form, and
the predominance of the Dorian, Aeolian, and Ionian modes
(all other modes were encountered, but to a lesser degree).
On the other hand, Dutch secular tunes tended to be of a more
florid nature than those of German origin. This was often
reflected in the text of the sacred as well as the secular song,
for the number of metrical feet per line often varied from one
strophe to another of a single hymn. In contrast, the form
of the strophe of a German hymn tended to be more stable.
In the singing of the Dutch hymn, single notes of the tune
were very likely repeated or a series of notes slurred in accordance

111

with the demands of the text. Melodies tended to be more free, less diatonic, and with more and greater melodic skips than in German tunes.

One hymn tune suggestion occurs in *Een Lietboecxken* which cannot be placed in either of the two above categories. This is the tune *Crux fidelis inter omnes,* which serves as the basis for the opening hymn of the martyr collection and relates the passion of Christ. It is significant that a hymn based on this subject was here linked to an old liturgical Latin hymn, just as, among the German Anabaptists, several passion hymns were linked with *Pange lingua.*

A significant change occurs in the type of tune suggestion printed with the twenty-nine hymns added to the first section of *Het Offer des Heeren* in the 1570 edition. In addition to the two main types of tune suggestions found in *Een Lietboecxken,* there is now a third type: the Psalm tune. Twelve of the twenty-nine hymns carry with them the indication that they are to be sung to Psalm tunes. This Psalm tune is generally supplemented, however, by the name of a secular tune. Investigation shows that, in the majority of instances, the Psalm and the secular tune had been linked in the 1540 publication of *Souter Liedekens.* The tune indication for the first of the twenty-nine songs, for example, reads: *Na de wyse: Von den eersten Psalm, Oft het was een Clerecken het ginck ter scholen;* the first Psalm of the *Souter Liedekens* was sung to this secular tune. Thus it is evident that at the time of the publication of the 1570 edition of *Het Offer des Heeren,* the Dutch Anabaptists were well acquainted with the Psalms of the *Souter Liedekens.* Why no Psalm tunes appear as melodic suggestions in *Een Lietboecxken* is not known. Although the singing of Psalms was given great impetus by the appearance of two versions of the entire Book of Psalms in 1566—one by Johannes Uitenhove and the other by Peter Dathenus—there seems little reason to believe that it was during this time that the *Souter Liedekens* first became popular among the Anabaptists, for these Psalms were largely replaced by the newer versions after 1566.

Six of the melodic suggestions made in *Een Lietboecxken* are repeated in the first part of *Het Offer des Heeren.* In addition to these and the secular tunes and their Psalm tune companions, there are again melodic indications making reference to earlier vernacular Reformation hymns, two of them German.

While the above-named hymn tunes are generally representative of those employed in Dutch Anabaptist hymnody, it should be noted that several Dutch hymnbooks incorporated tunes from a source not previously encountered—the French folk song. In the *Veelderhande Liedekens,* the oldest extant Anabaptist publication of which dates from 1566, there appear eight French tune suggestions. In *Een nieu Liedenboeck* and *Het tweede Liedeboeck* there appear seven French titles. The use of French folk tunes would seem to indicate that some songs in these collections originated in the southern part of Holland, where the folk were exposed to, and familiar with, the secular tunes of another linguistic group. The use of French words in some of these Anabaptist hymns further serves to illustrate that there was little attempt to retain a nationalistic or linguistic purity, but that language and melody were freely and indiscriminately borrowed. The French tunes adopted for use in Dutch Anabaptist hymnody are, generally speaking, also those encountered in French psalmody.

Whether or not any hymn tunes originated within the Dutch Anabaptist movement itself cannot be conclusively shown. While there are some tune indications that cannot be identified with any known sacred or secular tunes, it is not clear whether these were newly composed tunes, traditional secular tunes in which the sacred title had replaced the secular through long usage, tunes popular in the sixteenth century but now lost, or actually original melodies. No sixteenth century melody today extant has been proved to be of Anabaptist origin.

Stylistic Characteristics of the Hymns

The complete reliance of Anabaptist hymn writers on well-known contemporary tunes for the singing of their texts was coupled with an equally strong reliance on the stylistic patterns of the secular and sacred texts which their own writings sought to displace. It is doubtful that creative originality was ever a concern; rather, it would appear that the Anabaptist hymn writer consciously molded his strophe to fit the form of a familiar song (or songs), the tune of which was to be used for his text.   Thus it was the popular folk song which most often served as the immediate pattern for the Anabaptist hymn.

As in the sixteenth century folk song, the eight-line strophe was more frequently employed than any other in Dutch Anabaptist hymnody.   In *Een Lietboecxken,* for example, twelve of the twenty-five hymns follow this pattern.   Rhyme schemes within this group are somewhat varied; the most popular form is *ababcdcd,* employed for five of the hymns.   Other hymns employ the same pattern in the first quatrain, but vary the pattern of the second, producing the following schemes: *ababccdd, ab005bccb, ababbbab, and ababbcbc.*   As a whole, rhyme patterns are closely adhered to at the expense of natural word order and rhythm.   Iambic meter is generally employed, but the number of syllables per line varies greatly within the corresponding lines of the stanzas of a single hymn.   This freedom has already been noted in conjunction with the form of Dutch tunes.   Perhaps it is an indication that the rigidity of the Meistersinger forms had far less influence in shaping the pattern of the folk song of the Low Countries than of the German provinces.

Other strophic forms used were likewise those encountered in the folk song.   Three hymns are based on a strophic pattern of seven lines per stanza, with the rhyme schemes all slightly different: *ababccd, ababccc,* and *ababccb.*   Three hymns employ a form of six lines per stanza, with varied rhyme schemes: *abbbbb, abaaab,* and *aababb.*   Two hymns have strophic forms consisting of nine lines, with rhyme schemes both reading *ababcdccd,* and two hymns consist of four-line strophic forms, both with the alternating rhyme scheme *abab.*   A ten-line form, a five-line form, and a fifteen-line form are used once each.

Although the hymns of the first section of *Het Offer des Heeren* employ basically the same strophic forms, the four-line stanza here plays a more significant role.   This change was effected by the use of the Psalm tune, the metrical Psalm being most frequently cast in a four-line strophe with alternating rhyme scheme.

The linguistic instability of the period is evident in the hymns of the Dutch Anabaptists, as in most printed matter of this era.   Within any one book, a single word may appear with several different spellings, indicating that no standardization has been reached. Thus one finds *nieu* and *nieuw* (new), daer and daar (The *ae* combination is now obsolete), *wtgheloghen, uitgetoghen,* and *yutghetogen* (gone out), as well as many other inconsistencies.

The vocabulary, too, frequently appears today unpoetic and uncouth; one notes, for example, the incorporation of expressions now considered profane, or, at least, highly inappropriate for the worship service. It is, likewise, not uncommon to find words coined from the French language included in the Dutch phrase.

Both the opening and the concluding lines of Dutch Anabaptist hymns often clearly indicate the influence of antecedent secular ballads. In eight hymns of *Het tweede Liedeboeck,* for example, the poet begins with the popular folk song plea or command, "Hear ye," "Hear ye, brethren," or "Hear, friends." As in the folk song, too, the Anabaptist poet often becomes highly personal in the concluding stanzas of his hymn, sometimes giving his name, at other times at least hinting at his personal position or status, or the circumstances under which the text came to be written. Hymn No. 25 in *Een Lietboecxken,* for example, concludes with these lines:

Die dit Liedeken heeft ghedichtet
Jan Schut was hy ghenaemt

The author of a hymn in *Het tweede Liedeboeck* (p. 88) concludes in the following manner:

Die dit Liedeken eerst stelde
Die was in banden tot Ghent.

Many similar expressions could be noted. Sometimes a concluding stanza or stanzas naming the author appear to have been attached to a hymn after the writer's death.

Acrostic Verse in Anabaptist Hymnody

Writing in acrostic verse was a highly popular technique among all Anabaptist poets of the sixteenth century. This form of verse was by no means new, however; it had been used in the original Hebrew of twelve Old Testament Psalms. It was popular also among early Greek writers, as well as among monks of the Middle Ages. French poets from the time of Francis I (1494-1547) to Louis XIV (1638-1715) frequently employed this verse form, as did also writers in England, Sir John Davies (1565-1618) being the most prominent and prolific example.

Acrostic verse was, in general, so arranged that the initial letters of consecutive lines would spell out some name, title, or phrase, or follow the order of the alphabet. Anabaptist hymn writers frequently formed acrostics denoting the name of the poet; generally, however, the name was not formed from the initial letters of consecutive lines, but from the initial letters of consecutive stanzas. The authors of several hymns in *Het tweede Liedeboeck* can thus be identified: *Aensiet o Heer onsen strijt groot* (p. 69) spells the name *ANTONETTE LIEVENS* in acrostics; *Jubileert met vruechden te samen* (p. 78) spells out *JOEST JACOPS* in the same manner.

A number of hymns in *Veelderhande Liedekens* also bear acrostics: *Ghy Broeders al tesamen* (p. 104) forms the name *GISBERT DIRCUSOEN; Ich ben seer bedroeft in herte mijn* (p. 142) gives the name *JOEST JACAPSSOEN* (It is possible that the author here is the same individual who wrote the above hymn, spelling out *JOEST JACOPS*); another five-stanza hymn reads merely *JOEST* (p. 143) and is perhaps by the same author; the hymn *Met Menschelijcke tongen niet* (p. 200) bears the acrostic *MARRI TIENE*; and *Mijn siele verhuecht haer in dem heer* (p. 201) gives us the name *MACHIEL DEUNK*. In several other hymns there appear to have been acrostic forms which are now so badly disrupted that the names can no longer be distinguished.

The Pattern of the Martyr Ballad

For more than half a century after Martin Luther in 1523 commemorated the martyrdom of two Augustian monks at Brussels with his song, *Ein neues Lied wir heben an,* the martyr ballad continued as a highly popular means of eulogizing those who had sacrificed their lives for the sake of their religion; and Anabaptist writers produced an enormous volume of this form of hymn. It would appear that these Anabaptist hymns of persecution were largely modeled after a basic outline or skeleton, and that the individual writer merely filled in the unique details of each specific martyrdom. Undoubtedly this was the result of an unconscious, rather than a conscious, dependence on a given type.

The Anabaptist martyr hymn generally commences with a very brief introduction. Sometimes this consists of a one-line plea for attention, sometimes it is a one-or-more-line expression of the author's sorrow or joy, and at times it may be a prayer for strength or mercy, or an affirmation of faith. In this introduction there is almost always a subjective reference which may or may not be linked to the martyr story.

The introductory statements of Dutch martyr hymns most often set the mood of the sadness and lament characteristic of all Dutch hymns. Illustrative of this are phrases such as the following:

> O Godt ich moet v clagen
> Mijns hertzen droeuich leyt.
> (*Een Liedtboecxken,* No. 9, stanza 1)

> In bitterheyt der sielen
> Clage ich dit immer groot.
> (*Een Liedtboecxken,* No. 11, stanza 1)

At times the introduction is completely omitted, and the author plunges immediately into his sorrowful tale. Places and names involved in the tragedy are always given at the outset. After this the procedure is chronological, often with a brief description of the capture and imprisonment of the Anabaptist victim, followed by an account of his trial. Greatest length is usually devoted to issues forwarded at the trial and basic Anabaptist doctrine is defended. A brief statement then defines the sentencing, followed by a description of the execution itself. In some hymns this is quite brief; in others, the execution is presented in vivid detail.

Most martyr hymns give evidence of having been written by witnesses to the executions. Some hymn texts suggest that they were begun by the victims themselves while in prison awaiting execution and later concluded by witnesses to the fatal torture. All are filled with a deep sympathy for the victim.

117

From a survey of Dutch Anabaptist hymns it seems evident that their worth does not lie in originality, in excellence of rhyme and rhythm, or in beauty of language. In all these areas they fall far short of the standard of the best contemporary hymns. The lack of excellence in these characteristics is lamentable, but it by no means renders the hymns worthless or insignificant; for they present an invaluable insight into the cultural and musical standard of the average folk of the sixteenth century. But more important still, they are historical documents which express the convictions and sufferings of a significant segment of the Reformation movement. Doing this, they speak with great depth and force against those who would reduce the core of the Anabaptist movement to one of rebellious fanaticism.

HENDRIK W. MEIHUIZEN

Dutch Painters in the Time of Vondel and Rembrandt

WE MUST GUARD against drawing wrong conclusions from the fact that painters did not arise among the Anabaptists in the Lowlands until one hundred years after the founding of the first congregations. This lack of artistic expression was not due to a deliberate subordination of the arts among them, nor to the sobriety frequently attributed to them. The primary cause lay in the unfavorable religious climate of the sixteenth century. Though the Anabaptists felt inwardly compelled to share their talents for the enrichment of others, the spirit of the times made this impossible.

The period was one of unrest in the Netherlands, particularly for the Anabaptist-Mennonites. Living from day to day without security, a people on the move, they had little time or inclination even to decorate their walls with simple portraits or biblical paintings. The possession of portraits became a danger in itself. It follows, therefore, that the portraits of the early Anabaptists were prepared primarily by their enemies rather than by painters from within the group. With the decline of persecution in the late sixteenth century a new interest in portrait painting became apparent. Unfortunately, however, the Mennonites were not yet wealthy enough to permit the pursuit of this interest.

The seventeenth century did not greatly change the attitudes

119

toward the Mennonites, though it was eventually to become the century of tolerance. Mennonite artists would have found little recognition beyond their own circles. Roman Catholics and Calvinists inevitably looked upon the Mennonites with suspicion, frequently identifying them with the Münsterites. No good could come from such a movement. Perhaps these Anabaptist paintings would even mislead unwary admirers to accept the perverted biblical interpretations of the group. Beyond this, the Mennonite artists would hardly have fulfilled the doctrinal expectations of their fellow citizens—the Roman Catholics in their understanding of the fall, the Reformed in their interpretation of David and Bathsheba, or of Susanna and other apocryphal episodes.[1] Mennonite conclusions on reading the account of the fall would most certainly have been considered heretical by the other groups. David and Bathsheba and Susanna were not considered kindly by the strict Mennonite fathers themselves and a Mennonite artist, therefore, had no desire to bring their wrath upon himself by shocking them with his painting.[2]

With the coming of the twelve-year truce (1609-1621) in the Eighty Years War against Spain and in anticipation of continuing peace, the first paintings began to appear among the Mennonites. For a time they simply decorated the walls of homes and occasionally of churches, but the possibility of their being appreciated elsewhere now also existed. It is interesting to note that the earliest works to be discussed in the following pages fall precisely into this period.

The *Nieuwendijk* of Amsterdam seems to have held a particular attraction for the Mennonites of that city. The congregation, usually known as the Waterlanders, though it also contained many High Germans and moderate Frisians, met in a church near the *Jan Rodenpoortstoren* on the *Nieuwendijk*. Hans de Ries and Lubbert Gerrits left their spiritual imprint on this congregation.[3] The Mennonites who settled on the *Nieuwendijk* came primarily from Hoorn.[4] The spirit of Lubbert Gerrits, who died on January 12, 1612, continued to work among them, especially in those homes neighboring on the one which carried the sign of the Red Lion.

The influence of the broad-minded Gerrits on the congregation of which he was the elder can hardly be overestimated. He could already look back on an eventful life when he settled in Amsterdam in 1589. He did not play a major role at the unpleasant Harlingen meeting which was followed by the schism between the Frisians and the Flemish. It must have troubled him, however, to be in disagreement with Dirk Philips, the man who had ordained him to the ministry. From this dispute he had learned that the stubborn attitude of those who held their congregation to be the only true one led to despair. He became convinced that minor issues were the primary causes of divisions among the Mennonites. In a poem subsequently written by him he prays God to give his people "love in place of hate" and to grant to him, Lubbert Gerrits, strength "to end division."[5] This yearning for peace earned him the hatred of those members of his congregation who sought to place him under the ban in 1589, following the lead of Thijs Gerrits. Thereupon he moved to Amsterdam, where he was able to unite the High Germans with the moderate Frisians (also known as Lubbert Gerrits folk) on the basis provided by the Concept of Cologne.[6]

Lubbert Gerrits was the grandfather of Lambert Jacobsz, the first painter to manifest deep Mennonite convictions.[7] Jacobsz was most likely born in 1598, probably in a house on the *Nieuwendijk*. He died June 27, 1636. His father, Jacob Theunisz or Tonysen, though originally from Leer, won citizen status in Amsterdam on April 9, 1592, as a textile merchant. His marriage two days later to Pietertjen, the daughter of Lubbert Gerrits, undoubtedly strengthened the devotion to his father-in-law as elder of the congregation. In any case, when Joost van den Vondel declared himself unable to serve as deacon of the congregation in 1620 because of his emotional depressions, Jacob Theunisz declared himself ready to fill this post "for the sake of love." It is difficult to determine whether he did this out of love for the congregation or for his friend Vondel, who was a frequent guest at his house. It may be assumed that he was baptized by Lubbert Gerrits. On the occasion of the wedding of Lambert Jacobsz with Aeghtgen Anthonisdochter on July 28, 1620, he wrote a poem dedicated to friendship. From this poem we gather that Lambert's bride had lived in Leeuwarden, which may have been the reason for his settling in that city after their marriage.[8]

It is probable that the Waterlander congregation of Leeuwarden called him to be their minister, particularly in view of his relation to Lubbert Gerrits. His profession as painter was not considered an obstacle to this calling. There were other Mennonite ministers serving as art dealers also. Henry van Uylenburgh, related to Rembrandt's wife, was an art dealer. His family originally came from Leeuwarden. In keeping with the custom of that time Lambert Jacobsz served other congregations as well as his own. Out of this work probably grew his friendship with the Harlingen elder Yeme Jacobsz de Ring (1574-1627), whose portrait he also painted. The importance of this painting for the Mennonites becomes apparent with the work of W. Delff and J. Folkema, both of whom used it later to prepare engravings of de Ring. There was a ready market and great appreciation for these engravings among the Mennonites. This estimate of Lambert Jacobsz is not shared by Gerard Maatschoen, however, who refers to him somewhat condescendingly as "a certain Lambert Jacobsz."[9] Did this historian, who continued the work of Herman Schijn, consider painting and preaching an ill combination for a Mennonite? Or was he suspicious of Lambert's friendship with the Collegiant poet Dirck Raphaelszn Camphuysen?[10]

The Collegiants were frequently misunderstood. Their doubt as to whether any of the existing churches were justified in calling themselves the true church of Christ caused considerable commotion among the Mennonites. Camphuysen was much honored among the Collegiants because of his poetry and pleasing personality.[11] It is possible that Lambert Jacobsz felt drawn to Camphuysen and the Collegiants because he sensed there a certain affinity with the ideas of his grandfather.[12] The latter had likewise cautioned against a ready acceptance of those who claimed to have restored primitive New Testament church patterns, but who could not prove that they had received a call from God to this task.[13] To Maatschoen this must have appeared as an undermining of the very foundation of Mennonitism. In the meantime, as we shall see presently, the Collegiants stimulated numerous other Mennonite painters.

As a painter Lambert Jacobsz has not been discovered before this century. The three paintings in possession of the Leeuwarden congregation became important only with the discovery of another canvas in the National Museum. Painted in 1629, this canvas depicts the stubborn prophet of 1 Kings 13:11-23. Through the publicity given to this discovery other paintings were found.[14] In 1936 an art exhibit was prepared to commemorate the three-hundredth anniversary of the painter's untimely death. Though we may not go so far as to claim that his paintings are typically Mennonite, they nevertheless reflect the deep piety and devotion of their master.

This is not the first illustration of biblical motifs in Mennonite paintings. There were other paintings of this period which do not reflect a religious orientation of the artist nor seek to deepen the devotion of the viewer. Lambert Jacobsz succeeded in bringing this religious feeling to his paintings through the facial expressions and posture of the body. He chose primarily those subjects which reflect action, the spiritual background and meaning being provided by the posture and facial features. The nature of this action varied. It did not necessarily mean *doing*. In the Old Testament portraits he portrays primarily the decisive moments of an encounter: Jacob and Esau, the Widow of Sarepta, and others. In the New Testament themes he seeks to capture moments of liberation: Mary Magdalene, Peter and Paul, and others.

His paintings, however, can hardly be called "landscapes with biblical motifs" though this was true of his earliest works.[15] His landscape background reveals the influence of the great Italian masters, absorbed during a trip to Italy before his marriage. Soon this landscaping becomes no more than instrumental fill-in, focusing all attention on the portraits themselves. In this he was unique among his contemporaries.[16] How lovingly he treats these portraits. We think particularly of his Ruth and Boaz (now in Weenen),[17] of his Jacob and Esau (in Groningen), and the portrait of the Stubborn Prophet (in Lund). The animated facial expressions of these and other characters reveal, we dare to suggest, a character and personality deeper even than those whom he portrayed. These expressions reveal more than the artist; they point to a shepherd of souls who knew the inner workings of the spirit of man. When, in addition, his characters wear clothing considered typical of the Mennonites of that time, it is not without reason that he may be called a typical Mennonite painter.

It is clear that he transmitted something of this depth and love of his subject matter to his son Abraham, who as Abraham Jacobsz van den Tempel (1622-1672) made a name for himself as portrait painter.[18] Govert Flinck (1615-1660), however, was even more indebted to Lambert Jacobsz. The way in which the latter was able to secure permission from Govert's father, a bailiff of Cleve, for Govert to pursue an artist's career shows how completely he was both pastor and painter. Govert had such a burning desire to paint that his primary entertainment, even as a child, consisted in painting. To the father this seemed a sad waste of time and energy. Thus Govert was forced to paint secretly in his bedroom at night. In 1631 Lambert Jacobsz came to Cleve, presumably to visit the congregation. Though the High Germans belonged to Lambert's group, the whole duchy of Cleve could boast only one flourishing Mennonite congregation, the one at Rees.[19] During his visit to the Flinck home, Lambert Jacobsz was able to persuade the parents that art could also serve to the glory of the Almighty. Govert thereupon promptly accompanied him to his own home as apprentice.[20] Lambert Jacobsz had another apprentice, Jacob Adriansz Backer (1608-1651), originally from Harlingen. His father, Adrian Tjerks, soon moved to the *Nieuwendijk* in Amsterdam, becoming a deacon in the congregation near the gates.[21]

Thus we again become aware of the significance of the *Nieuwendijk* street for Mennonite life of that time. It is possible that Vondel thought of the virtues of these people, many of whom had come from Hoorn, when he characterized the citizens of that city as "quiet, upright and virtuous."[22] Vondel was also familiar with the chronicle of Theodorus Velius (Dirck Seylemaker), honoring this Mennonite physician and historian with a poem for the third edition of the chronicle.[23] Though the poet had become a Roman Catholic and dedicated the poem to the burgomasters and magistrates of Hoorn, it is clear that he thought of his friends on the *Nieuwendijk*. It was to these people that Govert Flinck also belonged in spirit, if not in the strict sense of the word.[24]

After a short apprenticeship (He probably did not stay with Lambert Jacobsz longer than one year), Govert came to Amsterdam to complete his studies under Rembrandt, together with Jacob Backer. It is true that he first went to the home of Hendrick van Uylenburgh in 1636, but he was soon introduced to the people of the *Nieuwendijk,* among whom the master Rembrandt himself was no stranger.[25] In 1641 and 1642 the latter painted the portrait of the minister Cornelisz Claesz Anslo. The youngest brother of Lambert Jacobsz, who called himself Henry Jacobsz Rooleeuw after the insignia of the house of his parents, married Catharina Hooghsaet. This Catharina, Henry's second wife, was also painted by Rembrandt in 1657.[26] The Mennonite family Hooghsaet likewise produced a painter from among them, Jan Cornelisz Hooghsaet (1654-1733) who, among other things, decorated the new city hall which had been built shortly before his birth.[27]

A primary characteristic of the spirit of the *Nieuwendijk* was personal freedom. While insisting on liberty within their own congregational life, the church near the gates was open to others and welcomed new relations. It is known, for example, that Vondel felt a certain attraction for the Remonstrants, eulogizing their new church on the Kaisersgracht (built in 1638) no less than four times.[28] Contacts were also maintained with Jews, certainly not in order to convert them. The contrary actually occurred sometimes. Flinck painted the chiliastic rabbi Manasse ben Israel, with whom Rembrandt also maintained cordial relations.[29] Beyond this Flinck painted not only Gosen Centen (1636), who belonged to the Flemish congregation of the Lamb—which had not yet joined the Waterlanders— but also the Remonstrant minister Johannes Uittenbogaert.

This desire for personal freedom was primarily responsible for the many contacts Govert Flinck maintained with high government and even military authorities,[30] though he continued to serve his own congregation faithfully.[31] This irenic spirit may have come, in part, as a legacy from the previously mentioned Dirck Seylemaker (Velius) who had been magistrate in Hoorn. According to the group at the *Nieuwendijk,* participation in local and state affairs was a personal matter that each one needed to decide for himself, particularly after the independence of the Netherlands had been established by the Treaty of Westphalia, 1648. In gratitude for this freedom and for religious liberties many Mennonites felt compelled to assume social and political responsibilties.

For these reasons Govert Flinck had little difficulty painting the portraits of magistrates and other high office holders, particularly in view of the high esteem in which he was held by them. During his early years he seemed to prefer painting historical scenes and referred those desiring portraits to Bartholemeüs van der Helst.[32] Later, however, under pressure from rich merchants he also turned to portraits, painting the burgomasters Cornelis and Andries de Graeff, the Elector of Bradenburg, and Field Marshal Joan Maurice of Nassau. Against all of these, nevertheless, he maintained his independence, painting them without flattery, just as they appeared to him. In his group pictures, on the other hand, he gave way to a certain sentimentalism as in Amalia van Solms' Mourning Over the Death of Frederik Henry (National Museum),[33] the Repudiation of Hagar (Berlin), Bathsheba with the Letter from David (Leningrad), and Samson's Imprisonment, among others.

Flinck was even able to win his independence and freedom over against his master Rembrandt. It seems to have been particularly difficult for him to find his own style in relation to the latter, but he succeeded.[34] His well-known illustration of Isaac Blessing Jacob (1639) shows the influence of Rembrandt, but cannot be held as a work of the great master.[35]

The significance of Flinck, however, did not lie in these paintings, though the burgomasters of Amsterdam commissioned him to paint eight large and four small panels in this style in 1656 for the adornment of the city hall. He was unable to complete these. Of the smaller panels he was able only to submit two summary sketches before Amalia van Solms came to visit the hall, but two of the larger paintings remain extant. These further reveal his spiritual orientation: the Consul of Rome, Curius Dentatus, Resisting the Temptation to Bribery, and King Solomon's Prayer for Wisdom. An unimpeachable man, he sought wisdom.[36] Perhaps he owed this integrity to his Mennonite faith with its emphasis on this virtue. His significance lay particularly in the faithful reproduction of living personality and features. Vondel praised this attention to detail, remarking that he was able to count each gray hair upon his head according to the portrait Flinck had painted of him in 1652, when Vondel was 65 years of age.[37] It is regrettable that so many of his male and female portraits have not yet been identified.[38] From these we could perhaps learn more about him and the congregation he attended: whether the church loved him as much as he loved the church.

A fellowship similar to the one Flinck knew in Amsterdam seems also to have existed in Delft. Here Michiel Jansz van Mierevelt (1567-1641) made his home. Mierevelt was generally considered more traditionally Mennonite than his younger contemporary Flinck. This may have been due to the fact that he painted portraits of both Hans de Ries and Lubbert Gerrits.[39] Though these paintings are lost they live on in the engravings prepared from them by his son-in-law Willem Jacobsz Delff. They had already aroused the attention of the Waterlanders while Mierevelt was still alive. Vondel, still a Mennonite at that time, called Hans de Ries a jewel from God and speaks approvingly of Lubbert Gerrits' longing for peace within the church.[40]

Little attention is generally paid to the varied Mennonite emphases of van Mierevelt. This variation must be attributed to his frequent contacts with stadtholder Prince Maurice, for whom he did much work, as well as his familiarity with Philip William, son of William the Silent, with the Duke of Mansveldt, Oxenstierna, Oldenbarnevelt and other courtiers and military leaders.[41] He was unable to accept an invitation to the English court since the pest raged there, and since Albracht van Oostenrijk, governor of the southern Netherlands, had invited him to Brussels.[42] It is significant that Carel van Mander reports the governor as guaranteeing van Mierevelt complete freedom to live according to his Mennonite faith though Roman Catholicism was the only religion tolerated in the South.[43] The Mennonite convictions of van Mierevelt were somewhat different, however, from those of the Old Flemish, which van Mander seems to have appropriated.

127

Van Mierevelt's religious convictions were those of the Amsterdam Collegiants, though he held them before the Collegiants had organized a college in Amsterdam.[44] We have already referred to the fact that the Amsterdam Mennonites did not keep themselves separate from other Christians, recognizing in them believers who also "sought perfection with all their heart."[45] Thus Vondel could write as a Roman Catholic to the Collegiant Joachim Oudaen that "if Christ is the center, the pivot around whom heaven and earth and all things revolve, there is no difference in our faith." Among all of these existed the hope for perfection for the achieving of which the "almighty may grant grace to you and to us."[46] This irenic spirit with its concern for all men appeared in van Mierevelt's last will and testament. He bequeathed considerable sums of money to the city for alleviation of need, but he also remembered the churches in his will for the same purposes. The poor of his own Waterlander church may have received a slightly larger share through the church than others, but he also remembered the Flemish, the Remonstrants, and the Lutherans.[47]

Van Mierevelt and Govert Flinck could be considered equals were it not for the more sober and subdued tone of the former. An aura of sadness hangs over the features of the van Mierevelt portraits, a seriousness bordering on melancholy.[48] He refused to exaggerate the greatness of the greatest who came to sit for him. Even the princes he painted lacked grandeur.[49] Like Flinck he painted many portraits, most of which compared favorably with those of his Amsterdam contemporaries. Those who know his work can hardly agree with the complaint of van Mander that his historical compositions showed neglect and confusion. We note with appreciation, however, van Mander's characterization of van Mierevelt as a "quiet, gentle man with a good mind."[50]

The first of these virtues prevented him from taking too seriously the homage paid him on every hand, the second stood him in good stead in his work. He enjoyed having his sons Pieter and Jan assist him with the many orders, entrusting the painting of the environment to them. His nephew Jacob Delff also helped him, being particularly adept at painting the clothing parts. The work of these helpers did not add to

Portrait of Joost van den Vondel • GOVERT FLINCK
Rijksmuseum, Amsterdam

The Inobedient Prophet of 1 Kings 13 • LAMBERT JACOBSZ • Rijksmuseum, Amsterdam

Stopping at the Inn • SALOMON VAN RUYSDAEL • Rijksmuseum, Amsterdam

Portrait of Hugo de Groot • MICHIEL JANSZ VAN MIEREVELT
Rijksmuseum, Amsterdam

his reputation. Nevertheless, in the praise given to his detail, and to the honesty of his characterizations,[51] we observe the same virtues as in Lambert Jacobsz and Govert Flinck, virtues which seemed to grow naturally out of their Mennonite way of life.

If van Mierevelt may be characterized as avoiding ostentatious displays, this is even more apparent in the work of Salomon van Ruysdael (1602-1670). He too seemed guilty of the charge of van Mander that he neglected the historical dimensions in his background painting. His primary love was the landscape, which he studied and portrayed with religious devotion.

Van Ruysdael waited long for the recognition due him. This was primarily because of the reputation of Jacob, the son of his brother Isaac, who wrote his name Ruisdael. Though Jacob's landscapes seem to be more appealing to the common people than Salomon's and capture more nearly the living scene, he himself left the Mennonite church for some unknown reason.[52] Salomon proved to have understood the Mennonite emphasis on good works as the fruit of faith. He went through life almost unnoticed, a quiet, dedicated artist, transferring to his canvases the fortitude and peace of the surrounding countryside.[53] Yet this quiet man who, according to his biographer, painted no less than six hundred items, had a deep compassion for those in need of help. Born in Naarden, he was registered in Haarlem at the Sint Lucasguild in 1623, becoming its dean in 1648.[54] Shortly thereafter he became the guardian of the three daughters of his deceased brother Pieter de Goyer (He himself assumed the name *de Goyer* for a time, after *Gooi,* the region of his birth), and in the following years many others who had any claim upon him came to him for help. The names of those he helped as executor and in other ways are primarily Mennonites as, for example, de Neufville, van Halmael, van Sorgen. These names identify them as belonging to the Lamists primarily, the group worshiping in the building at the Lamb. Under the leadership of Galenus Abrahamsz de Haan they became particularly concerned about unity among the Mennonites and for more cordial relations to the Collegiants. Their union with the Waterlanders finally became a reality on June 1, 1668, still during the lifetime of van Ruysdael.[55] This union effort met with more resistance in Haarlem than elsewhere, but van Ruysdael undoubtedly was sympathetic to the Waterlanders and furthered the union.

Though van Ruysdael did not move in the high social circles as did Flinck and van Mierevelt, he was as concerned as they for the social order. His portrayal of the sea voyage, his equestrian motifs, robberies, the storming of Roermond and other scenes of battle, show that while he himself could not participate in these activities he, nevertheless, took the world as it was.[56] He had been commissioned to create these scenes, his own inclination lay in the painting of dreamy, tranquil landscapes under a somber and cloudy sky.[57] A recurring theme in many of his works is the arrival of a tired traveler at his home or lodging for the night. Did this man, who helped others so much, live with a constant inner longing for his eternal home?

Van Ruysdael painted only two major biblical scenes. The first was the baptism of the Ethiopian eunuch, an attractive subject for Mennonite artists because of the evident practice of adult baptism and explicit emphasis on the importance of faith. At least five variants of this scene are extant. Yet he was not interested in using his painting as a means of supporting the practice of adult baptism. The figures of Philip and the eunuch are not close enough to encourage this assumption. His second biblical scene, painted no less than six times, is the disciples on their way to Emmaus. None of the figures, Cleopas, Christ, or the unnamed disciple are prominent enough in the foreground to make this a declaration of faith in the living Christ. The painting indicates the fear van Ruysdael held of displaying the holy to every casual observer. Only those who themselves come to these scenes with reverence and devotion find in them, in the posture and expression of the men, the piety and faith van Ruysdael here confessed.

It is interesting to note that we see van Ruysdael as Mennonite most clearly in his river landscapes. Several of these are unmistakably reproductions of the environment of Castle Nijenrode. This area, where many Mennonites built their summer homes, was commonly known as the "Mennonite heaven."[58]

Among the names of the Mennonites who have possessed homes in this area and during this time we find Alderwerelt, Bierens, de Neufville, and Rutgers, who were members of the Amsterdam community.[59] We can no longer trace the origin of the commission to paint this area, but it may be assumed that these Mennonites from Haarlem and other places loved to "see in winter the scenes of their summer pleasures. Salomon van Ruysdael gave them a remembrance of this quiet landscape in a reproduction so faithful that no one sought to change or improve it, for 'lo it was very good.' "[59] Most of his paintings, however, show quiet landscapes, painted out of a mood which would not change or improve the work of God, who had made all things good.

This honesty was characteristic of Mennonite artists. They desired to leave both portrait and landscape as God had made it. It may be said that the four artists discussed here supplement each other. Deep biblical and devotional roots were required for the fine arts to arise on Mennonite soil, roots as we found them in Lambert Jacobsz and the others. The artists had to be committed to openness and integrity as we saw it in Govert Flinck; they had to partake of the compassion for the struggling soul of man in the way van Mierevelt was never able to avoid; and they had to be carried by the same loving gratitude for life itself, which we found so characteristic of van Ruysdael. Perhaps one should expect more of Mennonite art, but certainly these elements should not be lacking. When we recognize that these men were in no wise ashamed of their Mennonite faith, we affirm that the time of Vondel and Rembrandt brought forth four major Mennonite artists. Though they did not assume a prominent place in the life of the Mennonite church, with the exception of Lambert Jacobsz, they, nevertheless, were significant representatives of Mennonite life and thought.

NANNE VAN DER ZIJPP

The Dutch Aid
the Swiss Mennonites

THE CRADLE OF Anabaptism was in Zürich, Switzerland. There, in January 1525, the first Anabaptist congregation came into being. Through persecution Anabaptism spread not only to other areas in Switzerland, but also to the surrounding countries, above all, also to South Germany. In Strasbourg, for example, there were soon large numbers of Anabaptists. It was there that Melchior Hoffman joined the congregation in the summer of 1530. Hoffman became the apostle of Anabaptism in East Friesland and in the Netherlands. In the fall of 1530 he baptized 300 persons in one day in Emden, the capital of East Friesland. From Emden Anabaptism reached out to the Netherlands. Hoffman himself had visited the Netherlands several times. In the fall of 1530 a congregation existed in Amsterdam. About the same time one was formed in Leeuwarden, while elsewhere in the provinces of North Holland, Friesland, and Groningen Anabaptism began to arise. Thus this movement in the Netherlands, although it had a history of its own and developed independently, still had its origin in Swiss Anabaptism through Hoffman.

Nevertheless, it appears that in the Netherlands they were not conscious of the original relationship. Even Menno Simons did not mention the Swiss Anabaptist brethren. When in 1552 Gellius Faber accusingly stated that Menno's church was still

136

only sixteen or seventeen years old and had started with the revolutionary *wederdopers* of Münster, Menno did not parry the attack by pointing to the origin of Anabaptism in Zürich, a decade before Münster. Apparently Menno did not know about this origin. Likewise Swiss-South German Anabaptism was practically unknown in the Netherlands. In the oldest Dutch martyrs book *Het Offer des Heeren,* first published in 1562, Michael Sattler appears as the only non-Dutch martyr. Sattler's *Brotherly Union* appeared in a Dutch translation in 1560 and the conclusion of Sattler's *Confession* was printed then in *Het Offer des Heeren.* Otherwise no Dutch translations of writings of that time from Swiss or South German Anabaptism are known to me. This also agrees with the fact that an assembly of Anabaptist leaders from Moravia, Zwabia, Switzerland, Württemberg, the Breisgau, and the Alsace, which met in Strasbourg in 1557, rejected the strict application of the ban and shunning which Menno and his followers advocated, after which Dirk Philips and Menno had broken the bonds of unity with the Swiss and South Germans. Soon the memory of these brethren was entirely lost by the Dutch Mennonites, although Hans de Ries had included in his martyrs book of 1615 a number of short reports of martyrs from Switzerland and South Germany, such as Felix Manz, Leonart Keyser, Leonhard Schoener (Schiemer) and others.

It was not until shortly after 1640 that the Dutch Mennonites were again reminded of the existence of fellow believers in Switzerland. Rumors of persecutions in the Canton of Zürich began coming to their ears. In 1642 Godefridus Hottonus, preacher at the French church at Amsterdam, wrote a letter to Zürich in which he asked whether the rumor was correct that the Anabaptists there were being persecuted. Johannes Jacobus Breitinger, the leader of the Zürich Evangelical Church, answered him on August 21 of the same year in an extensive writing. Also Izak Hattavier, who had earlier lived in Zürich and was now a salesman in Amsterdam (According to others, he was a preacher of the French church), asked and received information from which, I suspect, he made an announcement to the church council of the Mennonite congregation *Bij 't Lam* (By the Lamb) in Amsterdam.

In addition the knowledge of the sad circumstances into which the Zürich brethren had come was spread further by a war of words between Petrus Bontemps, preacher of the French church at Haarlem, and Joost Hendricks, preacher of the Amsterdam Mennonite congregation By the Lamb. Bontemps had asserted that the government of Zürich had complete right to jail the Anabaptists because they contended against the legal authorities. The measures that were taken there, he insisted, could not properly be called a persecution. Joost Hendricks and later also Abraham Davidsz Volboet of Haarlem (writing under the pseudonym Gerard van Vryburgh) defended the fellow believers, complaining about the inhuman treatment which they had to suffer in Zürich. Furthermore, the Mennonites at Amsterdam also received firsthand information through a report entitled *Ein wahrhaftiger Bericht von den Brüdern im Schweitzerland in dem Zürcher Gebiet wegen der Trübsalen welche über sie ergangen sind, um des Evangeliums Willen, von dem 1635sten bis in das 1645sten Jahr* (A true report of the brethren in Switzerland in the Zürich area concerning the tribulations which have come over them for the sake of the gospel from the year 1635 till the year 1645) written by Jeremias Mangold, one of the brethren there, in February 1645. It was used later with other reports by T. J. van Braght in his *Martyr's Mirror* and also printed separately.

J. H. Ottius writes in his *Annales* that the Mennonites in Amsterdam were very much impressed by what happened in Zürich and on March 3, 1645, sent 100 dollars (*rijksdaalders*) through the above named Izak Hattavier, together with a letter of help and comfort for the imprisoned Mennonites. With that the great relief program of the Dutch Mennonites on behalf of their Swiss brethren began. It was to last more than one hundred years.

The relief action was of five different kinds: direct financial support, moral support, political help by mediation of the Dutch government, colonization in the Netherlands, and often paying for the transport of emigrants to America. Unfortunately, there was little one could do for the Zürich brethren. The aim of the Zürich authorities was *die Täufersekte auszurotten* writes Ernst Müller, and neither the earnest urging of Hattavier at the Zürich church council, nor the letter which Hans Vlaming, Doopsgezind salesman and church council member, wrote to Zürich, nor the intercession of the States General of the Netherlands (February 1660), nor the attempts undertaken at the same time by the city magistrates of Rotterdam and Amsterdam, aroused and inspired to do this by the Dutch Mennonites, brought any results. Even less could the suggestion that all the Mennonites from the Canton Zürich should emigrate to the Netherlands, which suggestion did originate from the church council of the congregation By the Lamb in Amsterdam, find grace in the eyes of the Zürich authorities. By 1661 all the Mennonites from the Zürich territory had disappeared. Many of them had fled to the Palatinate in Germany.

But soon the attention and active relief work of the Dutch Mennonites were required for their brethren in another part of Switzerland, namely in the extended Canton of Berne, where numerous Mennonites lived in the Emmental and along the northern shore of the Lake of Thun. As the history and suffering of these brethren has already been treated in many books, I will confine myself in the following to the relief work of the Dutch Mennonites.[1]

In the beginning the relief activity proceeded from the church council of the then still undivided congregation By the Lamb in Amsterdam, in which also the church councils of Rotterdam and Haarlem were sometimes involved. After the splitting of this Amsterdam congregation (1664) into a Lamb and a Sun congregation, the church council, particularly of the latter, was continually and deeply concerned for the oppressed Swiss. The already mentioned Hans Vlaming was the soul of this action. On his insistence a commission for the Swiss affairs came into being at Amsterdam, of which he himself was the secretary and treasurer. Shortly after 1670 this commission was enlarged with representatives from the Lamists and the Waterlanders, while with the passage of time congregations outside of Amsterdam were also represented in the committee. Eventually a more general committee came into being, the General Commission for Foreign Needs, of which the leadership continued to remain in the hands of Amsterdamers and a sort of executive committee of members of the church councils from both Sun and Lamb took the initiative. By correspondence these remained in contact with the brethren in Switzerland as well as with those who emigrated to the Pfalz. When it was necessary they called for general collections which were then held in practically every congregation in the Netherlands, divided the money and made all other necessary arrangements. From time to time general meetings of the committee were held. At the meeting held on February 24, 1710, when the situation in Berne was critical for the Mennonites and radical decisions had to be made for which much money was necessary, the following congregations were represented: Amsterdam-Sun, Amsterdam-Lamists, Rotterdam, Leiden, Haarlem, Gouda, Alkmaar, Hoorn, Enkhuizen, Monnikendam, Zaandam, Koog-Zaandijk, Wormerveer, Krommenie, Wormer, Jisp, De Rijp, Graft, and Harlingen. Among those who gave their support for the work of the committee and primarily deserve to be mentioned are the Amsterdam preachers Dr. Herman Schijn and Dr. Wilhelm van Maurik in addition to Abraham Fries, Jan Willink, Jacob Vorsterman, Cornelis Beets, Joachim van Anklam and Albert Pronk, all from Amsterdam, together with Henrik Toren and Jan Suderman of Rotterdam.

In 1802 it was decided to abolish the funds for foreign needs, since after 1784 the activity had been stopped, no further payments being required. The amounts still in the treasury were repaid to the congregations in proportion to the gifts earlier given to the committee. A balance of about four hundred guilders, which was left over, was spent as a gift to the Waldensians in Italy in 1825. A total of more than half a million guilders was gathered from 1671 to 1740 through collections in church services for the relief of foreign fellow believers. The brethren in Switzerland, the Swiss brethren in the Palatinate and Alsace, and those who had emigrated to Pennsylvania in the first half of the eighteenth century, received about a fourth of this sum. The rest of the money was used for the benefit of the oppressed and persecuted Mennonites in Poland, Prussia, Moravia, and Hungary, to whom the care of the committee was likewise extended. Above all, much money came from Amsterdam. After 1690 the congregation there gathered about 84,000 guilders. Contributions from other churches, however, also remained liberal. The little congregation of Rotterdam, for example, at that time numbering about 375 members, collected 2700 guilders on Sunday, December 7, 1710.

When it became known that the Mennonites in the Canton of Berne were under persecution by the authorities—their religious services forbidden, they themselves thrown in prison, their property confiscated—the church council of the congregation By the Lamb took action. A certain Adolf de Vreede was sent from the Netherlands to Switzerland and on June 11, 1660, delivered three letters to the cantonal government, given to him respectively by the States General of the Netherlands, the city directors of Amsterdam and those of Rotterdam, which pleaded for toleration in behalf of their Mennonite subjects. The sending of De Vreede had no single positive result. Berne answered to the States General on June 15, 1660, that it considered its task and divine commission to keep and maintain the Evangelical Reformed Church in its territory pure, on which account it saw itself obliged to cleanse the territory of these headstrong, unconvertible members who were disobedient to the government and called themselves *Taüfer,* etc.

Already earlier, on October 24, 1659, Hans Vlaming, the active deacon in Amsterdam, had written extensively to Christoph Luthard, professor of theology at Berne and member of the city commission whose duty it was to draw up regulations against the Mennonites, to move him to clemency toward these people who desired nothing else but to serve God according to their conscience. Others also—for example, Abraham Heidanus, professor of theology at Leiden, and a certain member of the church council of the Waalse congregation at Amsterdam—pleaded in Berne for the Mennonites, attempting among other things to bring a stop to the confiscation of their property. When on August 27, 1660, a group of Bernese Mennonites were expelled, who according to an otherwise unestablished tradition emigrated to the Netherlands, a sharp protest was sent by the States General on request of the Dutch Mennonites. This was repeated in another writing dated September 10, 1668, in connection with another deportation. In 1670-71 Berne sharpened the regulations against the Mennonites. So many were imprisoned that they could no longer house the arrested

Mennonites. It was decided, therefore, to keep the older Mennonites in prison for life, to house the weak and sick in a certain place, and to send the healthy men to the galleys as quickly as possible. Many Mennonites who were still at liberty fled from Berne and emigrated to the Palatinate where they arrived poor and destitute. About the situation in Switzerland, the fate and condition of those who had been able to flee to the Palatinate, we read in five extracts from letters included in the *Martyr's Mirror* of Van Braght.[2] The third of these extracts is a letter to Hendrick de Bakker (probably the physician and preacher, Johannes Becker, of the congregation By the Lamb in Amsterdam) and written by Jacob Everling. I suspect that Everling was the author of all of these letters, dated April 7, May 23, October 13, November 2, 1671, and January 5, 1672, respectively. This Jacob Everling was elder of the congregation Obersülzen in the Palatinate. He later corresponded with the committee in Amsterdam and became the mediator between the Swiss emigrants in the Palatinate and the Dutch Mennonites. The Mennonites in the Netherlands were, of course, also informed of the need of their fellow believers. The congregation at Rotterdam received a letter from the church council at Krefeld, dated December 19, 1671, with the following contents:

Worthy and beloved brethren in God and fellow servants of the church of God at Rotterdam. . . .

We the undersigned cannot withhold from you gentlemen all that our Brother Jan Flos [It must be Floh] reported to us on October 21. While coming from Heidelberg to Mannheim in the Palatinate he met about twenty persons, brethren in the Christian faith, who had arrived there the previous day from Berne, Switzerland. It was heart-rending to see them. The greater part were old people fifty, sixty, seventy years of age, naked and destitute because they had not had a night's rest in their own houses for more than a year, as he said. They told him their sad and very miserable plight with bitter crying . . . explaining further that they no longer dared to remain in Switzerland on account of the severe placard, dire threats and anxiety. They explained further that they had still expected about forty persons, hoping that they had not been captured. The highways and passes were being carefully watched to prevent them from leaving the country. Some of the captives were put to the galleys, some lashed and branded. Among the latter was one admonisher [minister] who died after a few days. Some were thrown into prison where they had to suffer much misery, hunger and affliction.

Furthermore as we have received it by writing from the Palatinate, about one hundred households of our fellow believers from Switzerland have arrived in the Pfalz thus far. . . . We can understand very well that our fellow believers in Switzerland are too few and have too limited temporal means so that they cannot care for so many naked and poor refugees in this cold winter without assistance. Therefore we understand ourselves to be obliged to offer the helping hand to these poor refugees. We, therefore, also request our fellow members at Rotterdam to demonstrate mercy toward these our poor fellow members in the Christian faith and naked and sorrowful refugees according to ability even as Christ our Saviour and Redeemer said in Matthew 5:7. . . . Will you gentlemen please, if you agree with us that it is necessary, also share our writings with our fellow members at Dordrecht and Ter Gouw [i.e., Gouda], so that something can be sent to those poor sad refugees for the substance of their bodies and against this cold winter. We shall await your answer with the deepest interest.[3]

This letter was printed and circulated. Attached to it was a writing from two Swiss deacons from the Palatinate addressed to Hans Vlaming at Amsterdam. In addition a complete list of 76 families that had arrived in the Palatinate was enclosed, entitled: *The condition of the Swiss who for the sake of faith are being persecuted; their old age and what they have brought with them, who now reside between Brem and Bingen.* The total number of persons, adults and children, amounted to 227. This number would have been much larger if the families had been complete, but even this list shows the tragedy of being in flight, as we have also experienced it in Europe in the last quarter century. What misery this list speaks of can be seen from a few arbitrary selections:

Catrien Denzeler, seventy years old, has two daughters, the one still unmarried, has brought six rujksdaalders [dollars] with her; the other called Babe, has left her husband with four children, the fifth died during the journey. She brought two quilts with her.

Ulrich Kuener, sixty-two years old, and his wife fifty-seven, have a child with them and left five, whom they still expect to come also. The oldest thirty, the youngest fifteen. The oldest has a child twenty-four hours old.

Ulrich Liechte, thirty-two years old, his wife thirty-four. The wife and five children are left behind, hoping they may be able to follow. The oldest child is ten years of age, the youngest eight months. They brought four dollars with them.[4]

It was well understood in the Netherlands that help had to be given. Already at the beginning of January 1672 collections had been received here and there. The first contributions that came in were very satisfying and gave hope of good results. Amsterdam (the churches By the Lamb and By the Tower) raised nearly 15,466 guilders, Zwolle nearly 413, Alkmaar around 650 guilders. By early February it was already possible to transfer a considerable sum to Jacob Everling, who bore the responsibility for distributing the money. The church council of Rotterdam was of the opinion that one would do well to colonize the Swiss emigrants in the Netherlands, but this plan was not realized. One suspects that this plan failed because the Swiss preferred to remain in the Palatinate where they felt more at home among the few Mennonites who lived there. The language was similar and, above all, their more conservative point of view in matters of faith in contrast to the Dutch Mennonites—who in their opinion had wandered far from the old principles, also in their manner of living—led the Swiss to choose the Palatinate. At the end of February a committee of four Dutch Mennonites left for the Palatinate to visit the Swiss refugees and to speak with them about what should and must be done further. They were all Lamists, namely Frans Beuns, Dr. Johannes Backer and Anthony Rooleeuw from Amsterdam, and Johan Andriesz (Jan van Aken) from Utrecht. Once more they took a considerable amount of money with them to alleviate the need, the sum of 11,000 guilders.

For the brothers and sisters who sat in prison in Berne and for those who were not in a position to flee because of border watches, one could unfortunately do very little. Also for those who were "sold" by Berne as rowers to the galleys on the Mediterranean, one could not offer the helping hand at that moment. This appears from a letter by Duyvenstein, sent from Venice on September 23, 1672, reporting that the galley on which the condemned Swiss were located was at Corfu and that it was impossible to do anything for them.[5]

The committee remained in contact with the States General of the Netherlands, to whose Grand Pensionary they frequently delivered reports during this entire period, but the States General could also do very little at that time. Furthermore, it seems that in the following years the persecutions in Berne were no longer as severe as before. In 1687 a letter was received in Amsterdam reporting that four brothers who had been put in prison four years earlier were now released through the aid from the Netherlands.[6]   Out of this we see that in the course of time the suppression of the Mennonites in the Canton of Berne continued, as did the assistance of the Dutch Mennonites.

But the continued attention of the Dutch Mennonites was even more crucial for the situation in the Palatinate than in Switzerland.   To report here the relief aid to the Mennonites in the Palatinate is not outside of our subject.   Indeed, it has a direct relationship to it since the persecuted Pfalzers were primarily the emigrated Swiss Mennonites.   The Amsterdam Archives contain a very large number of items about this new relief program from the years 1690-97.[7]   The letters which the Dutch Stadhouder (stadtholder) William III of Orange, after 1689 also King of England, wrote to Johann Wilhelm, Elector of the Pfalz,[8] on August 11, 1694, and July 14, 1697, respectively, in order to intercede for the persecuted Mennonites are also significant sources.   In the years 1690, 1693, 1694, and 1699 collections were organized in the Netherlands for the Pfalzers by the Commission for Foreign Needs.

If the commission at Amsterdam had relative rest in the years 1672-1710, and if the minutes of the assemblies held in those years furnish little material, this must, unfortunately, still be understood as the calm before the storm.   The government of the Canton Berne had proceeded with further measures against the Mennonites.   Of this the Mandates and Restrictions taken by the cantonal government in the years 1693 to 1695 testify.[9] They contain complaints about the "ever increasing Täufer sect" (*immer zunehmenden Täufersekt*) and measures were taken "to correct such evil" (*wie solchem Übel abzuhelfen*).   To the latter belongs, among others, the decision to consider anyone who would not swear an oath as disobedient to the authorities and to punish him with forfeiture of his property and expulsion from the country.   Still it appears that these regulations were not applied directly in their sharpest form.   At any rate, we hear little of exile before 1710.   The Amsterdam Archives contain two important letters from 1708, both directed to Dr. H. Schijn, minister of the congregation By the Sun at Amsterdam.   The first dated January 6, 1708, originated with Jan Frerichs, a Mennonite salesman at Deventer, who had received extensive reports from Switzerland about the persecution of the brethren among other ways through the sending of men to the galleys. The second letter, addressed to Dr. Schijn and Wilhelm van Maurik, minister of By the Lamb at Amsterdam, originated in Mannheim in the Palatinate, reporting, among other things, the names of all who at that moment were in prison in Berne.[10]

Extensive reports, whether direct from Switzerland[11] or via the fellow believers in the Palatinate, kept the Dutch Mennonites well informed of the situation in Berne, where the persecution was very systematically organized in 1709. Sir Johann Ludwig Runckel, the representative of the Dutch States General in Switzerland, showed himself to be a great friend of the Mennonites and incessantly interceded for them and regularly kept the Mennonites in the Netherlands informed of what was happening in Berne. Between 1710 and 1717 he wrote no less than seventy letters to the Amsterdam commission about the situation. In his first letter of January 22, 1710, he reported that the need had risen greatly. This immediately compelled the Commission for Foreign Needs to renew its activity. The Berne government, which had inquired of the government of Zürich late in 1709 how they had gotten rid of Mennonites there, promptly received the cynical answer that at Zürich they had killed a number of them, thrown many into prison, and chased the rest out of the country. On the advice of the *Täuferkammer* they determined to take drastic measures against the *starrköpfigen und unverschämten Wiedertäufer*. They entered into negotiations with a certain Georg Ritter, who took it upon himself to transport a number of captive Mennonites to England for forty-five dollars (*thaler*) per person on condition that the Bernese government would provide serviceable ships. From England they were to be reshipped to America. The Mennonites *wurden von Ihrer Königlichen Majestät in Grossbrittanien zur peuplierung der amerikanischen Inseln begehrt* (were coveted by Her Royal Majesty of Great Britain for populating the American Islands). *Islands* is incorrect to the extent that it was the intention to transport these people to Georgia or Carolina where colonists were needed. The costs of the journey were to be paid out of the confiscated property of the Anabaptists.

146

On March 18, 1710, Ritter departed with fifty-five Mennonites, mostly men who were transferred to the ship from the prison in Berne. On April 6 the ship arrived in Nijmegen by way of the Rhine. In the meantime, neither the Berne government nor the committee in the Netherlands had been idle. The former had taken all the necessary measures to get the transport through quickly and among other things had acquired passes from French and German princes and cities for unhindered passage. But already after the departure they discovered that one thing had been forgotten, namely to request passage through the Netherlands from the Dutch government. Urgently the Swiss charge d'affaires, F. L. Pesme, Lord of St. Saphorin, was appointed to handle this affair. He directed a writing to the States General with the request for free passage for the transport, and supervision so that the exiles might not escape during their transfer in Rotterdam. It was asked that the requested authorization be sent speedily to Sir Ritter, in care of Dietrich Köster, Transport Concern [sic], Cologne. At the delivery of the memorandum the clerk of the States General, Francois Fagel, was polite, but received it coolly. St. Saphorin then had also to write to Berne that the "chancellor," i.e., Fagel, had spoken very excitedly with him about this affair, and had remonstrated him over the intolerance of the Bernese government. The chairman of the States General, whom St. Saphorin then visited, also gave him a less than friendly reception. We can at once add that the States General in its assembly of March 2 decided to refuse the requested license for free passage. From the minutes of the States General it appears that the decision for refusal was based on the fact that 1) in the Netherlands one is of the opinion that in the matter of religion each person must be allowed his freedom to believe and confess what he judges to be right for his own salvation, and that no one may be persecuted or punished because of his faith and confession, provided his life and doctrine do not harm the state or country, and 2) that the States General wished to witness through the decision to refuse that they rejected wholeheartedly the inhuman intolerance of the government of the Canton of Berne.

Sir St. Saphorin as well as the Dutch Secretary in Switzerland was informed of this decision. Space does not permit a full report about all the discussions that were held before and afterward at the diplomatic level in the Hague; also of St. Saphorin with Fagel, from whom he was not only to be told that they would give no pass but also that the Dutch would prevent the passage. In no event would a license be granted to Dutch ships to transport the prisoners from Rotterdam or Briel to England or America. Further discussions were pursued between St. Saphorin and the English ambassador Lord Townshend as well as with Fagel and with members of the States General. The decision of the States General was not changed by this, though the English minister threatened with war on account of the insult to the King of England. St. Saphorin ventured to say in his writing to Berne that from the very beginning the clerk of the States General had drawn the "Wederdoppers in his country" into the affair. This is correct. Fagel had immediately informed the commission in Amsterdam about the transport that was on its way, as also about the decision by the States General to reject the requested transit pass. The commission had immediately sent a deputation to the Hague which spoke repeatedly with Fagel as well as with St. Saphorin. The Rotterdam baker and preacher Hendrik Toren, a member of this deputation, has recorded the events from day to day, from hour to hour, in his diary.[12]

The zealous secretary of the Commission for Foreign Needs, Jacob Vorsterman, of Amsterdam, recorded everything that had any bearing on the relief assistance to the Swiss brethren in this and the years following in his *Relaas ofte Aanteijkening wegens het uijtsegghen en afvoeren der Doopsgezinden uijt Switserland*.[13] It was undoubtedly the warm intercession of the Dutch Mennonites that prevented the earlier mentioned deportation to America. When the ship of Ritter arrived in Nijmegen on April 6, the deportees—a part of whom had already been put off at Mannheim because they were sick or weak—were granted freedom. Most of them, after being cared for and strengthened by members of the congregation at Nijmegen, went to the Palatinate as free men to live near their fellow believers there. A few of them remained in the Netherlands and at one of the many gatherings of the commission held in those days in Amsterdam told of the situation in the Canton of Berne and of their experiences.

Thus the commission received firsthand reports from which it also became clear to them that even though the danger of deportation was past for this group, the lot of the Mennonites in Berne would continue to require much of their attention, time, and money.

So as to be ready to act intelligently in the difficulties anticipated in the near future it was decided to alter the composition of the commission so that all Mennonite denominations and all Mennonite congregations in the Netherlands would be involved in it. An executive committee of Amsterdamers was organized and given authority to take steps immediately when necessary. In addition to this an assembly of representatives who were to meet once or twice a year was organized so that the whole relief action received a firmer and more permanent character. Through the letters of Runckel from Switzerland and those from the Mennonites in the Palatinate they kept informed precisely of what happened in Switzerland, what regulations the government of Berne took or framed, and how the fellow believers fared. Runckel had been tremendously active, particularly in 1710 and 1711. The "Amsterdam gentlemen" also remained in constant contact with the clerk of the States General, Fagel, who was always on hand for the Mennonites. It was clear that the Bernese authorities wanted to be rid of all Mennonites and a repetition of the deportation was feared in March. For a while it seemed as if the matters could be arranged to the satisfaction of both the government of Berne and the Mennonites. The king of Prussia, Frederick I, it was learned, was inclined to allow all the Swiss Mennonites to come to his territory to settle down and drain the marshes. In Prussia they would receive complete freedom of religion, he assured them. The plan that had the sympathy of the Bernese authorities also, and that was already so far advanced that Cornelis Michielsz Kalff, a Mennonite salesman and shipowner in Zaandam, was found ready to effect the necessary regulations for the colonization in Prussia, finally ended in failure because the Mennonites in the Canton of Berne would not leave their fatherland, though the Dutch Mennonites and, above all, Runckel had taken it upon themselves to persuade the brethren to accept it. Even less came of other plans, such as the transferring of all Mennonites from Berne to a Prussian enclave near Neuchatel or to a district in Burgundy.

149

Then came the great plan to bring all the Mennonites from Switzerland to the Netherlands with the assistance of the Dutch Mennonites. This plan was presented in the (general) assembly of the Commission for Foreign Needs held at Amsterdam on November 5, 1710. It remained pending because of the plan to move the Swiss to Prussia, but when that failed to materialize, it came to the fore again. Thanks to the invitation of the Dutch and perhaps even more to the tenacious perseverance of Runckel, who not only had to win the Bernese authorities, but by endless reasoning persuaded the really very stubborn Swiss Mennonites, they left the fatherland and went forth into a new future in the distant Netherlands.

This plan finally succeeded, though not all the Swiss went along. A large number had withdrawn into remote Swiss valleys in the hope that sooner or later they would enjoy some tolerance. For Runckel it was a great success when the government of Berne permitted the emigrants to take with them the money from the property they had sold. Georg Ritter, who had led the unsuccessful transport in March and April 1710, was now entrusted with the organization and accompanying of the new transport.

The preparations required much care, and there were many difficulties, not only from the side of the Bernese authorities who, after issuing an amnesty declaration on February 11, 1711, which permitted the Mennonites to be registered without danger of imprisonment, still remained quarrelsome in all kinds of ways. The greatest difficulty, however, was due to divisions among the Swiss Mennonites. The followers of Hans Reyst did not want to be in the same ship as the followers of Hans Ammann, and vice versa. As a result, the number of those who went was much smaller than had been the original intention. Runckel still wrote to the committee in Amsterdam on May 16, 1711, that because of various circumstances he had little faith that the affair would be successful. It was in reaction to this somber letter from Runckel that the committee wrote on June 2:

We may not be able to hide from your honour how much anxiety the whole affair brings to us. Thus the conduct from one side or the other confuses and discourages us very much, so that we fear not only that no good, but an entirely terrible end shall come of it . . . for we see clearly that all the effort which the Mennonite Chamber, etc., put forth shall only have the consequence of making those poor peoples completely dependent and beggars for all things, and thus to drive them out of the country or to bind them around the neck with a cord which will certainly make them remain in the country. Thus the unmerciful shearers have the opportunity either to enrich themselves from the last penny of these miserable ones or to ban them to the galleys, to deliver them into eternal imprisonment or to deliver them to capital punishment and thus to make themselves guilty of their blood.

In order to make a long (and irritating) story short, the embarkation took place at Neuchatel as well as at Berne on July 13, 1711. All costs were paid by the Dutch Mennonites, who had held a special collection for this purpose. Three hundred and twenty-five Mennonites and twenty-one others who were not members of the congregation (members of the households or those who were sympathetic) could be taken on board the four ships; thus three hundred and forty-six persons departed from Basel on the evening of July 17. Sir Runckel, whose unselfish activity in the previous weeks is almost unbelievable, had come to Basel personally to take care of last minute details and to take leave of them. The sum of money which remained after deducting all the rather exorbitant costs was placed at his disposal by the authorities at Berne, along with the confiscated funds of the ones who had been taken prisoner and also the funds from the property which unfortunately had for the most part been sold at too cheap a price. After the departure of the group Runckel tranferred the total amount, 28,000 guilders, by bill of exchange to the gentlemen Vorsterman and Honnoré at Amsterdam. I can add to this that Runckel was able later on to send at least 14,000 dollars (*Reichsthaler*), so that a total of 60,113 Dutch guilders and 15 cents had been accumulated by the approximately 340 Swiss. From this we must subtract the 167 children that were with the group. Counting adults only, about an average of 350 guilders fell to each person, from which it would appear that according to the values of the time they would clearly be considered poor people.

In the meantime the committee in Amsterdam had not been idle. An important assembly of representatives met on March 18, 1711, after the declaration of amnesty had been published. They dealt principally with three things: First, an appeal to send to Switzerland to print and distribute among the Mennonites an invitation to come to the Netherlands. Dr. Schijn, minister of By the Sun congregation at Amsterdam, had drafted a resolution for this purpose and it was accepted by the assembly. Seven hundred copies of this circular letter were later printed in Switzerland and distributed among the Mennonites. The second very weighty point for the assembly was to consider where the Mennonites from Switzerland, should they come, could be colonized in the Netherlands. Since they were all agrarians, it seemed necessary to consider how to locate them in rural areas. Farm buildings and land would have to be bought or leased for them. Alle Derks, a Mennonite leader in the province of Groningen, suggested that they look for a satisfactory location there. Others offered locations near Kampen or Deventer, while there already was a standing offer from an owner of land in Friesland proposing to sell a large area of peat land in the neighborhood of Bakkeveen for 80,000 guilders. Definite decisions could not be made, seeing that they did not yet know how many would be coming. The third point was the question of where one could get the necessary funds for such a large program. They thought the Swiss would bring some money with them, but how much one could not tell. (As we have already reported above, it worked out agreeably and significantly.) The treasurers declared that there was still a considerable amount of cash, some 5,000 guilders, but a rather large amount would certainly be needed, so that it was clear that another general collection would be necessary. This was later and brought together exactly 50,000 guilders.

On August 3, 1711, the four ships with the Swiss arrived in Muiden, Holland, from where they were transported to Amsterdam the very same evening. A few who were sick had remained behind at Mannheim. Some others who had already left Switzerland earlier but now wished to go along to the Netherlands had boarded ship at Mannheim so that the total number, old and young, who arrived in Amsterdam, amounted to exactly three hundred and fifty.

At first they were housed in two neighboring warehouses "on the Zandhock" which had been furnished by the committee "as a large lodging and provided with the necessary equipment, bedding, blankets, and everything that was serviceable for setting up a household, for feeding and for refreshment."

The same evening and the following day, one of the commission members writes, the Amsterdamers and most of all the Mennonite brethren with wholehearted interest streamed to this temporarily furnished lodging to be witnesses of this heart-rending spectacle. It even seemed necessary to have the entrance properly guarded by the police. They also knew how to take advantage of the moment: boxes placed at the entrances finally delivered a contribution of 1045 guilders and 11 cents.

The following day they discussed what was to be done further. Three leading figures of the Swiss, the preachers Daniel Ricken, Hans Ancken, and Melcher Zahlen, carried on discussions with the commission members as representatives of the immigrants. First of all, the question whether they wanted to remain in the Netherlands was discussed. There was still the possibility of going to Prussia. One of the Swiss brethren, who had already come into the Netherlands with the deportation of 1710, Hans Bürki, had been in Prussia and brought a report about the political and economic situation in that land. After reporting back to the whole group, Ricken and colleagues reported on August 10, in the gathering of the commission with the representatives, that they preferred to remain in the Netherlands. Thereupon the commission members, Alle Derks from Groningen and Steven Abrahams Cramer from Deventer, announced that they were prepared to seek locations for a large part of the Swiss in the province of Groningen and near Deventer. The Frisian representatives had also looked around in their area. There were possibilities to locate near Harlingen and near Gorredijk. Options had been taken on a number of farms both in the province of Groningen and near Kampen. These offers were accepted. The commission decided to assume as their full responsibility the costs for relocating the Swiss brethren, the local establishment of the household and maintenance during the coming winter, and further to extend assistance or where necessary financial aid for the renting or buying of what they called "a decent livelihood" (*behoorlijke kostwinningen*). In Amsterdam the Swiss were also amply provided with all sorts of things which they lacked or would need before long and perhaps would not be available in remote areas such as Groningen and Friesland. Leafing through the still preserved books of the treasurers of the commission we gain a great respect both for the domestic attention and the almost motherly concern of the commission members. Every little thing appears on the books: bedding, ticking, blankets, pillow slips, different kinds of clothes, in addition to items purchased for them. A notable posting from the accounts during the time of the stay in Amsterdam is 23 guilders 10 cents for hooks and eyes. We need to remember that these conservative Swiss Mennonites would wear no buttons on their clothes, but fastened them with hooks and eyes:

Die mit Haken und Oesen	("Those with hooks and eyes
Wird der Herrgott erlösen,	Will be redeemed by God,
Die mit Knopfen versehn	Those with buttons appearing
Werden zur Hölle gehen.	Will toward hell be steering.")

After staying for seventeen days the immigrants left Amsterdam again. On August 20, 1711, the ships sailed from the Weepers Tower (*Schreierstoren*) through the Ijsselmeer to the Zuydersea with twenty-one headed for Harlingen, one hundred and twenty-six to Groningen, eighty-seven to Kampen, and one hundred and sixteen to Deventer.

It is not possible within the brief scope of my story to sketch extensively the fate of the four groups. Those in Harlingen remained only a short time. The prospects did not appear favorable to them. Also the large group that was helped to find housing in Deventer did not feel at home there. A part of them, just as those who had come to Harlingen, traveled to the Palatinate after drifting around for some time in our land. The rest of those who had settled in Deventer went to live near those in Kampen. In Groningen they received farms not far from the city in Hoogkerk, Noorddijk, and Helpman, but primarily on the Kalkwijk, southeast of Hoogezand and east of Sappemeer, in the Sap Lake which had been drained in the previous century.

A significant amount of financial aid was necessary to resettle the Swiss. Above that which they had brought with them and apart from the costs which resulted from the efforts of Runckel in Switzerland, transportation, and the costs of providing goods for them in Amsterdam, the Dutch Mennonites had to sacrifice much in those years, even though fortune was with them inasmuch as the prices for renting or buying land were especially low in that year. For some of the Swiss, farms (little ones?) were purchased for 2000, 1418, 1125, and even 400 guilders, and rent was proportionately low.

The settlement at Kampen was not only satisfactory for the Swiss and the committee; it was a success. That is valid in even larger measure for the settlement in Groningen. They had, nevertheless, held themselves more or less aloof from the Dutch Mennonites until the end of the eighteenth century—one group in Kampen even until 1826. Certainly they were thankful for what the brethren and sisters in the faith had done and sacrificed for them, but they were of another spirit. The Dutch Mennonites had gradually accommodated to their surroundings after the time of persecution and had more or less taken their place in the life of their nation. It seemed significant—and it is difficult to ascertain what has been cause and what effect in this case—that they had lost many of the old traditions and peculiarities of faith and life. The Swiss with their old-fashioned costumes, their hooks and eyes, and their round beards, had given the Dutch Mennonites the impression that they were people who lagged behind, while the Swiss, on the other hand, judged their Dutch fellow believers as having "almost completely lost their Mennonitism," as it has been characterized. In addition to the difference in language, this difference in cultural level and in religious concepts resulted in the Swiss organizing their own congregations where they continued their old Swiss traditions until they united with the Dutch Mennonite congregations, the one congregation somewhat earlier, others later.

Thus, as the excellent Alle Derks formulated it at an assembly of representatives from the commission in the summer of 1713, "the great work [was] taken in hand and completed, thanks be to God." What still remained to be done for the immigrants of 1711, we may call follow-up care. But with that the task of the Committee for Foreign Needs was still not finished. I do not refer so much to the great need of the Mennonites in Prussia and Poland, where later attention and much money had to be devoted during several decades—a chapter in itself—

but rather to the further development of the situation in Switzerland, and in particular in the Palatinate. After the departure of the above named group, not all the Mennonites had disappeared from the Canton of Berne. Many, particularly from the Amish faction, remained behind more or less secretly. Others, trusting in the declaration of amnesty, had turned back from the Palatinate and elsewhere. It appeared, however, and became clear from a strong placard of May 24, 1714, that the Bernese authorities were not done with the Mennonites. We read this placard:

Concerning the Wiedertäufer whom we have exiled from the country as also those who persist in hiding, here and there both men and women, we once more serve notice by the power of this our public proclamation that they depart from our lands, and forbid once and for all their return, since we have firmly resolved that all Wiedertäufer who may have been banned from the land in former times or presently and in the future shall be found or trapped among us, shall be condemned to the galleys without grace; but the old and the invalid, together with women, who are not fit therefore, shall be given another heavy punishment.

The (state church) congregations of the canton were to spy out the Mennonites and deliver them to the authorities. Whoever would give room and board to a Mennonite would be punished.[14]

What its meaning was appears not only from the increased activity of the Bernese *Täuferjäger,* but also from the fact that shortly thereafter fourteen Mennonites were arrested, sent to Savoy together with forty galley slaves with the intention of sending them to the galleys also.[15] Thanks to the furnishing of ransom by the Dutch Mennonites, they were spared from this fearful fate. It did not go so well with others. Nevertheless, the Dutch Mennonites remained diligent, and they sometimes had success with the king of Sicily in winning liberty for some in the following years.[16]

Under such circumstances Mennonites in Berne sought safety in flight elsewhere, in the Palatinate, in Alsace, in the Netherlands, but not all. The obstinate wanted to remain, and their progeny still live in the Emmental. In the fall of 1714 a small group arrived here. They also settled near Sappemeer, among whom was Samuel Peter, surnamed Maihuser, the progenitor of the Meihuizen family so well known among us. They were fairly well established and needed no appeal for help to the Commission for Foreign Needs. That also applies to individuals who arrived in the years 1715, 1716, and 1717.

I can end my theme here. After 1717 the troubles of the Dutch Mennonites with their brethren who lived in Switzerland or who had departed directly from there, ceased.

The chapter "Switzerland" in the books of the Commission for Foreign Needs is closed. But the chapter on relief aid to the Swiss brethren is still not finished. As we saw, they fled for the greater part to the Palatinate. They were also persecuted there, or their freedom was at least much hindered, and the books of "Foreign Needs" until about 1765 and hundreds of letters and reports preserved in the Amsterdam and Rotterdam Mennonite archives, inform us extensively about them.[17]

The following may be added to that account: Most of the electors of the Palatinate had little tolerance. There the principle of "who reigns, his religion" (*cuis regio, illius religio*) was applied with all its implications. If the elector was Catholic, the Lutherans and Reformed had to suffer for it; if the following elector was Lutheran, the tables were turned. But no matter how or how often the tables turned at the coming of the successive electors, the Mennonites were usually those who had to pay for the piper. The Swiss emigrants primarily after military ravage of the French in 1685 were welcomed heartily. They could well be used. But the old history of the children of Israel in Egypt was repeated. The people grew in number and Pharaohs appeared who had not known Joseph. Numerous irritating and ignominious regulations were made: *numerour clausus* (restricted numbers): 240 families, no more; the others must go away; special taxes were levied for the Mennonites, "expiatory money," prohibitions against holding religious meetings, prohibitions against marriage, even prohibitions against burying their dead.

Through the alluring offers of English shipping agents—the propaganda pamphlet of the English mintmaster Ochs from 1717 is well known—many turned their eyes in the direction of the New World, the English colonies in America, and especially to Pennsylvania, which must have seemed to them to be a land of milk and honey. From ca. 1709 until 1765 streams of "Swiss brethren" came from the Palatinate to the Netherlands, often destitute and certainly hoping to receive the passage money for the trip to the promised land from "the gentlemen from Amsterdam." That also placed high demands on the Commission for Foreign Needs. Although warnings from the commission were sent to the Palatinate time and again that assistance would certainly be given in the form of temporary housing and aid in seeking an emigration ship and such, but that no more money would be made available for the ocean journey and that everyone who did not have money with him would be irrevocably sent back to the Palatinate, in many cases their hearts nevertheless moved their hands to help.

The Mennonite congregation at Rotterdam put forth particular efforts for the Palatine-Swiss, and although later there were no strong bonds between the Mennonites in Pennsylvania and the Netherlands, men in America nevertheless did not forget the great work of the Commission for Foreign Needs. In 1872 S. W. Pennypacker spoke at a Mennonite commemoration as follows: "Next to God we owe much gratitude to the brethren in Rotterdam and the Mennonites in Holland. Without them the forefathers of many of us here would not have come."

FRITS KUIPER

The Discordant Voice
of Jan de Liefde

ONCE A FISHING BOAT was driven to the sea coast because of the negligence of the pilot. The sailors, happy because of the perfect calmness after rolling and tossing about on the deep sea, began to sleep quietly without worrying about the possibility of a coming storm. But an old pilot awoke immediately and, seeing the storm approaching, called out "Danger, danger!" He proposed that the boat be pulled still closer to the shore and harbored for the winter. The sailors awoke frightened, but another pilot eased their mind: they should simply proceed smoothly close to the shore. Then a third pilot arose. He said that if they wintered they would perish from want, and if they coasted, they would never get home. He called on them to use all their might to keep the boat afloat and to again bring it into deep waters. He snatched up hooks and punting poles to shove the vessel into the open waters. "Stop," they called to him, feeling the boat rocking and rolling, "stop, you are shoving too hard." "Alas," he replied, "if you had not drifted away even to the danger of sinking, I would not have to shove so hard." (*Waart gij niet afgedreven, ik sou niet overdrijvan*). Since then they called him "the Shover."

Thus Jan de Liefde concluded the preface of his pamphlet, *Danger, Danger, and No Peace,* which he published on his own in the year 1844 in Zutphen, where he was minister of the Mennonite congregation. He was not yet thirty years old at that time. In his pamphlet he criticized the Dutch Mennonites of his time very harshly. During the remaining twenty-five years of his life—until his early death in 1869—he felt himself obliged

159

to be just as harsh a critic of the whole body of Dutch Protestants.

The immediate cause for writing the above-mentioned pamphlet was the controversy between his older colleague, the Reverend Halbertsma of nearby Deventer, and his own teacher, Professor Samuel Muller, who was then nearly sixty years old and had reached the highest point of his influence in the Dutch Mennonite brotherhood. Halbertsma had published a series of sermons together with an introduction, in which he criticized Muller's leadership. Halbertsma feared that Muller's leadership would result in a return to rigid orthodoxy. Muller on his side had reviewed Halbertsma's sermons and denounced the author's complete lack of theological knowledge. Muller's friend Boeke, a Mennonite minister in Amsterdam, published an open letter to Halbertsma, defending the professor and declaring that the danger of orthodoxy was very small indeed. He contended that not more than one or possibly two students of Muller could be found to be orthodox.[1] In his pamphlet de Liefde then proclaimed that he himself should be identified as one of those students of Muller who had become orthodox.

The 110-page pamphlet is written in an excellent style. In my opinion it is by far the best prose of any religious work written by a Dutch Mennnonite in the nineteenth century. He gave it the subtitle: *A Word to Those Sleeping and Lulled to Sleep*. His harsh cry remained completely unanswered. In his own congregation, where the members did not like his sermons though many non-Mennonites of the lower classes were glad to hear them, his position became quite untenable. In the course of the next year he was obliged to retire voluntarily. De Liefde was later to deny that his resignation was voluntary, but formally it had indeed been his own decision to relinquish his position as a Mennonite minister.

In this article I will try to describe for the reader of the second half of the twentieth century, especially in America, what the harshest critic of the Dutch Mennonites in the middle of the nineteenth century had to say. He did not engage in discussion with his older colleague Halbertsma. He simply denied his Christianity, for he saw him as still completely under the power of Satan, as de Liefde himself had been until his conversion. In Halbertsma's sermons, "in which the Lord is abased and man deified," de Liefde found again the ideas that his own natural self would like to proclaim, that he would have proclaimed before his conversion, if only he had dared to do so. But de Liefde had been more prudent and preached his sermons so that they did not appear so openly to be godless. De Liefde said:

The Lord has not yet opened his eyes—with that one word all is said. For as long as he is still wandering in the darkness, what else can a man do than hate the light and stumble over the stone laid down in Zion? What else can he do except to slander, to err, to lie, to be proud, arrogant and bitter? Look at his opponents. What else is there to be seen in them, notwithstanding all the delicacy in their language—what else than throwing away from themselves and throwing at the guilty one?"

Jan de Liefde also did not want to enter into discussions with Muller and Boeke. But looking at the danger in which he saw the Dutch Mennonites of his time, he wished to make clear: 1) "that the central point for the unity of the Mennonites is untenable," 2) 'that this unity is not in Christ," 3) "that the means employed to consolidate and further this unity are not from God," and 4) "that the fruits produced by this unity contradict the Word of God."

In dealing with the first point he made clear that only a small minority of the Mennonites asserted that the Holy Scriptures are the word of God, whereas by far the greater part only accepted that the word of God might be contained within the Holy Scriptures. Since the content of the word of God is uncertain, the Scriptures do not provide the required central point for unity. Only the outward sign of adult baptism remained. But was there really a solid background for that sign?

Mennonites all give the same name to their Lord, namely Christ, but in their images of Him do not resemble each other at all. Some see Him as a perfect man raised to heaven by God. Very few will say Jesus is God himself revealed in the flesh. "He is a God-man, a single being, who has no peer, no equal in the whole of creation. . . . My heart burns within me when I am allowed to draw this picture," says de Liefde, "because he is glorious, the only one for whom all that belongs to him is quite desirable. Alas, the number of those who have such a Lord is relatively small among the Mennonites of our day." The third and by far the greatest party has still a different Lord. De Liefde then quotes the manual of Muller's close adherent, Boeke, "a sinless, holy, perfect man and also a higher Godlike being." De Liefde then says that this expression "makes you think of a high, elevated creature, an angel of the highest order, an inhabitant of heaven, who before he became man had trained himself in virtue and wisdom." And he concludes, "So much at least is clear, that to them he is not God, otherwise they would surely grant to God the honor that he deserves."

That there was not one faith among the Mennonites of his time de Liefde demonstrated by pointing to the differing views of the two professors of the Mennonite seminary, Muller and Cnoop Knoopmanns.[2] Recalling the time when he studied at the seminary he tells us, "While the first made us compose sermons in which we spoke to man as a being having sufficient power in himself to make himself perfect, with the help of the grace of God, and urged him to purify himself of all sin, the other spoke in his lectures on ethics about man and his depraved nature in a tone that surely would have edified Augustine and Calvin." In a note at the bottom of page 35 of his pamphlet de Liefde asks Cnoop Knoopmans to contradict this openly if he felt he had been misunderstood and did not really disagree with Muller. So far as I could tell, Knoopmans never did, but until his early death in 1849 he remained Muller's best personal friend.

On the lack of unity concerning baptism de Liefde says:

When in Ephesians 4:5 the apostle speaks of one baptism as a sign of the unity of the church, he surely does not have in mind only the baptism by one Spirit (1 Cor. 12:13). Where one denies the existence of that Spirit as a person, while the other glorifies him as God, and a third one contradicts his immediate influence by the spirit of man—how could they really be baptized by one Spirit and be drenched with one Spirit?

Having in this way demonstrated that no unity in Lord, belief, and baptism could be found among the Dutch Mennonites, de Liefde points to the French phrase *Esprit de corps* as typifying the Mennonite community.

This corporate spirit has three characteristics: first, that it does not submit itself to any fixed rule, but depends only on the meaning that is accepted by the majority; secondly, that it considers its own organization to excel all others because of its special exclusive prerogatives and for that reason places itself in a certain kind of empty opposition against any other organization; in the third place, it puts the existence of the organization above the existence of the whole to which the organization belongs.

In dealing with the third point concerning the means used to further Mennonite unity de Liefde analyzes the work of the Algemeene Doopsgezinde Societeit (ADS) at Amsterdam. On the one hand it aims at supporting needy, dwindling, or languishing congregations; on the other hand it seeks to train young men for preaching. With regard to the first aim, de Liefde criticizes the council of the ADS because it is an aristocratic body. "All are men of the upper class, rich capitalists or scholars from the principal towns of the nation." Concerning the second, he points to the fact that there is not only the question of aristocracy but also of a hierarchy (a reign of priests). Officially the professors and ministers in the council have no legal authority over the other ministers and the congregations. But "in spite of their own intention they become priests and popes and often before they are aware of it themselves, they have gripped the episcopal crosier with both hands." In addition to this de Liefde asserts that "the Mennonite Church is governed according to the metropolitan system. . . . On account of this all things are in, from, and by Amsterdam—so that among the Mennonites Amsterdam becomes what Rome is among the Catholics."

And then there is still a last means for unification that should be mentioned, says de Liefde. "It is money, that powerful cultivator of unity that can reconcile the greatest enemies, that may quell the most fierce uproar." De Liefde was especially critical of the fact that there was no public accounting of the funds used. Also that in the case of a disagreement between a congregation and a minister the congregation was always taken to be in the right and the financial responsibilities toward the minister were canceled. This was a bad thing in the eyes of de Liefde. He speaks of "a principle that, if it had been vigorously applied in the apostolic period of Christianity, would have left the Apostle Paul without the support which the congregations were sending him, for no one has ever given greater offense than Paul, de Liefde concluded. At the end of his section on the third concern, de Liefde says, "Far from pretending that the Mennonite Conference is engaging in such un-Christian practices on purpose, we have only demonstrated how the spirit and the whole organization of their ecclesiastical life has necessarily resulted in such practices."

Under his fourth and last point de Liefde begins by saying "that not only the ministers but every member of the congregation should pay attention to doctrine." He puts on record that every heresy is tolerated, except infant baptism. But, he adds:

Where there is no concern for doctrine, no force to enforce discipline, there is surely no bond nor bridle. But can freedom in Christ be the same as the lack of bond and bridle? . . . The apostles . . . did not hesitate to resist firmly any heretical tendencies and ideas. . . . There was certainty and conviction, on account of which the congregations could face eternity with unmistakable assurance, for they know that their salvation has been accomplished. . . . [Therefore] one of the following three must be true: either the Mennonite congregations are perfect and constitute a group that never takes offence at the truth; or the Mennonite ministers are more able preachers of the truth than the Lord Jesus and his Apostles, as is evident from their ability to preach the truth without giving any noticeable offence; or the Mennonite ministers preserve peace and quiet in their congregations at the expense of fair and faithful preaching of the truth itself.

Having thus made clear his four points, de Liefde acknowledges that all that he has become he owes to the help given by the Amsterdam congregation, and that he has received all of his education and training from the ADS and its seminary. Now, he says, "they desire evidences of my gratitude for the benefits I have received."

Well then, I cannot offer better ones than I have given in these pages. I see the conference in danger; I hear voices that are calling "peace, peace." What would be of greater value than to warn those who are sleeping of the danger that is imminent? Would I really love my benefactors if I allowed them to drop asleep at the brink of their ruin? But what good is it to be appointed as a minister within the conference if I do not warn, admonish, or give advice?

Having thus poured out his deep concern for his people, de Liefde concludes, "The cry has been 'peace, peace,' but in the midst of that peace I see grave danger. Now I have cried 'danger, danger,' in order that, if God wills, real peace may come in spite of these external dangers."

What was the effect of de Liefde's pamphlet? The answer to this question seems very simple. Whoever studies Dutch Mennonite history in the midst of the nineteenth century will find that practically no response was given. The brotherhood lost de Liefde as one of its ministers about a year after the publication of his pamphlet. Several years later he published a second pamphlet with the title, *Answer to Professor S. Muller*. The second was, in my opinion, not as arresting a proof of his ability to admonish as his first. He had lost his contact with the Mennonite brotherhood, the only community of faith in the midst of which his admonitions could have made real sense. Therefore it was a real tragedy for him to have left the brotherhood. Not that he was not listened to by others outside of the Mennonite congregations. On the contrary, his influence on the malcontents within the Reformed Church—and they were numerous— was very great. De Liefde showed them the way to act, to rebuild their church if it should become clear that it was no longer God's congregation. Quite a number of Free Evangelical Churches (*Vrij Evangelische Gemeenten*) that still exist in the Netherlands, came into being directly through the work of Jan de Liefde. Many others felt themselves strengthened by his activities. But personally I am quite convinced that all his work for Christian education in the family and the school, his ardent fight for the separation of church and state, his high spirited disavowal of the so-called Christianity of western civilization— all this should have been connected with the Anabaptist tradition, as the tradition should have remained alive among the Dutch Mennonites.

De Liefde made a mistake in leaving the Mennonite brotherhood. But the leading men of his generation made a still greater mistake in not trying to retain him. When the renowned merchant and man of letters, Willem de Clercq had left the Mennonite brotherhood some fifteen years before, Muller and Cnoop Knoopmans wrote him long letters. The latter expressed the hope that de Clercq would come back. De Clercq had succumbed to strong Calvinist influences, had favored infant baptism, and had become entangled in the typical non-Mennonite problems of H. F. Kohlbrugge's very remarkable theology.[3] But until his death de Liefde's orthodoxy remained typically non-Calvinist and non-Lutheran. He himself might have believed that he did not fit well into the Mennonite brotherhood; others should have declared energetically that he ought not to depart.

But in general the whole brotherhood remained silent. Nobody answered his pamphlet, and when de Liefde left the brotherhood a year later, there was also no protest in the congregations. In 1861 when the ADS celebrated its first fifty years, de Liefde's name was not mentioned. At the celebration of its first centennial nothing was heard about his harsh critique.[4] In 1947, however, Peter van der Meulen wrote his thesis for his theological doctorate on the genesis of the ADS, *De wording van de Algemeene Doopsgezinde Societeit* (Wormerveer, 1947), in which he tried to do justice to Jan de Liefde. And in 1961, at the time of the commemoration of the 150th anniversary of the founding of the ADS the writer of this chapter published a booklet *Twee dienaars van een Heer, Samuel Muller en Jan de Liefde* (Two Servants of One Lord . . .). The title derived from the viewpoint that the leading man of the nineteenth century Mennonites and his harsh critic should be seen as complementary to each other.

I have already said that de Liefde made a mistake in leaving our brotherhood. For the brotherhood his departure was certainly a kind of handwriting on the wall (*meme tekel*) that was not duly recognized. On the other hand, he not only made quite a number of tactical errors that might be understood as arising from various difficulties in his character, but he also had a serious defect in his theological insights. He had chosen for orthodoxy and against rationalism (of Halbertsma) and supernaturalism (of Muller and Boeke). In his orthodoxy he wished to be biblical and not ecclesiastical. And he really knew the Bible well. Therefore he understood the necessity of saying *no* to theological ideas which he recognized as false. But did he really see how Samuel Muller was also endeavoring to do justice to the whole message of the Bible? It is clear that he did not understand Muller mentally, although he certainly loved him. That Muller's supernaturalism was untenable and would be succeeded by a form of liberalism that would be unable to give due attention to the message of the Bible, de Liefde foresaw, though Muller saw it only after he was an old man of more than eighty years of age. But de Liefde did not understand that in the light of biblical revelation his own rigid orthodoxy was no more tenable than Muller's supernaturalism. De Liefde was right in saying *no* to the heresies of others. He was not critical enough of his own system. To have right insight into truth always remains a calling—it never has been nor ever will be an obtained possession. The New Testament could have taught him that. It may be necessary for a Christian to say *no* to his fellow Christian with full conviction. But de Liefde said it on rather formal grounds to nearly all of his fellow Mennonites.

For de Liefde the main issue was, Is Jesus Christ really God? That was surely no minor matter. And whoever denies that Jesus Christ is God has to justify his way of thinking, for it deviates from the main stream of Christian thought. But it has been proved that all orthodox theological words can be used in such a way that they do not mean anything. Within the Mennonite brotherhood things should be talked through all the way. The one should ask the other the exact meaning and content of the words he uses. That, however, was not done as often as it should have been done in the days of Muller and de Liefde, even as it is done too infrequently today. Although they could never forget each other—indeed, they seemed to have loved each other until the end of their lives—they did not find the way to full reconciliation.

It seems rather difficult to find out why they could not. Did they perhaps overestimate their respective differences and points of view? That is likely. But, as far as I can see, that was not the fundamental reason for their remaining discord. That reason, I believe, could be found in the fact that both of them failed to see the central importance of the Anabaptist implications of their position. Therefore, both identified themselves too much with the major trends within the Christian life of those days. De Liedfe stood on the right wing, and his influence stimulated the rise of Neo-Calvinist confessionalism, which he would not have approved at all. He died before this Neo-Calvinist movement expanded to become one of the major

167

trends of Dutch national life. De Liefde died in 1869, near the end of his fifty-fifth year. The great rise of Neo-Calvinism in the Netherlands did not take place until the last quarter of the century. Muller stood on the left wing, but he was upset —as I have shown above—when in the late 1860s he saw how the modernist movement was developing. He was then more than eighty years old and his former pupils did not listen to him any longer. He died in 1875, at the age of ninety, personally respected but considered as a man of the past. Only in his private *Memoirs* could his children and grandchildren read how far he had rejected the modernist development of his later days.

In our day, more than a century later, the time may have come when the heritage of Jan de Liefde can be accepted by the Dutch Mennonites and made fruitful for the whole of our world-wide brotherhood. May there be found among us on both sides of the Atlantic those who are willing to study more profoundly than I did what the harsh critic in the midst of the last century had to say. In the situation of our days, in which the heritage of the Anabaptists is of more value than ever before, we should listen to Jan de Liefde, who was surely one of us to a much greater degree than he himself knew.

Part Two

GERHARD LOHRENZ

The Mennonites of Russia and the Great Commission

ANABAPTISTS FOUND their way to the Vistula Delta shortly after the origin of the movement. Some apparently came as early as 1530. Though the swampy terrain was considered unfit for settlement, they came in search of freedom of worship. Three generations were to labor before the region became habitable. The high price paid by these pioneers is indicated by the report that eighty per cent of the settlers during the first years died of swamp fever.[1] Many political restrictions were placed on them. Over two hundred years had to pass before they were permitted to build their own churches—in 1768. They were forbidden to accept ethnic non-Mennonites into their church. No preaching outside of Mennonite circles was permitted. Though they were not actually persecuted, they did suffer under the constant oppression and severe restrictions placed on their family and corporate life. This was particularly true because of their practice of biblical nonresistance. Eventually the burden of intolerance became almost unbearable. In this dark hour of the eighteenth century the Mennonites were offered a refuge by the Russian government.

The exodus to southern Russia began in 1788 and continued, with some interruptions, to 1865. According to Ehrt a total of 1609 families, comprising some 8000 individuals, came to Russia.[2] The reasons for emigration, however, were not ex-

171

clusively religious. A high birth rate, together with a pro-
nounced rural-agricultural orientation, had led to a considerable shortage of good land for the younger generations. Beyond this many considered the Prussian cultural environment a
threat to the values of the Mennonite faith. The Russian government, on the other hand, was eager to settle its vast southern
lands with potentially prosperous farmers. Attractive offers were
consequently made to new settlers.

A great deal has been written, particularly by P. M. Friesen,
about the special privileges granted to the Mennonites by the
Russian government.[3] Unfortunately, Friesen was a rather un-
critical admirer of Russia and his interpretation of the intentions of the Russian government are not penetrating. Actually,
the Mennonites were granted only the rights granted to all
foreign settlers with the exception of military service. Whereas
other settlers were given some freedom from military service,
up to twenty years exemption, the Mennonites were to be free
from military service *for all eternity*. Ehrt, a non-Mennonite
historian, has come to the conclusion that the supposed privileges granted to the Mennonites have been misunderstood and
overestimated.[4] A Russian writer states:

The privileges granted by our government were not so much a lure
for the settlers as simply a necessary, realistic requirement without which
settlements could not have taken place. These privileges were granted
equally to all those who cared to settle in the regions set aside by the
government for this purpose.[5]

Concerning this problem Cornelius Krahn has stated:

In truth, the territory of the Ukraine where the Mennonites built their
temporary miserable mud huts, had only recently been acquired by
Russia and was a place of exile from Moscow, where wild Nomads
pastured their herds. Not a shrub could be seen and never had a plow-
share torn the soil.[6]

The Mennonites were required to live in areas assigned exclusively to them. Since southern Russia was only gradually
being penetrated by the Russian people, the Mennonites of
the first and second generations found themselves completely
surrounded by other alien cultural elements, primarily roving
Mohammedans. Thus the requirement to remain in their
area simply reinforced the Mennonite tendency to isolation.

Separated from their environment by government decree, by culture, language, social status, and religion, and separated by many miles from their former home, the new colonies remained isolated communities forced to shift for themselves as best they could.

The cultural level of these first settlers was low. Though the German language was used in all church services, it was understood rather poorly, the Low German (platt Deutsch) constituting the primary medium of communication. There were few books. Few leaders of intellectual and spiritual stature had accompanied them to their new home. The ministers were elected from among the laity, without formal training. Since no remuneration was given for their services they struggled, as did all the others, to wrest a living from the hostile soil.

Under these circumstances a slow stagnation crept into the intellectual and spiritual life of the group. When missionary David Schlatter visited the colonies in 1825 he reported that the church had "lost its salt."[7] But the spiritual life was to sink even lower during the next two decades. What impact could have come from Russian culture was lost since the settlers did not know the Russian language. By 1845 only one item had been printed by the Mennonites in Russia, a polemical tract on the *Kleine Gemeinde*.[8] Continued intermarriage within the group led to a unique self and group consciousness. To be a Mennonite meant not primarily religious but ethnic relations. To censure or condemn the group for this decline, however, is unwarranted in view of the circumstances we have just considered.

Slowly the positive forces began to assert themselves. Many longed for a more intensely dedicated Christian life. The schools were reformed. Even more, this new restlessness found expression in the emerging of *new Christians,* the origin of the Mennonite Brethren Church, an event which shook the very foundations of the Russian Mennonite community. So strong was the impact of this *renaissance* on Mennonite life that by 1924 Karl Lindemann, a non-Mennonite, could say:

The high level of economic and intellectual development among the Mennonites is the inevitable legacy inherited from their fathers, a heritage they have increasingly developed and perfected. Among these qualities the striving for further development of the mind and the intellect are particularly conspicuous. This is true also of their diligence and perseverance, their social sensitivity and their subsequent altruism. The latter finds expression in a host of welfare institutions, in general charity, and in a deep religiousness which penetrates and regulates both their familial and social relationships.[9]

THE FULFILLING OF THE GREAT COMMISSION

A Promise Not to Evangelize?

The Mennonites of Russia have repeatedly been accused of having promised not to evangelize among the Russian population. Such a promise was never made. It is true, of course, that a quarter century before their coming, on July 22, 1763, the Russian government categorically forbade all proselyting among members of any Christian denomination within the Russian realm.[10] To persuade a member of the Russian Orthodox Church to leave the establishment was considered a criminal offense.[11] It has been argued that, since such laws existed in Russia, the Mennonites should not have settled there. But where else could they go? They not only needed more land, but had lived under very similar restrictions in Prussia for over two centuries.

The Mennonites of Russia have also been accused of accepting a system of privileges which were not bound to qualifications of faith but of blood.[12] This charge is difficult to understand. Wherever in history people have fought or bargained for liberty they have always sought to secure this benefit for their children as well as for themselves, hoping, of course, that their descendants would share their convictions. Is it wrong to discover this same concern among the Mennonites? Lindemann, in discussing the agreement between the Mennonites and the Russian government, wrote, "In these negotiations the problems related to freedom of conscience took first place."[13]

Beyond this it has been suggested that the internal decay which blighted the Mennonite communities in Russia for a time resulted from "the dry rot of cultural egotism."[14] Again we must point to the circumstances that led to this decline. The decay which did come was not due to cultural selfishness but simply to the fact that, as is so often the case in history, a great

174

truth was contained in "earthen vessels." The environmental and traditional problems led to where these vessels for a time bore too eloquent a testimony to their earthiness. This was not deliberate, though it was sin; the decline arose from the inability to be and to do otherwise because of human weakness. As such, the spiritual ebb, while not excusable, is a persistent historical and existential problem.

Yet even in the times of lethargy there were those who had not lost the vision. The old Anabaptist concept of the church as a fellowship of believers and the concern for the Great Commission was never lost completely among the Russian Mennonites. Though the fires burned low a breakthrough here and there, on the part of individuals or small groups, bore evidence to the depth of life beneath the surface. In its own time the fire was to break forth with a clear, consuming light.

Growing Concern for Home Missions

One sign of this breakthrough was the growing concern for the spiritual welfare of the unregenerate within the colonies, focusing in the work usually referred to as *Innere Mission*. A number of the settlers had come into contact with evangelical pietism in Prussia, resulting in a clearer understanding of the Scriptures, in a more vital Christian life, and in a new love for schools and mission work.[15] Among these new leaders was Tobias Voth who, converted at the age of twenty-seven, became a pioneer educator among the Mennonites. Thus Friesen wrote that, "since the time of Voth and Bernhard Fast a new understanding of the Christian life, enriched through inner experience and growth, never died out in the Ohrloff congregation."[16] Similarly new life flourished in the Rudnerweide, Alexanderwohl, and particularly the Gnadenfeld churches. Mission festivals were conducted. Contrary to common practice the ministers of these churches did not read their sermons, but presented them freely.[17] It was this warm, personal Christianity of which Voth was the first representative, that became the forerunner of what was known as *Brudertum*. Representing a synthesis of the more positive aspects of pietism and Mennonitism it continued among the so-called *Kirchengemeinde* even after the founding of the Mennonite Brethren Church.[18]

175

The advocates of this deeper life were at the same time those who carried a concern for all nonbelievers, Mennonite and others. They offered their help to the Russian Bible Society, founded in Leningrad in the nineteenth century, to distribute Bibles among the native Russians. The orthodox Russian historian C. D. Bondar reports that "many of them [Mennonites] felt compelled to assist in the distribution of the Scriptures."[19] A branch of the Bible society was organized in the Molotschna settlement and officially recognized in 1821. Here the Mennonite elders Fast, Goerz, and Wedel took an active part.[20]

The interest of the Mennonites in the welfare of their Russian co-citizens became apparent in other ways. During the Crimean War (1854-56), and the Russo-Turkish War (1877-78), thousands of wounded Russian soldiers were voluntarily taken into Mennonite homes and nursed back to health. Large sums of money were collected to assist the bereaved families of Russian soldiers. According to the records of the Russian government the Chortitza settlement alone contributed approximately 100,000 rubles for the aid of needy Russians during the years from 1853 to 1892. During the Russo-Turkish War the Molotschna settlement cared for many Bulgarian refugees. When the Russian government offered to reimburse them in the amount of 50,000 rubles the Mennonites declined. Instead, they lent some 33,000 bushels of seed grain to the refugees. Similar help was given on other occasions as N. B. Kamensky also reports in his book, *A Question of a Misunderstanding?*[21]

Kamensky reports an interesting and illuminating incident. The Mennonite, Herman A. Bergman, had donated a large sum of money for the repair of the Orthodox Church in the Russian village of Solonenenko in 1889. He had, however, attached one condition to the gift, a condition which the village had accepted. No alcoholic beverages, said Bergman, were to be sold in the village for a period of six years. Kamensky added, "the beneficial results of this act are already noticeable."[22]

There were many evidences of concern also on the part of well-to-do individuals. One of these, Peter Heese (d. 1911), supplied several Russian villages with all necessary food during a year of famine.[23] During the Russo-Japanese War dozens of Mennonite young men served as volunteers in Red Cross units at the front. Several of them lost their lives, including a medical doctor, Nikolas Friesen.[24]

Nevertheless, the Mennonite church found itself in a dilemma. The Great Commission clearly urged "Go Ye"; the law of the land said, "Don't you dare." For this predicament the Mennonites found a solution known as *vertical mission work.* This meant, essentially, confining themselves to the task of training and evangelizing their own children and young people. Since the total number of Mennonites doubled approximately every twenty-five years, this was indeed a formidable task. A minute of the all-Mennonite meeting held on January 24 and 25, 1883, points out the concern for this home mission work:

In the interest of our home mission work we desire and feel compelled to see that the following be achieved: a) That Christian nurture, family worship, prayer, and above all, genuine piety be pursued in the home. b) That the schools seek these same ends through able, humble, and pious teachers supported both by pupils and by parents. c) That all congregations pursue these ends through Sunday schools for children, activities for young people. These must be taught to carry on a proper Christian conversation. Also, a thorough catechetical instruction must be provided in order that d) a common bond of love may unite our congregations and all scattered brethren. To all the gospel message must be brought, first through the placement of teachers and elders as necessary and possible; second, through the itineration of visiting preachers. . . .[25]

The conference of the following year decided, among other things, to discourage entertainments "which run contrary to a life of sanctification, to wit: indecent songs, card playing, dancing, and etc. . . ."[26] The conference of 1890 took a stand against excessive drinking of alcoholic beverages as well as sale of the same, against dancing, card playing, and other ills. It suggested that the best means of combating these evils is the forceful preaching of God's word. It was decided to establish good libraries and to organize church choirs and Christian youth groups.[27]

In discussing the admission of people from non-Mennonite background into the church, the conference of 1889 spoke as follows:

It is not contrary to our articles of faith to admit individuals from other denominations if they wish to join our church. Our circumstances in

Russia are such, however, that our right to admit them is limited. No one can be admitted from the Orthodox Church, nor are males from Lutheran, Catholic, or Reformed churches eligible, since they and their sons are obliged to render military service. It is permissible to accept females from the last three churches. This is not contrary to our confession of faith.[28]

It is interesting to note that the conference of 1887 recognized the necessity of establishing a theological school for the training of Mennonite ministers. The repeated emphasis on this need in subsequent conferences indicates a sensitivity to the needs of the church and a vision for its welfare and growth.

A new and vigorous church had emerged with the founding of the Mennonite Brethren Church in 1860. With it came a new sense of mission. Whereas the old church had lost most of its zeal and contented itself with a peaceful coexistence, the new church soon found ways of implementing the Great Commission. Both Ehrt[29] and Bondar testify to this, the latter saying that "in common with the German Baptists the New Mennonites have played a prominent role in the development of the South Russian baptism . . ."[30] He continues by relating how the authorities found a group of evangelical believers in the Russian village of Ostrikovo, and that the new Mennonite Gerhard Wieler of nearby Liebenau had been their teacher. Wieler had been able to explain the Bible to them in their own language. The meetings in Ostrikovo had been held in private homes, attended by some twenty to thirty-five persons. Several of these Russian believers had also attended the prayer meetings of the new Mennonites in Liebenau.

Since this work was illegal, the risk involved was considerable. The law provided that "for the seduction of a member of the Orthodox Church to any other confession the guilty party will be condemned to the loss of all personal property as well as of his rights and privileges. He will be exiled to Siberia or else condemned to serve in corrective penal institutions."[31] The law published in 1894 against the *Stundists*, an evangelical-pietistic movement, was equally rigorous and more explicit. All children were to be taken from parents who confessed to be *Stundists*. Worship services were forbidden, as were private schools. Their membership had to be registered and published to prevent their employment by orthodox believers. They were not allowed to own or rent property. If found reading the Bible or praying with others the *Stundist* was to be arrested immediately and sent to Siberia without process of law. Finally, no funerals were allowed for them, nor were they to be buried in hallowed, i.e., cemetery, ground.[32]

The new converts of Ostrikovo, however, not only rejoiced in their new faith but spread it to other villages. Some of them removed the icons from their homes, a blasphemous action punishable with from eight to thirty-six months imprisonment. To destroy an icon meant lifelong exile to Siberia, yet the new converts felt that to retain them was a sin in the light of the second commandment. When several converts stopped attending the Orthodox Church further trouble, including court action, followed. In his work with this group Wieler was assisted by the new Mennonites John Klassen and Jacob Reimer. Particular emphasis was placed on the distribution of copies of the New Testament.

Many other instances of effective work among the native Russian population are evident. In 1863 Evrosina Morosowa, who had been employed by Henry Huebert, was baptized by a Mennonite minister, encouraged by the congregation of Liebenau of which Huebert and Benjamin Bekker were leaders.[33] In 1862 Henry Neufeld, Abram Unger, Gerhard Wieler, and Peter Berg, all new Mennonites, were cited before the court for spreading sectarian, i.e., Mennonite, doctrine. Though the charge could not be proved, they were placed under strict police surveillance. In October 1863 Wieler baptized Mathvey Serbulenko, a Russian boy in the employ of new Mennonite Willms. On April 22, 1864, Wieler baptized twenty-two-year-old Andrew Pedacenko in the village of Einlage. For this deed Wieler was sent to prison in 1865. The other leaders remained under police observation. In June 1865 Peter Froese, also a new Mennonite, was cited before the court to answer charges of having influenced the Russian Jacob Sarany to leave the Orthodox Church.

A revival had broken out in the Lutheran villages of Old and New Danzig in 1864, through the work of the Chortitza new Mennonites. On May 10 some twenty persons were baptized there. A similar impact was made on the Swedish vil-

179

lages of Schlangendorf and Muehlhausendorf on the Dnieper River, and even in the Jewish village of Dobraja. In these efforts Wieler, Neufeld, Unger, Klassen, Bekker, and others took the initiative. Their very boldness forced government intervention. Aaron Lepp, a new Mennonite who had preached while in government service, was dismissed from his post. In spite of these difficulties the Einlage Mennonites retained intimate contact with the Danzig group, preaching to them and breaking bread with them. On July 11, 1869, Johann Unger, the brother of Gerhard—who was to play an important role in the history of baptism in southern Russia—baptized some thirty individuals of the Danzig group. Among these was Efim Cymbal who soon assumed leadership among the new group. It was he who baptized Ivan Raboshapka, though the latter had been converted by the new Mennonite Martin Huebner. Raboshapka later baptized Ratushney. These two were to become the primary evangelists among the native Russian population of the South, gaining wide recognition in evangelical circles for their ministry.

Thus Wieler carried on an effective ministry from 1870. In 1871-72 he worked in the Odessa region. For a time he made his home in the Lutheran village of Rohrbach. The Russian peasants came to him from far and wide and, as Bondar states, he "seduced" them to the new faith. Within this new fellowship cultural walls disappeared. The Russian converts took part in Mennonite services and shared their hospitality. After their organization as independent congregations these converts, as well as the German Baptists, took part in the church conferences of the new Mennonites. At the Rueckenau (Molotschna) conference of May 21 and 22, 1882, for example, nineteen Russian Baptists and several German Baptists participated together with the delegates of the four new Mennonite congregations: Molotschna, Einlage, Friedensfeld, and Kuban. The latter four sent more than fifty delegates. Items of both common and specific concern to the *Russian Brethren* and the *German Brethren* were discussed. It is evident from the minutes of the conference that the South Russian Baptists and the new Mennonites had one missionary committee and a common treasury at this time.

John Wieler was deeply involved in work with the Baptists. In 1884 he called a conference of Russian Baptists at Novo-vasilevka to organize *The Union of the Russian Baptists.* In 1886 Wieler was elected first chairman, a position he held until his flight to Romania in order to avoid exile to Siberia.[34] He translated the Oncken (German Baptist) confession of faith for his Russian Baptist brethren. It was used as the official state-ment, being printed in 1906 at Rostov under the title *The Con-fession of Faith of the Russian Evangelical Christian Baptists.*[35]

The new Mennonite publishing house *Raduga* was estab-lished at this time to aid in the circulation of literature in the German and Russian languages. Thousands of books, brochures, and tracts carrying the spiritual concerns of the new Menno-nites were circulated through its work. A sales outlet was estab-lished in Leningrad, with the well-known evangelical Christian minister I. C. Prochanov in charge.

The ecumenical activity of Wieler, the *Raduga* press, and others continued on every hand. The new Mennonite Gerhard Braun addressed a conference of evangelical Christians in Lenin-grad in September 1909; P. M. Friesen represented the Men-nonites at the all-Russian Baptist Congress held at Rostov in 1909. In 1906 an *Alliance House* was opened in Halbstadt, Molotschna, to serve as a house of worship for all true believ-ers.[36] Mennonite preachers found ready acceptance among the Russian Baptists. One of the latter, Balachin, wrote that "the brethren J. Reimer and P. Unruh are especially gifted and very useful at Bible conferences. Wherever these are to be organized I would recommend that these brethren be invited."[37]

That this work with the Baptists and other evangelicals did not crowd out Mennonite concern for the established church is seen from an article appearing in the *Friedenstimme*:

During this year 1910 we have already experienced great blessings in Barvenkovo. Many have turned to the Lord. The Spirit of God is active among the Russians, though too slowly, as it seems to us. The Russian brethren gather in the house of brother Golub on Sundays. How happy we would be if we could build a beautiful house of worship for our Russian brethren here in Barvenkovo. This year we have appointed eleven brethren to work among the Russian people.[38]

It is clear that not all Mennonites approved of these activities. Their objections varied. A number of the concerns commonly stated, however, are given by Elder Heinrich Dirks of Gnadenfeld, who opposed the new zeal, as follows:

In late 1910 government officials began to search for Baptists among our people. The members of the Mennonite Brethren Church, as also members of the other new churches that have arisen among us, are suspected of being Baptists. The investigating officials clearly wanted to hear us say that the others were Baptists.

Among the old Mennonites there are indeed those who consider the new Mennonites to be Baptists. Such conclusions seemed logical since the new churches are in closer fellowship with the Baptists than with us. While they refuse to celebrate communion with us they take it with the others. As far as I know, however, no one has officially called them Baptists. We have stated that they too, are a part of the Mennonite people.

That this would happen could be foreseen. . . . Our people have been warned not to take action which would make it appear that we are non-Mennonites, since this would surely lead to a loss of the privileges granted only to Mennonites. . . . The Scriptures warn against a zeal that is not according to knowledge (Rom. 10:2). To initiate propaganda in existing churches is against the counsel of the Apostle Paul (Rom. 15:20). . . . Every Christian church must renew itself from within. Of late certain religious liberties have been restricted. . . . Is this not the result of zeal without judgment which some new churchers and their sympathizers have engaged in? Shall we all now pay for the folly of these few? So long as the Lord, who holds the key which opens and closes doors, has not opened the door to free and open evangelism in Russia we of ourselves are not permitted to break that door open. Such action can have serious consequences for us all.[39]

Nevertheless, the work continued. In many ways the Mennonites provided the major evangelical thrust in Russia. Thus Ehrt concludes that "the Mennonites were important carriers and leaders of the evangelical movement. Mennonitism was the midwife and tutor of Russian evangelicalism. . . . In the historical-spiritual field this is the most significant contribution of the Mennonites in Russia."[40] Lindemann adds: "The German settlers have . . . taught their Russian fellow citizens to organize their family life as well as their entire household according to the German pattern and have taught them to lead a life in accordance with human dignity." The whole world knows, says Lindemann, that the German settlers instigated the evangelical movement in Russia.[41] Saloff-Astakhoff wrote: "Yet though they [the Mennonites] could not evangelize openly they had a strong influence upon the surrounding Russian population, helping to spread the evangelical Protestant movement in this country."[42]   When the Russian Baptist delegation visited America in 1956 it was reported that "the visitors spoke of the Mennonites as evangelical pioneers, the first sowers of the truth of the gospel in their land.   Mennonites have had a great influence upon the evangelistic movement, and their preachers today are helping the Baptists in the evangelization of the many who are only nominally Christian."[43]

It has become clear that much mission activity was carried on.   That this was carried on primarily by the new Mennonites is obvious.   Both Ehrt and Bondar agree that the old Mennonite Church (*kirchliche*) did no mission work among the native population.[44]   That many of the old church joined the new Mennonite movement because they shared the rising vision for evangelism together with a longing for deeper spiritual life is self-evident.   Thus, while the Mennonite Brethren Church comprised only 4.3 per cent of the total Mennonite population in Russia in 1888, they had grown to include 22.5 per cent by 1925.[45]

The preceding discussion has been based on the written sources.   Much quiet witnessing was carried on by thousands of Mennonites in their daily living during their entire stay in Russia.   I remember vividly how my mother would talk to our native Russian workers about spiritual things.   Since many of the girls were illiterate, Mother bought a book with many illustrations.   It depicted the human heart, full of evil, of pride (a peacock), impurity (a pig), etc.   It showed how the word of God could shine into the human heart to cleanse it by the power of the Spirit and ended with the picture of a clean heart in which Christ could dwell.   I remember, too, that as a young lad I saw my parents and our Russian maid kneeling together in prayer.   These influences have not been recorded but form a part of the total witness given within the land.   The effects of this *living of the faith* can, of course, not be measured.

Participation in Foreign Missions

Another sign of spiritual vigor among the Russian Mennonites was their participation in foreign mission work.   Tobias

Voth must be considered the pioneer. He organized mission study groups, secured mission literature, and received offerings, which he forwarded to the Mission Society at Barmen.[46] A letter written to Voth on June 30, 1827, by Moravian Bishop Gottlob Schneider testifies to the cordial relations with other mission bodies, as does a letter written by a missionary Salet of Tiflis to Elder Bernhard Fast on July 27, 1825[47] Salet had apparently visited the Mennonite settlement earlier. Another missionary, Moritz, had visited Lichtenau in 1825.[48] The Swiss missionary Schlatter visited the Mennonite settlements repeatedly.

Stimulated by these contacts the churches, particularly the church at Gnadenfeld, soon organized mission meetings, festivals, and other activities, including women's missionary societies. A formal missions association was organized at Gnadenfeld around 1850. By 1854 they had established contact with the Amsterdam Mennonite mission society, as a result of which their interest began to center primarily around the support of the Dutch program in East India. Annual offerings were also sent to other places, however—to orphanages in Armenia, to the Syrian Orphanage in Jerusalem, to the Rhenish Mission, to St. Chrischona, to the Mission to the Jews, the Russian Bible Society, and to the Russian Red Cross.[49]

Following the schism of 1860 the old Mennonites continued their support of the Dutch work until 1914. The arrangement seems to have been satisfactory to both parties. The Dutch had good educational institutions, political experience, and the necessary contacts in the Indies. The Mennonites of Russia in turn supplied most of the workers and by 1914 the major share of the financial support. While the Russian Mennonites had a representative on the Amsterdam board, the policy decisions were carried out primarily by the Dutch.

The first missionary from Russia was Heinrich Dirks. Born in Gnadenfeld in 1842, he graduated from the secondary school of the colony and enrolled at the Mission House in Barmen, Germany. He spent four years at Barmen, followed by one year of language study (Dutch, English, Javanese, Malayan). Thereupon he came home, married, and was ordained as elder and missionary. He arrived in Sumatra in 1871, opening a mission station in Pakantan. Ten years later he returned to Gnadenfeld and assumed the eldership of the congregation. In this capacity he exerted a wide influence in favor of foreign mission work, traveling widely not only in Russia, but also in Holland, Germany, and America. He remained a primary force in creating new vision for the work until his death in 1915.[50]

Dirks was followed by no less than nine other couples and eleven single persons from Russia, all of whom carried on significant work in Java and Sumatra, except Maria Reimer, who went to Egypt.[51] Individuals also gave financial support independently. Thus Peter Schmidt of Steinbach supported two native evangelists in Java.[52] In addition to this several Russian Mennonites had gone to America for their training and entered the mission field under American Mennonite sponsorship. Among these were P. A. Penner, J. F. Kroeker, P. J. Wiens, and Agnes Wiens whom P. J. Wiens later married. All of the Mennonites who had come to America in the 1870s had come with a keen sense of mission as Kaufman also states: "They brought with them an interest in education and mission."[53] Most of them retained their contacts with the Russian brotherhood, the Wienses visiting Russia in 1904-5 and Kroeker retiring there. It is clear that these brethren helped to bring a sense of mission to the American brotherhood.

The Mennonite Brethren Church also took an early interest in foreign missions. No sooner had they set their own house in order than they arranged for a mission festival, in 1867. The offering was sent to the German Baptists. In 1885 their first missionaries, Abraham Friesen and his wife, volunteered for foreign service. While studying at the Baptist Theological Seminary in Hamburg-Hoorn, Friesen came in contact with the American Baptist Missionary Union of Boston and became convinced that he should work with the Union at their mission in Nalgonda, India. His home congregation approving, he and his wife sailed for India, arriving at Nalgonda among the Telugu people in 1890. Most of the Mennonite Brethren missionaries consequently followed Friesen to India, totaling six couples and eight single persons from Russia, of which two went to Africa under non-Mennonite boards.[54]

The relation of the Mennonite Brethren to the Baptist Union

185

was a happy one. The Mennonites enjoyed almost complete freedom in the field assigned to them, and the churches enthusiastically supported the work. After 1902 women's mission societies were organized in numerous congregations. A missionary paper *Erntefeld* appeared in 1900 together with an annual pamphlet *Unter den Telugus*. In relation to missions the contacts of the Mennonite Brethren with the old church were also cordial. Thus missionary Dirks wrote:

Even though the old Mennonite Church does not agree with the Mennonite Brethren on all points, and even though we must endure being the objects of their missionary activities, nevertheless, a number of the old church, including this writer, rejoice in the blessed work of the Mennonite Brethren missionaries in British India. There is no tension among us as far as the work among the heathen is concerned.[55]

From these accounts it has become apparent that the Mennonites of Russia did carry on an extensive program of foreign missions, supported by a large part of the brotherhood. The sense of mission was nourished through preaching, mission meetings and festivals, itinerant missionaries, women's missionary and sewing circles, letters from the field, mission papers, and pamphlets. In addition to the *Erntefeld* and *Unter den Telugus,* Heinrich Dirks included an extensive section on foreign missions in the yearbook annually. Much of the literature read was non-Mennonite. Missionaries from other denominations also visited the colonies from time to time. Financial support of this work has been assessed as follows:

One of the sure signs of the existence of a wide interest in foreign missions among the people is the financial support that was given to the missionary cause. It is difficult to find any figures on this as on Russian Mennonite donations for benevolent causes generally. In all their giving the Mennonites of Russia seem to have favoured the principle laid down in Matthew 6:3. . . . There was no broadcasting of one's 'good stewardship'. . . . Without doubt, however, the Mennonites in Russia gave comparatively freely to the mission cause.[56]

Zeal for Missions

In the light of the tremendous mission outreach within Protestantism and among the Mennonites of America during the late nineteenth and early twentieth centuries it has sometimes appeared as though the Mennonites in Russia had little mission zeal, little spiritual life, little concern for their non-Mennonite neighbors. It is important, however, to see each generation in the light of its own problems, intentions, and milieu as I have attempted in the preceding. While this does not preclude analysis and evaluation, it does prevent quick judgment based on a superficial comparison with our own values from which we have not gained the necessary perspective. Perhaps the Russian Mennonites of earlier decades would be as critical of us as we have at times been of them, if they had the opportunity to see us in perspective. To reproach the Mennonites of Russia too severely from our point in history is, in a sense, to reproach them for being human.

It has frequently been pointed out that the Mennonites permitted or actually created a situation in Russia, according to which Mennonitism had primarily ethnic connotation. Mennonite culture and social order left no real option to young people other than that of also becoming Mennonites, an approach which violates our Anabaptist understanding of the nature of the church. This was largely true, unfortunately, yet there was no other alternative. To find the necessary land and freedom our fathers had to settle lands that were lonely and alien. Consequently their colonies became cultural islands in the wilderness, or hostile regions, leading to almost complete self-sufficiency and the inevitable in-group culture. The first two generations, ca. 1800-1850, were forced to devote all their energies to the task of conquering the frontier. Mothers carried their infants to their work in the fields, children of ten worked all day, a boy of fourteen was considered a full-grown laborer.[57] Emergencies, such as the famine year of 1833, increased these pressures of existence. While the loss of life among the native population was severe, the Mennonites were able to help each other by buying grain valued at 403,000 rubles in distant provinces and hauling it to the settlements at great cost and effort. Thus no Mennonites starved to death, but in the concern over their very existence the spiritual life hardened and was often neglected.[58]

That the Mennonites were nevertheless concerned for their neighbors has been the conclusion of this study. Numerous instances were mentioned, but many others were omitted. Mrs.

187

Maria Klassen's will provided a sum of 5000 rubles to endow the cost of an itinerant minister to bring the gospel to the scattered Mennonites.[59] Johann Cornies (d. 1848), probably the most outstanding personality among the Mennonites of Russia, became a benefactor to the Hutterites and the Nogais, helping them to become established and earning for himself their title, the Father of Our People. When the Dukobors were to be exiled to Siberia Cornies interceded for them and saved them from this fate. Many Russian boys and girls were taken into the Cornies' home and given thorough training in farming and housekeeping.[60]

It has also been shown that the Mennonites generally felt their primary responsibility in the nurturing of their own large families and settlements. Materially they cared for each other in times of need. A particular problem was the securing of more land for the young couples. For a time a Mennonite proletariat did develop, but after much struggle ways and means were found to resolve this problem also.[61] That this struggle meant the overcoming of a great deal of "selfishness and rudeness of the human heart and a narrow intellectual horizon" is obvious,[62] but that such a genuinely Christian solution was found and that it remained in force up to the revolution deserves a great deal of credit. Finally, however, understanding and love triumphed. The same was true of the alternative service program—forestry work. From 1881 to the Revolution some 1000 young Mennonite men had served in forestry work in lieu of military service. Their maintenance and other costs had to be borne by the brotherhood at an average (1913) annual cost of 350,000 rubles.[63] This willingness to sacrifice cannot be explained except in terms of Christian motivation.

The spiritual concern for the brotherhood, in addition to the home missions activities already referred to, manifested itself in a vast institutional program. A splendid educational system was established. By 1910 the Russian Mennonites had established some 400 public (primary) schools, thirteen secondary schools, four schools for girls, two trade schools (*Handelschulen*), two pedagogical institutes, one school for the deaf and mute, and one business school (*Kommerzschule*).[64] The maintenance of these schools ran into hundreds of thousands of rubles annually. Added to these were the orphanges, deaconess home, institution for the mentally ill, three hospitals, and two old people's homes. There were, in addition to these, many similar institutions supported privately. If it were possible to add into one sum all the monies given for these causes, it would undoubtedly have exceeded several million rubles annually. While some of this work may have been supported because of indirect social pressure, it is fair to state that most of the contributions were made, often at great sacrifice, out of a deep desire to serve the Lord and to be obedient to His word.

Particular spiritual activity became evident during the last twenty or thirty years before the revolution. Thorough religious instruction was given in all Mennonite schools. All pupils had to participate since religious instruction was not optional. The biblical truths were simply hammered into the young minds and lives. In recalling the years during which I myself was subjected to this discipline, I do not remember a single pupil who resented this religious instruction. Most enjoyed it. The fortitude with which most of the Mennonites met the difficulties of the post-revolution era must in considerable measure be attributed to this early, thorough teaching. Short courses for ministers and church workers were held regularly prior to the revolution. Prominent Mennonite and non-Mennonite ministers were invited for these occasions, among them Professor Stroeter, Fritz Oetzbach, Dr. Baedecker, a Rev. Broadbent from England, Adam Podin, prison chaplain from the Baltic, Baron Uexkuel from the Baltic, missionary Jacob Vetter, and others.[65] All these activities and contacts had a tremendously invigorating and stimulating influence upon the Mennonite churches.

With these contacts, however, other influences also came into the settlements. Among these influences were certain elements of pietism, elements which have sometimes been considered detrimental to the Anabaptist affirmations. Yet it can be said that Anabaptism, with all its depth and beauty, does not inevitably constitute a final revelation from God in every respect. There was, and needs to be, continuing room for *becoming,* not for self-satisfaction, both on the part of individuals and churches. Pietism helped the heirs of Anabaptism to gain new insights into biblical truths, thus leading them to further spiritual growth.

The Russian Mennonite understanding of the nature of the church was not nearly always clear. Many were *political* or *ethnic* Mennonites. This created a tension between the concept of the church as a brotherhood and the concept of the church as an ethnic people (*Volk*). Whether this was a less fortunate situation, however, than the rampant denominationalism of modern times is debatable. There are probably as many un-churched *ethnic* Mennonites in American cities as were proportionately in Russia during the spiritual ebb among the Mennonites. This, of course, is not to deny the problem. Every individual must confront the claim of the cross personally. There are no *grandchildren* of the Lord. Yet the *birth-right* pattern in Russia was unavoidable. Nevertheless, it is perhaps better to let the close church community create an environment favorable to spiritual decision, as was the case in Russia, than to have this decision made in an indifferent or secular context such as we find almost inevitable today.

While it is difficult to make a fair comparison between the missionary interest of the Russian and American Mennonites, a cursory survey seems to favor the Russian Mennonites. In spite of the fact, e.g., that more Mennonites originally came to America than to Russia, in spite of the fact that they came considerably earlier (1683), and in spite of the fact that they have always enjoyed complete freedom to evangelize in America, the number of Mennonites in America in 1914 was not substantially greater than the number of Mennonites in Russia. Names of non-Mennonite background were seldom found on American Mennonite church rolls. In spite of a greater cultural affinity, or perhaps because of it, the Mennonites of America had lost great numbers either to other churches or to secularism.

This is not intended to minimize the work of American Mennonites. A marvelous mission program has grown up through their work in the twentieth century. It must be remembered that the growth of missionary, educational, and other phases of church work among the Mennonites in Russia ended in 1914. For this reason a comparison with the work of the American brotherhood up to 1914 provides the proper perspective. At

190

this time there were approximately 106,235 Mennonites in Russia.[66] What growth might have occurred among them in the fulfillment of the Great Commission, had circumstances remained normal, remains conjectural. The potential, in any case, was great.

HORST QUIRING

Die Danziger Mennoniten:
Der Stand der Herkunftsfragen

UNTER DEN BEGRIFF *Danziger* fallen im Sprachgebrauch auch die im Danziger Werder ansässig gewesenen Mennoniten. Darüber hinaus stellt die Stadt Danzig den Kristallisationsort für das westpreussische Mennonitentum dar. Hier und in Elbing ist Menno Simons persönlich gewesen und hat die ersten verstreut angesiedelten Täufer gesammelt und sie in seinem bekannten Brief an die "Gemeinden in Preussen" 1549 mit seinem Zuspruch bedacht.

Ich darf dabei an meine ersten Veröffentlichungen zu diesem Thema anknüpfen. Archivstudien im *Archief der Vereenigde Doopsgezinde Gemeente"* in Amsterdam brachten mir das umfangreiche Briefmaterial zu Gesicht, das die Beziehungen zwischen den Glaubensbrüdern in den Niederlanden und den Ostlanden betrifft. Die Akten beginnen mit dem Jahr 1583, führen also in die Zeit der ersten Einwanderergeneration und handeln von den leitenden Predigern der Mitbegründer unserer Freikirche mit und nach Menno. Ein Teil der Urkunden ist in dem sogenannten *Urkundenbuch der Gemeinde Heubuden* in Abschrift vorhanden. All das ist noch längst nicht im einzelnen ausgewertet, und die Arbeiten des Verfassers stellen nur einen ersten Versuch dar. Manches, was dargestellt wurde in "Aus den ersten Jahrzehnten der Mennoniten in Westpreussen,"[1] ist durch die neueren Arbeiten überholt. Darauf ist hier übersichtsweise einzugehen.

Aber vorab kann doch mit Befriedigung festgehalten werden, dass zwei Forderungen als Arbeitsgrundsätze sich als richtig erwiesen haben: 1. Die Unterschriften bei den Briefen mit den zahlreichen Ortsbezeichnungen als Beigabe zu den Namen können wertvolle Hinweise auf die Herkunft der Einwanderer geben, da die Abgeordneten eine Reihe ihrer Heimatgenossen vertreten. 2. Die Bedeutung des südniederländischen Elements ist bisher nicht genügend gewürdigt.

Die Forschung ist an beiden Punkten weitergegangen. Gustav E. Reimer und Horst Penner haben die entscheidende Quellenforschung getrieben, auf denen Kurt Kauenhoven und B. H. Unruh weiterbauen konnten.

Von niederländischer Seite kamen neue Studien durch N. van der Zijpp, Johan S. Postma, von den Belgiern durch A. Verheyden und Jules Lambotte.

Die Namen

Es war hilfreich, dass der unter Mennoniten schon immer gepflegte Familiensinn zur regelrechten Sippenkunde führte und bei einzelnen Namen fast lückenlose Linien bis zur Einwanderung erarbeitete. Dies ist auch der sicherste Weg, um zu überzeugenden Resultaten zu kommen. Es ist zu viel auf diesem Gebiet gefolgert worden, ohne die Beweise zu haben. Die Ergebnisse lassen sich kurz zusammenfassen: Die Annahme, dass die meisten westpreussischen Mennoniten aus den "drei Frieslanden" kommen, ist nicht mehr zu halten. Der friesische Anteil wird etwa ein Fünftel der Einwanderer betragen haben. Der Hauptbeweis liegt in der Namensgebung: bei den Patronymika fehlen die typisch friesischen Genitivendungen fast völlig (inga, ma oder na). Da der Friese konservativ ist und seine eigenen Namen verwendet, liegt hier ein schlüssiger Beweis vor. Die anderen Folgerungen sind ebenfalls bei Postma[2] nachzulesen, wie er auch ein eigenes Namensverzeichnis aufgestellt hat, das in vielen Fällen das von Reimer[3] korrigiert.

Wenn also achtzig Prozent aus den anderen Provinzen der nördlichen und südlichen Niederlande stammen und damit fränkischen und sächsischen Stammes sind—auf die geringe Zahl von Ober- und Niederdeutschen, Schweizern kommen wir

noch zu sprechen—ist das allgemeine Urteil erlaubt: die westpreussischen Mennoniten sind überwiegend niederländischen Ur-
sprungs, wobei der südniederländische, heute belgische Teil einen
grösseren Prozentsatz stellt als bisher angenommen wurde.

Die Flamen

Es lag nahe, die beiden Gemeinderichtungen der Friesen und
Flamen auf ihre Verkoppelung mit ihrer jeweiligen Heimat zu
untersuchen. Wenn sich auch die Spaltung nach der Ansiedlung ereignete und dann erst auf die neue Heimat übergriff, so
legten es die Erfahrungen der Neuzeit nahe, zu vermuten, dass
sich hinter glaubensmässigen Entscheidungen "nichttheologische
Faktoren" verbergen, also familienhafter Sinn für Stammeszu-
gehörigkeit. Dazu kam, dass der Ausbruch der Verschieden-
heiten in Harlingen tatsächlich zunächst die stammesmässigen
Friesen und die nach Friesland geflüchteten Flamen betraf.

Hier war eine Beobachtung Reimers bis heute durchschla-
gend. Er folgerte gedankenscharf:

"Wenn aber zum Beispiel im Grossen Werder die Glieder der friesischen Gemeinde Orlofferfelde mitten unter den Gliedern der flämischen
Gemeinde siedeln, aber dieselben Namen haben wie die Glieder der
friesischen Gemeinde Thiensdorf im Kleinen Werder, so legt das die
Vermutung nahe, dass hier auch schon vor der Trennung zwei hinsicht-
lich ihrer Herkunft verschiedene Gruppen bestanden haben."[4]

Zweifellos finden sich Landsleute mit gemeinsamer Sprache,
Herkunft und Lebensschicksalen schneller auch in religiösen Fragen zusammen, besonders wenn sie schon ohnehin beisammen
wohnen. Auf der anderen Seite ist das Kuriosum festzuhalten,
dass es bis ins 18. Jahrhundert hinein in Amsterdam und Haarlem eine Gruppe "Danziger Flaminger" gab, die auf diese Weise
ihrer Verbundenheit mit den örtlichen Geistesverwandten Ausdruck gaben.

Der stammesmässig flämische Anteil an den Ostsiedlern ist
durch die neuere Forschung höher als bisher angesetzt. Die
Tatsache, dass die Verfolgung aller Nicht-Katholiken in den
südlichen Niederlanden einer fast vollständigen Ausrottung
gleichkam, liess die dortigen zahlreichen Taufgesinnten alles
Hab und Gut verlieren und in die nördlichen Provinzen fliehen.
Als auch dort die Verfolgung begann, waren diese Heimatver-

triebenen die ersten, die wiederum zum Wanderstab griffen.
Es gab 1566 zum Beispiel in Antwerpen zirka 2000 Taufge-
sinnte unter 86,000 Einwohnern, und alle Evangelischen mussten
fliehen. Insgesamt verliessen 100,000 evangelisch Gesinnte
das belgische Land.

Viele blieben in den nördlichen Provinzen und wurden hier
sesshaft. Manche Namen sind in den Gemeindearchiven festgehalten, wie de Wale, Couwenhoven, van der Smissen, Weyns,
Cranen; ihre Namensträger begegnen uns auch in Westpreussen.[5] Der fähigste unter den Taufgesinnten seiner Zeit, Hans
de Ries, stammte aus Antwerpen. Aus Alkmaar korrespon-
dierte er mit dem zweiten Ältesten der Danziger Gemeinde (nach
Dirk Philips), Quirin Vermeulen, der schon 1598 auf seine Kos-
ten in Danzig eine Bibelausgabe drucken liess. So deutet sich
auch in der leitenden Schicht das überragende flämische Ele-
ment an. Beruflich waren die flämischen Flüchtlinge wohl
meist, aus den Städten stammend, gewerblich tätig. Da sie
in Danzig und Elbing zunächst Schwierigkeiten hatten, Ge-
werbezulassungen zu erhalten, sind manche in landwirtschaft-
liche Berufe abgewandert. So ist es zu erklären, dass viele städ-
tische Berufsnamen unter einer rein bäuerlichen Gemeinde zu
finden sind, wie in Montau: Becher, Boettcher, Deckemaeker,
Kerber, Kliewer, Kopper, Krüger, Schwegler. Übrigens ver-
danken manche aufblühenden Gewerbe den tüchtigen Einwan-
derern ihren Aufschwung. Nicht ohne Humor haben die Stadt-
räte die Ausweisungsbefehle der Krone oder die neidischen An-
feindungen der Zünfte zurückgewiesen, mit dem Vermerk, es
sei doch christlicher, die Seelen der Menschen zu retten als
sie fortzuschaffen.[6]

Auffällig bleibt, dass der starke flämische Einschlag der Flüchtlinge in den Nordprovinzen Hollands und in Westpreussen so
schwer an den heutigen Namen nachzuweisen ist. Sie haben
wohl die Schreibweise ihrer Namen schnell der Umgebung an-
geglichen, manche Namen erloschen, und als Städter waren
die Familien wohl nicht so kinderreich wie die bäuerlichen. So
wurde aus de Wale — Wall, aus dem Vornamen Gillies —
Julius und aus Noé von Antwerpen wurde Kordt Noweh in
Danzig, Quirin van der Meulen wurde gebildet aus Krijn Vermeulen.[7]

Da in Westpreussen über 200 Jahre lang die standesamtlichen Eintragungen von lutherischen oder katholischen Geistlichen vorgenommen wurden, kann man sich ihren Stosseufzer vorstellen, dass "Derk ein unaussprechlicher Name" sei, und wie man das *friesische* Tiart schreiben kann, sieht man aus unzähligen Abarten.

Da ist es den Krefeldern besser ergangen. Aus dem flämischen van der Leyen wurde nur von der Leyen. Aber ob aus Hans Quins, der 1570 Flandern verliess, ein Wiens wurde, ist noch zu untersuchen.[8] Am sichersten ist immer noch die persönliche Unterschrift, wie sie unter zahlreichen erhaltenen Briefen in Amsterdam nachzulesen ist. Die meisten Auswanderer konnten lesen und schreiben und wussten sich auch in schwierigen Dingen auszudrücken.

Ausblick

Eine weitere Hilfsquelle hat sich erschlossen durch die Schülerverzeichnisse höherer Schulen. Kurt Kauenhoven[9] hat die Söhne von Mennoniten, die das Elbinger Gymnasium von 1598 bis 1786 besuchten, herausgeschrieben. Wir stossen auf einen Abraham Meckelburg; Daniel Stobbe, Colbergensis Pomeranus; Thomas von Tongerlohe, Belga. Hier sind die spärlichen Spuren der Herkunft aus Pommern, von denen auch Reinhold Heuer schreibt[10] und aus Mecklenburg, worüber J. ten Doornkaat-Koolman umfassend berichtet hat.[11]

Es bleibt schliesslich noch übrig, den kargen Hinweisen auf anderen Herkunftsgebieten nachzugehen. Von Mecklenburg nahm man bisher den Namen Warkentin an. Aber Postma deutet auf den alten seeländischen Vornamen Warrekin.[12] Aus Mähren stammen Josephus Hauser und Darius Hein.[13] Hier begegnen wir oberdeutschem oder schweizerischem Einfluss. Nachweislich bestanden lose Verbindungen zu Mähren und Oberdeutschland, und aus Westfalen nach den Niederlanden geflüchtete Täufer mögen sich dem Zug nach dem Osten angeschlossen haben, aber an diesem Punkt sind die Quellen spärlich. Es kann sich nur um einzelne Personen gehandelt haben, die rasch in den vorhandenen Gemeinden Westpreussens aufgingen.[14]

196

J . F . G . G O E T E R S

Das älteste rheinische Täuferbekenntnis

WÄHREND WIR FÜR das erste Jahrzehnt des Täufertums am Niederrhein seit 1533 als Quellen im wesentlichen nur obrigkeitliche Mandate, Verhörsprotokolle und ähnliche Gerichts- und Polizeiakten besitzen, bescheren uns bisher nahezu unbekannte Akten zum Reformationsversuch des Kölner Erzbischofs Hermann von Wied ein Glaubensbekenntnis aus Kempen, einer Stadt im gleichnamigen Amt des Niederstifts. Da es—beim bisherigen Stande der Forschung—das erste Bekenntnis dieser Art am Niederrhein ist, verdient es eine Veröffentlichung im vollen Wortlaut.

Von den geschichtlichen Umständen schicken wir vornehmlich aus Akten, die später einmal veröffentlicht werden sollen, einige Nachrichten voraus, die zum Verständnis nötig sind. Die Reformation in Kempen ist seit 1543 im Gange. Ihre Vorkämpfer sind Wilhelm von Rennenberg, kurkölnischer Amtmann von Kempen, und der evangelische Prediger Dietrich Vollebier. Unter den Adligen ist vor allem Gottfried von Haes, Herr von Hüls, zu nennen. Die Täufergemeinde in Kempen, deren Bekenntnis wir hier kennen lernen, ist 1545 klein. Sie beträgt etwa 12 Männer, wozu teilweise noch die Familien hinzuzurechnen sind. Interessant ist, dass die Mehrzahl von ihnen 1542/43 in einer Petition evangelischer Bürger von Kempen erscheint, sie sind also zuvor evangelisch gewesen, bevor sie zum Täufertum übertraten. Aus Verhören geht hervor, dass keine dieser Personen sehr viel länger als ein Jahr getauft ist. Entweder sind sie im benachbarten Gladbach (dem heutigen Mönchengladbach) oder von Gladbacher Lehrern in Kempen getauft worden. Diese Lehrer sind Thönis von Jüchen bzw. Sasserath (beide Dörfer liegen bei Rheydt, Sasserath gehört zur kurkölnischen Herrschaft Odenkirchen, Jüchen zum Herzogtum Jülich, Amt Kaster) und Michiel Oistwart. Näheres von diesen beiden wissen wir nicht. Die Kempener Gemeinde kommt meist im Hause des Schlossers Reynar (Reinhard) Piper zusammen, allerdings nicht zu regelmässigen Versammlungen, sondern nach Gelegenheit. Sie feiern untereinander das Abendmahl als brüderliches Gemeinschaftsmahl. Meist sind es jüngere Ehepaare. Ein Mitglied hat zwei seiner Kinder nicht kirchlich taufen lassen, zwei Ehepaare sind der kirchlichen Trauung ferngeblieben und haben sich von den genannten Täuferlehrern einsegnen lassen. Gemäss den Bestimmungen des kurfürstlichen Reformationsbedenkens von 1543 werden sie vom Amtmann vorgeladen und am 28. März 1545 verhört. Als Rechenschaft ihres Glaubens geben sie das Bekenntnis ab, das von Thönis von Sasserath verfasst ist. Wir dürfen also annehmen, dass wir in diesem Bekenntnis nicht nur den Glauben der kleinen Gemeinde in Kempen, sondern den der Täufer in der weiteren Umgebung vor uns haben. In einem Dokument des gleichen Jahres wird für die Umgebung die Zahl von 1,000 Täufern genannt, das Zentrum sei Gladbach.

Am 17. Juni 1545 wird — wieder nach den Bestimmungen des Reformationsbedenkens über das Verfahren mit Täufern — in Gegenwart des Amtmanns, der Beamten und einiger Adliger des Amtes ein Glaubensexamen mit den Täufern abgehalten. Vergebens hatte man sich bemüht, dazu aus Wesel den Theologen Nikolaus Buscodensis herbeizurufen. Statt seiner amtieren als Theologen die Prediger Heinrich Zell aus Bonn und Johannes Praetorius aus Andernach. Die täuferischen Wortführer sind, da die beiden Lehrer in Gladbach nicht zu erreichen waren, ein Goldschmied Georg und der Steinmetz Tewes Ruebsam, beide aus Kempen. Sie, wie auch alle anderen vorgeladenen Täufer, bleiben standhaft bei ihrem Glauben. Mit dem Gebot, von ihrem Glauben abzustehen, und dem Verbot, weiter Zusammenkünfte zu halten, zu lehren und zu predigen, werden sie bis auf weiteren Bescheid entlassen. Was daraufhin geschehen ist, wissen wir im einzelnen nicht. Dr. Albert Hardenberg, kurz darauf evangelischer Prediger von Kempen, hat noch manche Auseinandersetzung mit Täufern gehabt und die Mehrzahl von ihnen zum Abfall bewegt. Er betont, dass sie bescheidene und stille Leute seien. Eine kleine Täufergemeinde hat sich in Kempen noch bis ins 17. Jahrhundert erhalten und ist erst von der Gegenreformation in Kurköln zur Auswanderung gezwungen worden.

Wir lassen hier das Bekenntnis im niederdeutschen Original buchstabengetreu folgen. Dabei setzen wir die Marginalien (Bibelstellen) in Klammern in den Text. Die Versnummern ergänzen wir ebenfalls in Klammern. Ebenso haben wir die Numerierung der Artikel hinzugefügt. Das Aktenstück besteht aus acht handgeschriebenen Blättern und ist sichtlich die Originalfassung, wie sie übergeben wurde. Der erste Abschnitt mit den äusseren Angaben bildet das Titelblatt und stammt von der Hand des Amtsschreibers, ist also später hinzugefügt. Die Titelrückseite ist unbeschrieben.

DAS KEMPENER TÄUFERBEKENNTNIS

Dusse articulen hait Reynar Piper ubergebenn hern Wilhelmen, frigheren zu Rennenberch etc., voirdt dem hern von Huls, zosampt dem schulthissen, kelner, in bywesende borgermeister und raidt der stadt zu Kempen anno etc. 45., Saterdages am hilligen Pfingstavende. Und sindt die articulen ires gelovens, darbei sie, bis sie eins besseren uis dem reinen wordt Gottes berichtet werden, zu pleiben gedennckenn.

Eyrwerdyger, gnedyger heir und junckerr Rennenburch. . . . Wyr armen, guetwyllge undersayssen geven E. L. zo erkennen unseren gelouven in Jesum Christum, der uns geoffenbaret is doer die barmhertzicheit Gottes, und wir ouch vor Got und E. L. denselvygen selichmakende gelouven in Jesum Christum goetwyllich synt to bekennen, (1. Pet. 3 (V. 15))[1] ja ouch vor allen mynschen, die es van uns begeren zo horen, up dat E. L. mach upmyrken und kennen leren, dat wir neyt anders en begeren zo suechen dan allein unser selen selicheit und ouch aller mynschen wayllfart an lyff und selen, glich wie ouch Christus gesocht hayt. (Mat. 5

(V. 11). 10 (V. 17-22). 19 (V. 27-30)) Und uns ouch also im
hayt heyschen navolgen in aller guedyger leyffden byss in den doet,
ja ouch van allen mynschen druck und smach zo liden, wie ouch
Christus geleten hayt, der uns ouch hayt geleirt und geboeden, all
unsen vyanden goedes zo doen, na gezeuchnis der hylger schryfft,
Mat. 5 (V. 44). Luce 6 (V. 27-28). Rom. 12 (V. 14) etc.

(1.) BEKENTENYS VAN CHRISTO UN SYNER HYLGER
MYNSCHWERDUNGE

Wyr bekennen und bezeugen myt dem hylgen Paulus, dat der
mynsch Jesus Christus is der heir vonn hymmell und hymmels, wie
Paulus 1. Cor. 15 (V. 47) klair genoch gezeucht hayt. Wie ouch
der hilge Petrus gezeuchnis van ym gegeven hayt Mat. 16 (V. 16)
Luce 9 (V. 20), da er spricht: Du byst Christus, der levendyge
son Gottes. Also bekennen wir ouch Christus, wie in der hilge
Petrus bekant hayt, dat er sy der levendyge son Gottes. Und
bekennen wir ouch, dat dieser eynyge son Gottes der eyrste is
geboren ouss Got van evycheyt (Colo. 1 (V. 15)). Und is dieser
eynyge son Gottes ouch dat krefftyge wort des vaters geweysen,
dairdurch er ouch alles hayt gemacht, ja hymmel und erde und
alles, vat dair is, glich wie Joh. 1 (V. 1-3), Col. 1 (V. 16), Heb.
1 (V. 2) geschreven steyt. Und is na der schryfft fleysch geworden,
glich wie Joh. 1 (V. 14) darvan spricht und beteigt: Dat wort
wart fleysch, ja ouch wie Paulus dair bouven myt Petrus bekennet,
dat er eyn hymmelsmynsch, ja ouch der heir vam hymmell, als
der levendyge son Gottes is erkant und erfunden geworden, der
untfangen is vam hilgen geyst, Mat. 1 (V. 18.20), geboren ouss
Maria, na der hilger schryfft Luce 1 (V. 35).

Ja ouch gelick also, wie Christus van im selver spricht und
bezeucht Joh. 6 (V. 48. 51. 53-58), also bekennen wir in ouch, to
syn dat brot vam hymmell, ja ouch dat rechte hymmelbrot, dat ja
ouch Christus selver bekent, dat dytselvyge hymmelbrot is syn
fleysch, dat gegeven wart vor dat leven der werlt. Also synt wir
hy im gezeuchnis van Christo und syner mynswerdinge myt Christo
und synen apostelen recht vereynyget, wie myt korten worden
erkant is, da wir ouch myt Gottes hulpen in betruen to bleven und
uns ouch gein schriftgeleirten noch hellenporten (Mat. 16 (V. 18))
aff sullen trecken. Der heir wyll ouch syne schaffgen in der rechter
wairheit behueden un bewaren, Amen etc.

(2.) Unser bekentenys vam hylgen doep Jesus Christy.

Zom anderen mayll bekennen und bezeugen wyr, dat Christus Jesus in sinen hylgen worden und ordnungen evych bestendich is und ouch bliven sall, ouch hymmel und erde vergain solde, ee syner worden eyns solde unwairafftich off ouch to neyten bevonden werden, die es gelouven, Mat. 5 (V. 18).

Weyll dan seyn hyllich wort evich is und neyt verandert en mach werden, so moyssen wir ummers ouch myt Christo und sinen hylgen apostelen bekennen und bezeugen, dat gein ander douff im wasser en is noch gebrucht en mach werden dan allein der douff des gelouvens, der up den gelouven van Christo bestediget is, aller gerechticheit inzotreten na dem willen und wayllgevallen sines hymmelchen vaters, gelick wie Mat. 3 (V. 6. 11), 28 (V. 18-20), Mar. 16 (V. 16) klair genoch erkant und bezeucht is van Jesu Christo.

Gelick wie ouch die hylge apostelen bezeugen in alle iren breven, die den hilgen douff gegeven, geleirt und gebroucht haven allein an den gelouvygen. Die hant sy gedoufft na dem bevell und gebot ires meysters Jesu Christy, gelick wie oven genoch verklairt is. Also synt wir myt Christo und sinen hilgen apostelen im gebruck des dupsels up den gelouven eyndrechtych und eyns, syns, gelick wie Acto. 2 (V. 38), 8 (V. 35-38), 10 (V. 44-49), 16 (V. 31-33), 19 (V. 2-6), Rom. 6 (V. 3-11), 1. Cor. 12 (V. 13), Tito 3 (V. 3-7), 1. Pet. 3 (V. 21) geschreven steyt.

Und gelick wie Christus, unser myster, myt sinen hilgen apostelen geinen ungelouvygen kinderdouff geleert, geschreven noch gebraucht en haven, also en moyssen noch en dorren wirs by unser selen verdomnys ouch neyt leren, schriven noch gebruchen, weyll alle die verflucht moyssen syn, dye synem gesatz aff-ader zodent, gelick wie Deut. 4 (V. 2), Apo. 22 (V. 18-19) und Mat. 15 (V. 13) geschreven steyt und ouch alle planssen, die neyt van Got en synt, oussgerodet moyssen werden. Der almechtige Got help uns im rechte gelouven bestendich zo bliven doer Jesom Christum, Amen.

(3.) Bekentenys vam hylgen nachtmayll Jesu Christy
und wem es im rechte gebruck gegeven un bevolen is.

Wyr gelouven und bekennen, dat Christus Jesus sinen lieven, hylgen jungeren hait gegeven und ingesatz eyn heylich nachtmayll, to gebruken myt brot und wyn, synen doet dairby to gedencken und to verkondygen, byss dat er kompt, gelick Mat. 26 (V. 26-28), Luce 22 (V. 19-20), 1. Cor. 5 (V. 7), 10 (V. 16-17), 11 (V. 23-26) geschreven und verklairet is.

Weyll nu Christus dyt hylge nachtmayll nemans en hait gegeven
noch bevolen dan allein synen hylgen, lieven jungeren, die ouss
dem hilgen geyst geboren, alles affgesacht hatten und im under
dem krutz synt nagekomen in allem druck, smag und liden, gelick
wie er ouch geboeden Mat. 10 (V. 16-25), 16 (V. 21), 19 (V. 27-
30), Mar. 8 (V. 34-38), 10 (V. 28-31), Luce 14 (V. 26-27) etc.

Derhalven moyssen wir ouch bekennen, dat sulchen hilge nachtmayll Jesu Christy geinen unboessverdigen, ungelouvygen son-
deren, gotzendienars, rouvers, mordeners, girigen, hoemoedigen,
hoerers, ebrekers, loegenafftygen, drockers eyrgens ist gegeven off
ouch zo eurer selicheit neyt en konnen noch moegen gebruchen,
sonder zo eurer eygener verdomnys und unselicheit, wie der Judas.

Und vermoegen ouch sulchen falche christen und gylsner geyn
christennachtmayll halten noch anrichten numerme, weyll sy geine
rechte, gehorsame junger Jesu Christy en synt, ouss im geboren
1. Pet. 1 (V. 3.23) und synen hilgen geyst ouch neyt en haven
noch ouch sych neyt en leven, dairby man sy soldte erkennen
Joh. 13 (V. 35), weyll sy dan ouch dem hilgen geyst van bouven
neit en synt geboren Joh. 3 (V. 3-6) noch ouch van sinem hylgen
geyst neyt en werden gedreven Rom. 8 (V. 14), so en synt sy
ouch die neu creatur Gal. 6 (V. 15) noch neyt geworden, dae
der fredt Gottes myt syner barmhertzicheyt over is gesprochen,
weyll sy neyt geystlich, sonder fleyschlich, girich und ertz gesinnet
synt, neyt rein van hertzen, sonder unreyn, ouch selver neyt myt
gedult under dem krutz Christy en komen noch vandeln, sonder
synt verfolger der christen und fyant des krutz Jesu Christy, denen
der bouch ir Got is und ir ende die verdamnys, glich als Phylip-
peren am 3 (V. 18-19) geschreven is.

Also is dyt unser orsach und gezeuchnis, dat sulchenen falchen
christen in irem verkeirten gelouven gein nachtmayll en is gegeven
van Christo, ouch in neyt geboeden noch bevolen, nachtmayll zo
halten, en konnen noch en vermoegen ouch nummerme dorch brot
und weyn in irem hertzen gerynyget werden van iren sunden,
(Luce 24 (V. 31-32), Acto. 2 (V. 39.40), 4 (V. 32), 10 (V. 38),
13 (V. 38)) sonder moyssen in iren sunden sterven und verderven,
weyll sy neit im rechten gelouven doer Christum en suechen, ir
hertzer und selen zo reynygen van iren sunden, dat sy selich wurden
und sych affsunderten van den falchen christen 1. Cor. 5 (V. 9-13),
2. Cor. 6 (V. 14-18). Und weyll dyt nu neyt by innen en is, darum
en haven sy ouch geine christengemeinten, weyll sy Christo selver
neyt gelouven noch gehorsam syn wyllen. Darum en konnen sy

ouch dat vorgemelte hylge nachtmayll Jesu Christy neyt haven noch gebruken, dat Christus sinen gelouvygen, rechte jungeren hayt gegeven und bevolen zo halten, wie oven genoch dairvan myt hilger schryfft bezeucht is. Dyt is ouch unse orsach und gezeuchnis, warum wyr neyt myt euch verkeirten krysten en konnen nachtmayll in sulcher glysnery halden on sundt, weyll sy dat rechte, hilge nachtmayll Jesu Christy neyt en haven noch gebruken en konnen na gezeuchnis der hilger schryfft 1. Cor. 5 (V. 8), 10 (V. 20-21), 11 (V. 27-32).

(4.) Wairum wir dieser werlt predycanten neyt en sullen noch moyssen horen off ouch ire junger neyt geseyn konnen.

So wyr horen, myrken und ouch gruntlich kennen leren, dat der nemans en ist, der Christo zogehort dan allein, die ouss im synt geboren 1. Pet. 1 (V. 23) und synen geyst moyssen haven, durch den sy gedreven werden, gelick Paulus zo den Romeren am 8. capyttel (V. 14) dairvan bezeuch, dye ouch alles moyssen affgesacht haven, wat up dieser werlt sichtbar, zytlich und vergencklich is und moyssen im also nafolgen under dem krutz, druck, smagh und lyden, gelick wie Christus selver dairvan spricht und bezeucht Mat. 5 (V. 11), 10 (V. 16-25), 16 (V. 24-25), Mar. 8 (V. 34-35), 10 (V. 21), 13, (V. 9-13) etc.

Also moyssen alle christen in Christo zo eyner neuer kreaturen werden, dae dat alte leven der sunde inne is vergangen, und moyss ouch all new syn geworden, als im 2. Cor. 5 (V. 17) und Gala. 6 (V. 15) gruntlich verklaret is. Und en mach ouch nemans in der wairheyt christen genompt werden dan sulchen upgemelte neugeborene, geystliche mynschen, die ouch alle teyt an iren fruchten erkant und geprobeirt moegen werden, glick wie ouch Mat. 7. cap. (V. 15-19) geschreven is.

Darum is ouch dytselvyge unse orsach vor Got und allen mynschen, dat wyr der werlt predycanten neyt horen en moegen noch ouch ire junger neyt geseyn konnen, weyll sy van bouven ouss Got neyt en synt geboren Joh. 3 (V. 3.5) noch ouch van Got neyt en synt gesant, darum ouch syne gotliche krafft noch art in syner gotlicher naturen neyt en begennen (Joh. 10 (V. 3-5)). Weyll sy noch fleyschlich, gyrich und erdychs gesynnet synt und verkopen ir wort un leer um eynen zeytlichen, vergencklichen jairlon, dat doch Christus umsuss hayt heyschen geven, Mat. 10 (V. 8).

Und darum en synt sy ouch geyn rechte hyrden, sonder huyrling (Joh. 10 (V. 12)), weyll sy die rechte ordynung Christy verkeren und ir eygen gesatz und mynsliche ordnung underhalden in dem verkeirden, schentlichen doup, nachtmayll und ban etc., lasteren und schelden dairby ouch die rechte, frome kinder Gottes und verraden un verfolgen dyegenen, die ir leer und leven neyt vor recht geconsyteren en konnen, wiewayll sy des neyt all en doent und noch etlichen in gueder naturen synt, so moyss noch glychewayll der allerbesten bekennen, dat er neyt en wandelt in der rechter, apostolicher leer, gebruck und ordnung Jesu Christy.

Und vermeinen, Got also zo dienen, wie ouch bouven gemelt is, myt eynen groten, sorgfeldygen, gyrygen ongelouven, verkeirterweyss gehurt und gedyngt um eynen vergencklichen jairloyn. O lieve fronden, wie weyt und vern synt die sachen van Got und synen rechten jungeren noch verscheyden etc.

Weyll sy dan ouch den hylgen worden Gottes inwendych noch outwendich neyt gelyck en werden befonden im hilgen geyst vereynyget, so ist ummer wair, dat sy ouch van Got noch synem hylgen geyst neyt gesant en synt und, wie sollen sy predygen, wen sy neyt gesant en weren, Rom. 10 (V. 15) etc.

Weyll sy dan ungesant lopen und des heren wort unstrafflich in leer und leven neyt gelick en synt noch dairin ouch neyt en wandelen, so vermant uns Got und syn hylger geyst, van sulchen to fluen, vermeyden und neyt to horen, ouch neyt in to groten noch in unse huyser to nemen, glich wie Mat. 7 (V. 15-23), Joh. 10 (V. 5), Rom. 16 (V. 17-18), 2. Tess. 3 (V. 6), 2. Tym. 3 (V. 13-14), 2. Joh. 1 (V. 10).

Allso moyss man die rechte lerers erkennen leren na getuchnis und anwysung der hylger schryfft, 1. Tym. 3 (V. 1-7), Tito 2 (V. 6-9), die van Got gesant synt und bliven in synem outgedruckten wort, leer und ordnung Christy. Sy schuen ouch alle vernofft und affgoederey und driven ouch dat wort ter boeten und gnaden frymoedich in reinem hertzen myt aller klairheyt und straffen ouch heren, vorsten, hoych und neder, geleert, ungeleert, man, vrau sonder eynych anseen der perschonen, weyll sy ouch wyssen, dat dat krefftyge doersnydende wort Gottes moyss gayn over alles fleysch, Joh. 17 (V. 6-8), 1. Cor. 1 (V. 17-29), Heb. 4 (V. 12).

Want alle, die sich neyt under dat hylge wort Gottes en buegen noch myt gelouven upnemen, die moyssen alle dadurch gericht und geordel werden, Joh. 12 (V. 48), Deut. 10 (V. 17), Rom. 2 (V. 11), Acto. 10 (V. 34), 1. Pet. 1 (V. 17), Apo. 20 (V. 12). Hey sy ouch, wer das hey sy, keyser, konynck, doctor off lerars, dan by Got en is gein anseen der perschonen. Darum gebruken sy ouch doep und nachtmayll myt aller gotlicher ordnunck, wie es Got doer syn hyllich wort gegeven und bevolen hayt, idt gerack to

leven off to sterven, in irem leven synt sy unstrafflich, ir wandel is
in Gottes fruchten und reiner leyfften, sy sterven alle daeg myt dem
hylgen Paulus um der broeder wyllen und werden um ires gotlichen
gezeuchnis wyll geachtet und gehalden vor slachtschapen, Rom. 8
(V. 36).

Ja alsodanyge lerars synt van Christo und synen lieve vater vor
und na alle teyt gesant und geschyckt in synen wyngart, zo wylchen
hey spricht: Seyt, ich sendt euch gelick die schapen mytten under
die wulve, Mat. 10 (V. 16), Joh. 17 (V. 18). Und alsulchenen
truen dieners und gotselige leyffhavers aller wairheyt myt eynem
oytmoedygen, reynen hertzen des gelouvens in Jesum Christum
hait der hylge Paulus Tymotheo und Tyto (1. Tymo. 3 (V. 2-7),
Tyto 1 (V. 5-9)) zo lerers over die gemeynten heyschen bestedygen
und uptonemen, up dat sy myt rechter, gesunder leer leirten und
ouch dairinne dem volck, ja iren schapen vorgingen in allem
gotseligen, leyfflichen wandell des hylgen, fromen levens in Jesu
Christy. All sulchenen lerers nompt Christus Joh. 10 (V. 2-4) vor
die rechte heirten, (Acto. 2 (V. 38-40), 1. Pet. 1 (V. 23), Colo. 2
(V. 10-13)) die die schapen myt eynem rechten, boussverdygen
leven bekeren und myt Gottes wort in irem hertzen reinygen und
besnyden van allem ungelouven des sundygen levens und dan also
myt gelouvenserkentenis oussfueren ousser der unreyner gemynschaff
der falcher wederchristen, aller mysbruchen, irer sunden und myn-
schengesatzen gereynyget zu bliven durch den erkanten gelouven
in Jesom Christum, in wylchem diese rechte lerers den schapen
vorgaint zom evygen leven und ouch die rechte schapgen in also
nafolgen in die frauden des evygen levens, und dyt is ouch der
rechte syn und leer Jesu Christy, Joh. 10 (V. 4), vairby man die
rechte lerars sall kennen leren by iren fruchten, Mat. 7 (V. 16-17).

Herbeneven en moyssen wyr geyne lerers van Got bekennen
anders dan uns die hylge schryff leirt und anzeicht, dan et moyss
alles na dem getuchnis der hylger schryfft geleufft, erkant und
gehalden werden, wie ouch Christus und sine hilge apostelen dairvan teugen myt allen rechten propheten und alle die lerers, dair
die hilge schryff neyt van en teuget, synt nach Christus wort deyff
un morder, Joh. 10 (V. 1), blynde verfuerer und glisner, Mat. 23
(V. 13-16), falsche propheten, Mat. 7 (V. 15-16), die man an
iren fruchten sall erkennen. Zo den Romeren 16 (V. 18) nompt
sy Paulus bouckdiener, die man fluen und vermyden sall. 2. Cor.
11 (V. 13) nompt sy Paulus falsche apostelen und bedrochliche
arbeyter, Phyl. 3 (V. 2. 18-19) nompt er sy hundt und boes arbey-
der, darzo fyant des krutz, eur eyrs zo schanden, dairzo ir ende die
verdomnys. 1. Tymot. 4 (V. 1) nomp er ouch etlige lerer der

duvelen. 2. Tymo. 3 (V. 8) nompt er sy den tzuveren in Egypten gelick, die da schinen eynes gotseligen levens und doch Gottes krafft verlouven. 2. Pet. 2 (V. 17) nompt sy Petrus bronnen on wasser, die myt evyger duysternis synt bevangen. Apoca. 9 (V. 3. 5) nompt sy der hylge geyst heuwschrecken, die dat gewyssen pinygen, qwellen und martelen, aver nummerme in der sunden reynygen und gesont machen. Wat der nu is, die iren eygen nutz und neyt Gotz eir, nutz und pryss gesocht haven und ouch noch neyt en suechen, die moyssen ouch noch alle na der hilger schryfft van Got verworpen und vor sine doer gesloten syn, Mat. 25 (V. 11-12) und ouch glich dem unnutzen knecht gebonden zom evyge fuyr verordelt werden, glich Christus selver dairvan gesprachen und geteucht hayt im selvyge capyttel (V. 30) etc.

So dan nu alle die lerers und predycanten dieser werlt dat wort in der ordnung Jesu Christy und sinen hilgen geyst neyt en haven, als bouven erkant is, vern bouten dat getuchnis Pauly 1. Tymo. 3 (V. 2-7), Tito 1 (V. 5-9) getreden sint und van den heren und vorsten dieser werlt gesant werden, begafft myt groten renten, und neyt gesant van Christo und sinen hylgen, lieven vater begayfft myt geystlichen gaven und suechen dat schentliche gewyn Balaam und den eygen bouck aff Got, als oven erklairt is, weyll sy neyt die schapen suechen to weyden, sonder alle teyt verleyden und wyllen ouch alle teyt gedienet haven, aver selver nemans neyt dienen, verkeren und neyt leren, doeden und net levendich maken, Mat. 12 (V. 30) verstrauen und neyt samlen, suechen sych alteyt selver in irem eygen nutz und neyt den nutz Jesu Christy und ires neysten etc.

(Die fruntschaff der werlt is ein fiantschafft weder Got. Jaco. 4 (V. 4).)

Also moyss Christus myt sinen lieven jungeren van diesen predicanten der werlt gesmacht, gelastert und verstoten syn, up dat sy gern wulden ir eygen eyr vor der werlt behalden und nomen darum die werlt christen und die christen ketzer, handelen allso jemerliche vern bouten dat reine, hilge, selichmakende wort Gottes in leren und leven. Darum heyscht uns ouch die hylge schryfft (1. Cor. 10 (V. 14), 2. Cor. 6 (V. 14-17), Apo. 18 (V. 4)) van in wyken, vermyden, schuen und fluen, wie bouven genocht myt hilger schryfft bezeucht is.

Alsus staint wir arme kinder int myddel tuschen Got und der overycheyt in aller bangscheit durch die orsach der schryfftgeleirten, die ouch alle teyt die overicheit haven angerouffen, gedreven und gedrungen, up dat unschuldygen blot to vergeyten Apo. 6 (V. 9-11), wylches ouch sall in in off ouch by in erfonden werden, gelich Mat. 23 (V. 29-35), Apo. 18 (V. 24) geschreven steyt.

O ir lieve heren und fursten, so ir uns nu zo den schryfftgeleirten und falsche propheten wylt driven und dryngen, da uns
Got und die hylge schryfft heyscht affwyken, fluen und vermyden,
als ouch oven genocht verklairt is, wem sollen wir nu dat meyste
gehorsam syn, dem evyge Gott off euch sterffliche mynschen. Ich
acht ummer, E. G. wirt selver richten, dat Got boven all der prys
zogehort und ouch van uns haven wylt, weyll er ouch zeytlich und
evych in die hell verderven kan, (Mat. 10 (V. 28)) aver die
mynschen neit dan dat leyff nemen konnen, so is dyt nu uns
gezeuchnis und orsach, warum dat wir diese predycanten neyt en
horen off ouch eure junger neyt gesyn en konnen, wie ouch oven
genocht myt hilger schryfft verklairt is.

Synt wir nu Got und sinem hilgen wort gehorsam, so vallen
wir in E. G. hant und straff. Synt wyr nu E. L. gehorsam, so
vallen wir in den torn Gottes und syn straf, dairaff geschreven
steyt Hebreo. 10 (V. 31): erschrecklich is et fallen in die hende
des levendygen Gottes. O evyger Got, wyll uns im gelouven
stercken, dat wir doch in geiner pynen van dyr geschreck en moegen
werden, Amen.

(5.) Bekentenis unsers gelouvens van der liever overicheyt.

Wyr gelouven, bekennen und bezeugen vor Got und ouch allen
mynschen, dat die overicheyt is ingesat und ouch is geordinert
van Gott na dem gezeuchnis der hylger schrift, zo den Rom. am 13.
(V. 1-7), 1. Pet. 2 (V. 13-17), wie ouch Christus selver dairvan
bezeucht und geboden hayt Mat. 17 (V. 24-27), 22 (V. 15-22)
dem keyser zo geven, das im zogehort, und Goede, dat Got zogehort,
wie ouch Christus myt Petrus dem keyser hy den zyns hant gegeven.
Also gelouven und bekennen wir ouch, dem keyser und ouch aller
overicheyt ouss dem gebot der leyfften schuldich zo syn, schatz,
toll und stuyr zo geven, up dat sy ir ampt, van Got untfangen,
bedienen konnen.

Wylcher ampt in gegeven is, den gueden und fromen to be-
schutzen und to beschirmen, dae der buess mit gewalt over in
wylt heyrschen, im lyff ader guet myt gewalt zo nemen off zo
berouven, solche deyff off mordener, rouver, mortbrenner und vat
van sulchen oveldederen off ouch boesswychteren synt, die synt
ouch altomayll der overricheit in gericht, ordel und straff gefallen,
wie ouch die hilge schryfft dairvan bezeucht, als oven gesacht is
zo dem Rom. 13 (V. 1-7) etc.

Darum bekennen wir ouch, dat wir vor Got schuldich synt,

vor sulche overicheyt to bydden, up dat wir eyn gotselich leven
under in in allem styllen vreden moegen haven, wie ouch der hylge
Paulus dairvan geschreven hayt 1 Tymo. 2 (V. 1-2), wie ouch
Gottes wyll is, der dae woelte, dat alle mynschen zo gotlicher
erkentenis komen mochten, up dat sy dairinne lefften und selich
worden. Got wyll es ouch gonnen und geven, die es van rinen
hertzen begeren zo beleven, Amen.

Ouch gelouven wir und bekennen myt rinen hertzen, dat sych
ouch nemans en mach erheven noch wederstreven myt eynyger
gewalt off ousserlichem wapen, weder die overicheit zo stryten,
er en moyss ouch fallen in den torn und straf Gottes und ouch in
die straff der overicheyt. Der almechtige Gott wyll uns weysheyt
geven in allen dyngen, up dat wyr Got syn rechte eir moegen
geven und ouch der liever overicheit eur recht eyr und gehorsam-
heyt moegen geven und oussrichten in allen dyngen, up dat wir
am strengen ordell Gottes gerecht und unstrafflich befonden
moegen werden, dae ederman sall loin untfangen na sinen wirken,
glich Christus Mat. 25 (V. 14-46) gruntlich gesprochen hayt.

Also is dyt unser gelouff und bekentenis van der geordyneirten
gewalt und overricheyt, den dat swert is van Gott gegeven over
die buessen zer straff aller oveldeder. Der evyge, almechtyge Got
wyll der overicheit weyscheit und verstant geven, ir ampt recht zo
bekennen und ouch vor Got recht bedienen moegen und sich neit
me to verunreynygen an dem unschuldigen blot der gerechten
durch radt der schryffgeleirten, die alle teyt den gerechten up
die fleyschbanck hant geroffen und gekrsyyen, wie sy ouch myt
Christo und allen rechten propheten und apostelen vor und na
alle teyt gedayn haven. Got wyll der overycheyt gnedich syn und
vergeven, die sych myt unwyssenheyt an eynygem unschuldygem
blot vergryffen haven, und gnadt van Got begeren, sich zo besseren,
geyn unschuldych blot me zo vergeyten noch up sich to laden vor
Got eventlich.

Wyr en begeren ouch geine upruerige, valche, duveliche geyster
to veranteren, dye myt dem swerdt fechten und stryden wyllen,
et sy ouch en tegen die overicheit off ouch eynyge ander mynschen,
dan wyr gelouven und bekennen, dat sulchenen boesen alltomayll
der overycheyt und ouch Got tsamen int gericht und straff gefallen
synt, wen sy schon ouch hundertmayll gedoufft weren. Dan wem
dat swert neyt en is gegeven, der en sall es ouch neyt angrypen,
sonder den es Gott hayt gegeven, die sullens alleyn bedyenen, glich
wie oven myt der hilger schryfft genocht dairvan erkleirt und
bezeuget is.

(6.) Wam dem wapen der rechter geleuvygen in Christo.

Dyt wapen der geleuvygen, dae wir uns myt sullen zom strydt rusten, ist allein dat krefftyge, hyllyge, selichmakende wort Gottes, dat moyssen wir im gelouven myt reinem hertzen antrecken und stryden dairmyt untegen die fyant unser selen, wylcher synt all duvelche geyster, die myt falcher leer mynschlicher weysheyt uns wyllen afftrecken van Christo und sinem hylgen wort des levens. Ja vor sulchen duvelsche geyster und glissnerey moyssen wyr uns wayll bewaren myt dem hylgen wort des levens, dat uns kan erhalden und selich maken.

Also bekennen wir ouch, dat uns ouch geyn ander ousserlich wapen en is gegeven noch bevolen, dan alleyn dyt geystliche swert, vylches is dat wort Gottes. Und alle dye wederwerdyge mynschen oder fyant, dye wir myt diesem hylgen wort Gottes und gelouvens-wapen im hilgen geist neyt en konnen noch en moegen gestyllen, van dennen moyssen wir liden, ja ouch alle smagh dragen byss in den doet, wie ouch unser myster Jesus Christus vor is gegangen in allem liden, der uns ouch allso hayt heyschen nafolgen under aller smagch, druck und liden. Des wir ouch eyn exempel haven bey allen hylgen, die ouch hant moyssen liden byss in den doyt, ja ouch alle smach der werlt hant moyssen dragen um der wayrheyt willen, die sy van Christo gezeucht haven. So wir dan Christus selver myt sinen lieven hilgen zom vorbylt des krutz und lidens haven, so wyll der almechtyge, leyffhavende Gott uns ouch stercken im gelouven, dat wir unser krutz und liden ouch geduldych moegen dragen durch Jesum Christum, Amen.

Weyll Christus spricht: Wer mych bekent vor den menschen, den wyll ich werderum bekennen vor mynem vater im hymmel, Mat. 10 (V. 32), so hant wir ouch hymyt unse bekentenis van der wairheit Jesu Christy gegeven, dairin man erkennen mach, datt wir neyt en suechen dan alleyn Gottes eir, pris und ouch der liever overicheyt gehorsam to sy, gelick uns Christus und syn apostelen (Rom. 13 (V. 1)) dairvan geleirt haven, und ouch aller mynschen wayllfart an lyff und selen, up dat wir ouch selich werden und eyn unvergencklich ryck moegen beerven, dat hymmels is, glick ouch Christus dairvan bezeucht, dat sin rick neit van dieser werlt en sy.

Derhalven en begeren wir ouch neyt myt eynigen ousserlichen, ertzen wapen uns to weren off uproer to maken. Und alle, die sulches gedain haven off ouch noch vornemen wolden zo doen, die bekennen wir, glich wie ouch boven bekant ist, dat sy alle synt gevallen int gericht der overicheit.

O ir lieve richter und heren, wilt doch den unschuldygen un-

schuldich layssen bliven und richtet eyn recht gericht, up dat ir
ouch van Got neyt gericht en werdt, glich Christus Mat. 7 (V. 1-2)
geleirt hait. Der almechtige Gott help uns durch syn guetigeit,
im rechten gelouven to bliven, durch Jesum Christum, Amen.

Menno und das Kempener Täuferbekenntnis

Überblickt man die Aussagen dieses Bekenntnisses, so fällt
die Verwandtschaft mit der Lehre Mennos sofort ins Auge.
Das lässt sich an den einzelnen Punkten noch näher erläutern.
Der erste Artikel von der Menschwerdung ist gerade zu dieser
Zeit ein wichtiges Thema in Mennos Schriften. Im Januar
1544 hatte Menno darüber ein Gespräch mit Johannes a Lasco
in Emden, an das sich mehrere Wechselschriften anschliessen.
Im Frühjahr 1545, kurz vor unserem Bekenntnis, erscheint in
Bonn, also im Kurfürstentum Köln, a Lascos Buch gegen Menno
über die Menschwerdung, das der Bekämpfung des Täufertums
in Kurköln dienen soll. Noch deutlicher ist die Abhängigkeit
des zweiten Artikels von Mennos Tauflehre. Die Disposition
findet sich in Mennos Schrift "Verklaringe des christlycken
doopsels" (Opera 1681, pag. 401 b) wieder. Der Abendmahls-
artikel legt dar, dass das Abendmahl nur von gläubigen Jün-
gern bei gleichzeitigem Ausschluss der Gottlosen stiftungsge-
mäss gefeiert werden kann. Er gipfelt — das ist die aktuelle
Situation des Bekenntnisses — in der Feststellung, dass die Evangelischen von Kempen keine Christengemeinde sind und nicht
das rechte Abendmahl halten. Der vierte Artikel über das
Predigtamt weist wieder deutlich auf Menno. Auch darüber
hatte er sich in Emden mit a Lasco nicht einigen können. Leben
und Lehre der Prediger, besonders ihre Besoldung und Anstel-
lung durch die Obrigkeit, mangelnde Zuchtübung in der Gemeinde und Inanspruchnahme der Obrigkeit gegen die wahren
Christen, das sind Argumente, die auch Menno in diesem Zusammenhang verwendet. Die Artikel 5 und 6 von der Obrigkeit und der Waffe des Glaubens richten sich gegen Vorwürfe,
die in "Warnung und Befehl wider die Irrtümer der Wiedertäufer" im Kölner Reformationsbedenken von 1543 erhoben
werden, wo den Täufern Verwerfung der Obrigkeit und auf-
rührerischer Geist im Stile der Münsterer Täufer zugeschrieben
werden. Ganz deutlich ist dort auch die Auseinandersetzung

mit den Batenburgern. Insgesamt sind diese Artikel eine eindurcksvolle Darstellung frühen mennonitischen Glaubens. Es verdient Beachtung, dass der Schriftbeweis bis auf zwei weniger wichtige Stellen ausschliesslich dem Neuen Testament entnommen ist. Der leitende Gesichtspunkt ist der der Nachfolge Christi.

Dieses Bekenntnis ist für unseren Raum insofern interessant, als er vor einer evangelischen Obrigkeit abgelegt wird. In ihm bezeugt das niederrheinische Täufertum, warum es sich mit der Reformation durch einen Landesfürsten nicht vereinigen kann und seinen eigenen Weg gehen muss. Bisweilen, besonders im Abschnitt über die Prediger, hat das Bekenntnis eine scharf antievangelische Tendenz.

Cornelius Krahn hat uns in seinem Buche über Menno dargestellt, dass dieser um diese Zeit im Rheinland gewirkt hat.[2] Einzelheiten darüber sind nur wenige bekannt. Der Grund für Mennos Übersiedeln an den Rhein liegt einmal in seinen Auseinandersetzungen mit den ostfriesischen Predigern, zum andern aber darin, dass die Reformation durch den Übertritt des Kurfürsten und Erzbischofs Hermann von Wied zum Protestantismus im Rheinland einen grossen Aufschwung gewinnt, an dem auch das Täufertum Anteil hat. Wenn Menno den Fürsten später mit dem Zusatz "loffelyker gedachtnisse" erwähnt, ist dies freilich kein Ausdruck besonderer Hochachtung, sondern die damals übliche Redeweise für einen christlich Verstorbenen in hoher Stellung. Krahn erwähnt Mennos Versuche, mit den Predigern von Bonn und Wesel, den beiden Zentren der Reformation am Rhein, zu Glaubensgesprächen zusammenzukommen.[3] Es wird dies mit den hier geschilderten Vorgängen in Kempen unmittelbar zusammenhängen. Der Bonner Prediger Heinrich, mit dem Menno korrespondiert, ist der obengenannte Heinrich Zell. In der Stadt Köln, wie Krahn anzunehmen scheint, dürfte Menno in dieser Zeit kaum gewesen sein, da sie fest im katholischen Glauben beharrte und die Reformation streng bekämpfte. Auch scheint es um diese Zeit keine Täufer in Köln gegeben zu haben. Vielmehr hat Menno wohl im Osten des Herzogtums Geldern, im Herzogtum Jülich und im kurkölnischen Niederstift gewirkt. Einer der Kempener Täufer und einer ihrer Wortführer im Gespräch mit den Predigern, Tewes Ruebsam, bekennt: dass ehr nu verlitten Martini Episcopi (= 11. November 1544) van eynem unbekanten, aver uiss Friesslannt der buerdich, ime binnen der stadt Kempen in Reynar Pipers huyss wedergedeufft. . . . Wenn auch diese Angabe nicht sehr deutlich ist, so dürfen wir doch vermuten, dass Menno in dieser Zeit in Kempen gewesen ist und dort sogar getauft hat.

Jedenfalls zeigt unser Bekenntnis, dass das rheinische Täufertum um 1545 dem Geiste Mennos folgt. Vielleicht werden in Zukunft bei weiterer Forschung noch deutlichere Spuren von Mennos Wirken am Rhein ans Licht treten.

HEINOLD FAST

Hans Krüsis Büchlein über Glauben und Taufe

Ein Täuferdruck von 1525

IM SOMMER 1960 fand ich in E. Wellers "Repertorium typo-graphicum" (Nördlingen 1864) unter Nr. 3583 folgenden Titel:

> Von dem Glawbenn / Gotes Der allein selig /machett, vnd nur/von hymel geben/würdt:/Von dem Tauff Christi. / Von dem Wasser, das vns nit selig machen mag. / Hanns Nagel vonn / Klingnaw / Ain Ledergerber / MDXXV

Ich gestehe, dass mich eine grosse Erregung überfiel, als ich diesen Titel las. Denn erstens war hier von der Taufe die Rede, und zwar in einer Art, die sofort auf die Nähe zu den Täufern schliessen liess. Zweitens war im Zusammenhang damit die Jahreszahl 1525 ein verblüffend frühes Datum. Drittens las ich — und ich traute meinen Augen nicht — den Namen "Hanns Nagel von Klingnaw". Ich wusste, dass es der Name des Ende Juli 1525 in Luzern verbrannten zweiten täuferischen Märtyrers war, der gewöhnlich Hans oder Johannes Krüsi genannt wurde und der in der St.-Galler Täuferbewegung eine führende Rolle gespielt hatte. Dass er etwas geschrieben habe, war mir nicht bekannt. Überhaupt gab es meines Wissens nur zwei Täuferdrucke aus dem Jahre 1525, beide von Balthasar Hubmaier. Es war mir klar, dass es sich hier um ein rarissimum handelte, von dem noch niemand eine Ahnung hatte.

Bei E. Weller ist als Fundort München angegeben. Ich bestellte also das Büchlein sofort von Zürich aus im internationalen Leihverkehr. Nach zwei Monaten Wartezeit, die mir sehr lang wurde, erhielt ich meine Bestellkarte zurück — unerledigt. Nach den zahlreichen Stempeln zu schliessen, war die Karte nicht nur in München gewesen, sondern an mehrere grosse westdeutsche Bibliotheken weitergereicht worden. Alle — einschiesslich München — hatten ihren Stempel "Nicht vorhanden" hinterlassen. Die Kriegszerstörungen hatten anscheinend auch hier ihre Wirkung getan. Es war eine grosse Enttäuschung. Ich tröstete mich bereits mit dem Gedanken, dass schon der von Weller zitierte Titel manche Schlüsse zuliesse. Doch dann versuchte ich es noch einmal mit einem direkten Brief an die Bayrische Staatsbibliothek, unterstützt durch ein persönliches Telephongespräch mit der Fernleihe in München. Nach vier Tagen konnte ich das Büchlein in der Zentralbibliothek in Zürich einsehen.

Ich berichte zuerst, was man ohne Wissen um das Büchlein aus den Akten und Chroniken über seinen Verfassser erfährt, um dann den neuen Fund zu untersuchen.

Hans Krüsi als Täuferführer

Nach dem Zeugnis des St.-Galler Chronisten Johannes Kessler war Hans Krüsi "von St. Georgen gebürtig".[1] Das Dorf St. Georgen lag einen halben Kilometer südöstlich von St. Gallen oben in der Senke zwischen der Bernegg und dem Freudenberg. Politisch gehörte es zur Gemeinde Tablat und damit zum Gebiet des Abtes von St. Gallen; kirchlich war es der Pfarrei von St. Laurenzen in der Stadt St. Gallen mit einer Kaplaneipfründe untertan.[2] Mütterlicherseits war Krüsis Grossvater hier "Praefekt" gewesen,[3] d.h. entweder Kaplan von St. Georgen oder Ammann von Tablat.[4] Das Tablater Lehenbuch zeigt, dass die Familie Krüsi in St. Georgen sehr zahlreich war und grosse Ländereien als Erblehen bestellte.[5] Personen mit dem Vornamen Hans sind dabei so oft verzeichnet, dass eine Identifikation mit dem späteren Täufer unmöglich ist.[6] Doch scheint es ziemlich sicher, dass es die mütterliche Linie war, von der er den Namen "Krüsi von St. Georgen" empfangen hatte.[7]

214

Seinen zweiten Namen, Hans Nagel von Klingnau,[8] verdankte er dann wohl seinem Vater. Dieser war nämlich Schulmeister in dem kleinen aargauischen Städtchen Klingnau gewesen[9] und hat wahrscheinlich [Mathias] Nagel geheissen.[10] Wie Krüsi auch noch zu einem dritten Namen, Hans Kern von Klingnau, kam, ist unbekannt.[11] Vielleicht war es nur eine Verwechselung.[12]

Hans Krüsi ergriff den Beruf seines Vaters und wurde Lehrer. Die einzige sichere Notiz über das Leben Krüsis vor seinem Übertritt zum Täufertum besagt nämlich, dass er "anfänglich zu Wil Proviser (=Unterlehrer) gewesen sei".[13] In dem Städtchen Wil, 30 Kilometer westlich von St. Gallen, befand sich eine Lateinschule, deren Lehrer 1516 Meister Michael von Pforzheim wurde.[14] Wie lange er blieb, ist unbekannt. Krüsi war entweder sein Nachfolger oder (wahrscheinlicher) sein Gehilfe; denn "seit der Mitte des 15. Jahrhunderts stand dem Schulmeister im Provisor ein Gehilfe bei".[15]

Über Krüsis Konversion zum Täufertum wusste 1538 Johannes Rütiner zu berichten, dass sie unter dem Einfluss von Johannes Ramsauer und Martin Baumgarter geschah.[16] Das muss Anfang April 1525 in St. Gallen gewesen sein. Die beiden gehörten nachweislich zu den ersten Täufern in St. Gallen. Hans Ramsauer, Altersgenosse Zwinglis und Sohn des gleichnamigen Zunftmeisters und Ratsherrn, war schon Anfang 1524 bei den Bibelstunden von Johannes Kessler, die für den Fortgang der Reformation in St. Gallen entscheidend waren und dann den Mutterboden für das von Zürich eindringende Täufertum bildeten, dabeigewesen.[17] Martin Baumgarter taucht in den Akten gleich in den ersten Täuferverhören Ende April 1525 auf.[18] Selbstverständlich hatte Krüsi dann sofort mit allen andern namhaften St.-Galler Täufern Berührung. In seinem Geständnis werden sie alle als seine Gefährten erwähnt: Uliman und Rugglisberger, Beda Miles und Nikolaus Guldin, Antoni Roggenacher und Gabriel Giger. Entscheidend war aber doch wohl die persönliche Begegnung mit Konrad Grebel. Sie beweist zugleich, dass Krüsi vor dem 9. April, an dem Grebel St. Gallen wieder verliess, zu den Täufern stiess. Der junge Grebel habe das Täufertum als erster aufgebracht, heisst es in Krüsis Geständnis. Ja, er habe ihm persönlich ein Büchlein gebracht und es erklärt. Das Büchlein sei geschrieben gewesen und nicht gedruckt.[19] Man hat angesichts einer solchen Aussage den Eindruck, dass Ramsauer und Baumgarter bei der Bekehrung Krüsis lediglich Zubringerdienste leisteten, der entscheidende Einfluss aber von Grebel selbst ausging.

Schon jeder einfache Täufer hielt es für seine erste Pflicht, das Evangelium weiterzusagen. Wieviel mehr ein zu den Täufern übergetretener Lehrer, der lesen und schreiben konnte! Krüsi scheint zunächst nach Wil zurückgekehrt zu sein, um dort für das Täufertum zu werben. In seinem Geständnis nennt er drei Wiler Bürger, mit denen er besonders eng verbunden war.[20] Ausserdem verkehrte er dort mit dem späteren Täufer Michael Wüst.[21] Im "Schneckenbund", einem Niedergericht im Amt Wil, fand er als Gefährten Hans Nüsch, der auch predigte und mit dem er seine Erkenntnisse austauschen konnte.[22]

Wahrscheinlich verlor Krüsi durch diese Tätigkeit sehr bald seine Hilfslehrerstelle in Wil. Er kehrte nach St. Gallen zurück und stellte sich dort mit Lesen und Predigen in den Dienst der Bruderschaft. Er verhandelte auch einmal mit dem St.-Galler Schulmeister Dominik Zili über seine Predigttätigkeit.[23] Zili war Mitglied der Kommission zur Überwachung der Predigten und Laienlesungen in St. Laurenzen.[24] Vielleicht hat Krüsi ihn in dieser Eigenschaft angesprochen. Jedenfalls musste sich Krüsi bald auch nach einem neuen Gelderwerb umsehen. Er entschloss sich, das Weberhandwerk zu erlernen. Zu diesem Zweck erhielt er von mehreren Täufern eine Unterstützung an Geld und Realien. Wann er seine in diesem Zusammenhang erwähnte Frau geheiratet hatte, ist unbekannt.[25]

Ende Mai und Anfang Juni 1525 drängten die Dinge in St. Gallen auf eine Entscheidung hin. Sowohl in der Stadt als auch im umliegenden Gebiet des Abtes von St. Gallen bereitete man sich auf eine Unterdrückung der Täufer vor. Die Täufer aber hatten bereits so viele Anhänger gewonnen, dass es zu ernsthaften Zusammenstössen kam. Krüsi sollte dabei eine führende Rolle spielen.

In der Stadt hatte der Rat bereits am 12. Mai zu einer öffentlichen Auseinandersetzung zwischen der täuferischen und der reformatorischen Partei aufgefordert. Auf Bitten der Täufer zögerte sich diese Auseinandersetzung bis Anfang Juni hinaus. In der Zwischenzeit holte man sich beiderseits aus Zürich, dem Zentrum der Auseinandersetzung, Hilfe; die Predikanten von Zwingli, der seine erste antitäuferische Schrift der St.-Galler Obrigkeit und Gemeinde widmete; die Täufer von Grebel, der brieflich bei Vadian protestierte und seine Brüder ermunterte. In den Pfingsttagen, vom 5. bis 7. Juni, fiel in mehreren öffentlichen Verhandlungen die Entscheidung. Taufe und Abendmahl, wie die Täufer sie feierten, wurden verboten. Zuwiderhandlungen sollten mit scharfen Geldstrafen oder gar mit Ausweisung geahndet werden. Ja, wegen der Unruhen, die diese Verhandlungen und Beschlüsse begleitet hatten, sah man sich am 8. Juni sogar genötigt, eine Bereitschaftspolizei von 200 Mann aufzustellen, die den Rat gegen allfällige Übergriffe schützen sollte.[26]

Diese Massnahme stand sicherlich auch im Zusammenhang mit den Ereignissen, die sich zu gleicher Zeit vor den Stadtmauern im Gebiet des Abtes zutrugen. Die Täuferbewegung war sehr bald auch auf dieses Gebiet übergesprungen und hatte dort einen durch wirtschaftliche Not vorbereiteten Boden gefunden. Die Bauern der Gemeinden Rotmonten, Tablat, Straubenzell und Bernhardszell, wie auch anderer Gemeinden des äbtischen Untertanenlandes, lebten in drückender Abhängigkeit vom Abt von St. Gallen. Ihr Hass hatte sich auf den geistlichen Advokaten des Klosters, Dr. Christoph Winkler konzentriert, der über die Einhaltung der äbtischen Rechte wachte. Als sich ihnen im März 1525 die Gelegenheit bot, nahmen die Tablater ihn gefangen, mussten ihn aber bald wieder herausgeben. Ihr Prozess gegen ihn lief noch ohne grosse Aussichten bei den Eidgenossen.[27]

In dieser gespannten Atmosphäre wirkte die Täuferbewegung wie entladend. Bereits im Mai war es zu Unruhen gekommen, bei denen Krüsi nicht unbeteiligt gewesen sein mag. Denn als Ende Mai in Frauenfeld ein Tag der eidgenössischen zwölf Orte stattfand, fasste man dort den Beschluss, gegen die aufsässigen Untertanen des Abtes, vor allem auch gegen die Täufer vorzugehen. Und als der für das äbtische Gebiet verantwortliche Hauptmann Melchior Degen mit diesem Beschluss Anfang Juni nach St. Gallen zurückkehrte, musste er hören, dass Hans Krüsi in St. Georgen, der Kirchengemeinde von

Tablat, "wiederum" seine Bibelstunden ("Lesungen") abhielt und taufte.[28] Er begab sich sofort mit einigen Knechten hinauf nach St. Georgen, um dort den Beschluss des Frauenfelder Tages auszurichten. Aber er erlebte eine üble Abfuhr. Als er nämlich anfing, von der Obrigkeit zu reden, fiel man ihm ins Wort und sagte, man hätte keinen Herrn oder irgendeine Obrigkeit ausser Gott und auch das Erdreich, auf dem sie lebten, gehöre Gott. Der Hauptmann möge sich hinwegscheren, sonst würde man nachhelfen und ihn den Bach hinunterjagen. Andere forderten den Hauptmann auf, zu bleiben und das Wort Gottes zu hören. Als er nicht darauf einging, verspottete man ihn: Er wolle das Wort Gottes nicht hören; sie selber würden sich schämen, wenn sie das Wort Gottes so fliehen würden. Inzwischen hatte sich eine grosse Menschenmenge gebildet. Das Gedränge wurde immer grösser. Als dann sogar ein Stein auf den Hauptmann geworfen wurde, bekam er Angst und ritt mit seinen Knechten von dannen.

Ich habe diese Szene nach dem Bericht des Hauptmanns erzählt. In seinem späteren Geständnis rechtfertigt sich Krüsi selber so: Als er auf der Gemeindeversammlung gepredigt habe und der Hauptmann gekommen sei, habe er gesagt, man solle für den Hauptmann beten, dass auch er zum rechten Glauben kommen möge. Christen seien in ihrer Erkenntnis und in ihrem Urteil nicht den Tauben und Gottlosen unterworfen. Man sei Gott mehr schuldig als den Menschen, und nach dem lebendigen Wort Gottes brauche niemand den Zehnten oder dergleichen zu geben etc. — Diese Aussage wirft gewiss ein milderes Licht auf die Szene. Krüsis Anliegen war primär ein religiöses.[29] Aber es wird auch deutlich, wie leicht solche Gedanken sozial-revolutionär missverstanden werden konnten. In der Lage, in der man sich in der Gemeinde Tablat befand, war die Versuchung dazu sehr gross. Jedenfalls wird das Zusammenfallen von religiösen und sozialen Reformbestrebungen die Ursache sein, dass die Täuferbewegung auch vor den Toren St. Gallens zu einer Massenbewegung wurde.[30]

Während am 6. Juni 1525 die St.-Galler Obrigkeit das Taufen und die täuferischen Abendmahlsfeiern verbot, protestierte man ausserhalb der Mauern mit einem demonstrativen Akt dagegen. An diesem Pfingstdienstag wurde Hans Krüsi trotz der

Warnungen des Hauptmanns von der ganzen Gemeinde Tablat als Prediger gewählt: Er solle taufen, lesen und auch "den Tisch des Herrn" mit ihnen feiern. Ausdrücklich wurde bestimmt, dass man auch weiterhin diese Feiern beibehalten und auf keine Obrigkeit Rücksicht nehmen werde.[31] Es leuchtet ein, dass die Obrigkeit in der Stadt sich durch eine Bereitschaftspolizei gegen Übergriffe auch von ausserhalb zu sichern suchte.

Krüsis Tätigkeit als gewählter Prediger von Tablat währte nicht lang. Er selbst bestätigt, dass er gegen die Heiligenbilder und die Reliquien predigte und dass daraufhin einige Gemeindemitglieder den Altar aufbrachen und die "Schelmenbeine" hinauswarfen. Auch habe er dort so viele getauft, dass er die Zahl nicht mehr wisse.[32] Eheschliessungen übernahm er ebenfalls.[33] Gütergemeinschaft wurde nur in einer freiwilligen Form durchgeführt, so dass, "wenn einer etwas hatte, er es mit andern teilte".[34] In Krüsis eigenen Worten: Man wollte Gott untertänig sein, sich nicht abweisen lassen vom Wort Gottes, nicht auseinandergehen und von der Lehre abfallen, sondern alle beieinander bleiben. . . . Es solle alles gemeinsam sein in der Liebe Gottes und im Glauben.[35]

Johannes Kessler hat uns überliefert, Hans Krüsi habe auch im nahen Teufen gewirkt und es dahin gebracht, dass man den bewährten, zwinglisch gesinnten Pfarrer Jakob Schurtanner abgesetzt habe.[36] Die Gemeinde Teufen liegt etwa dreieinhalb Kilometer südlich von St. Georgen. Auch wenn sie schon zum Gebiet von Appenzell gehörte, war sie leicht zu erreichen. Es ist deshalb durchaus möglich, dass Hans Krüsi seine Tätigkeit bis nach Teufen ausdehnte. Man hat das Zeugnis von Kessler darum stets für zuverlässig gehalten.[37] Jetzt hat sich aber in St. Gallen eine Zeugenaussage gefunden, auf Grund derer der Sturz Schurtanners nicht Krüsi, sondern Wolfgang Uliman zugeschrieben werden muss.[38] Es mag sein, dass Krüsi dann seine Dienste auch der Gemeinde in Teufen gelegentlich zur Verfügung stellte. Aber den entscheidenden Schlag führte Uliman. Darin muss sich Kessler geirrt haben.

Nur wenige Tage nach seiner Wahl in Tablat geriet Krüsi in die Hände der St.-Galler Obrigkeit. Bei einem Besuch in der Stadt, wo er das Weberhandwerk erlernte, gab er abfällige

Reden über die Obrigkeit von sich: Die Obrigkeit wolle das
Evangelium neun Klafter unter die Erde verbieten, und Ähnliches. Sofort griff die Obrigkeit zu und legte ihn ins Gefäng-
nis. Hier muss sich nun etwas Ungewöhnliches begeben haben.
Denn als Krüsi am 16. Juni gegen Urfehde wieder entlassen
wurde, musste er in seinen Eid die Bedingung aufnehmen, nie-
mandem etwas von dem zu sagen, was man mit ihm während
seiner Haft verhandelt habe.[39] Das ist ungewöhnlich und
muss einen Grund gehabt haben. Einen Hinweis gibt vielleicht
Johannes Rütiner, wenn er berichtet, Krüsi sei, nachdem er
von Johannes Ramsauer, Martin Baumgarter und anderen
für das Täufertum gewonnen war, "durch Johannes Kessler
wieder auf den rechten Weg geführt worden, weil Kessler ihm
wie einem Freund über die Aufdringlichkeit der Täufer vor-
klagte."[40] Kessler stand als ehemaliger Leiter der Bibelstunden
der Sache der Täufer sehr nahe. Vielleicht konnte er Krüsi
Versprechungen auf Besserung der kirchlichen Verhältnisse in
St. Gallen machen, die dem Abt und den katholischen Orten
nicht zu Ohren kommen durften. Aber das ist eine Vermutung.

Die Stadt entliess Krüsi am 16. Juni mit dem Bescheid, er
könne in der Stadt bleiben, wenn er nur das Handwerk lernen, vom Taufen, Predigen und Abendmahlfeiern aber ab-
lassen wolle. Wolle er jedoch weiterhin predigen, dann müsse
er das Hoheitsgebiet der Stadt meiden.

Hans Krüsi entschied sich fürs Letztere. Wie er später ge-
stand, forderte besonders Beda Miles, der mit ihm im Gefäng-
nis gesessen hatte und mit ihm entlassen worden war, ihn auf,
"dass er wieder lese." "Er solle nicht so vom Glauben abfallen."
Als auch die andern Brüder in St. Georgen ihn drängten, konnte
er nicht widerstehen.[41] Bald predigte und taufte er wie zuvor.

Nun aber schritt die äbtische Obrigkeit ein. Vom 26. Juni
an tagte in Baden die Jahresabrechnung der Eidgenossenschaft
über die Gemeinen Herrschaften. Da auch das Gebiet des
Abtes von St. Gallen dem Schutz von vier eidgenössischen Orten
unterstand, wandte man sich an die Versammlung und bat um
Hilfe gegen das Treiben Krüsis. Die Versammlung sagte sie
zu und schickte am Schluss der Tagung, am 6. Juli, je ein
Schreiben an Appenzell und an die Stadt St. Gallen. Man wies
auf das erneute Treiben Krüsis in St. Georgen hin — nicht

ohne den leisen Vorwurf, dass die Stadt St. Gallen ihn wieder
freigelassen habe — und bat, ihn unverzüglich festzunehmen,
wenn man seiner habhaft werden könne.[42] Doch war das nicht
mehr nötig. Denn ungefähr zur gleichen Zeit oder doch nur
wenig später gelang es dem Hauptmann Melchior Degen, Krüsi
in seiner Wohnung in St. Georgen nachts im Bett zu über-
raschen und gefangen zu nehmen.[43]

Die Anhänger Krüsis hatten so etwas gefürchtet und sich da-
rauf vorbereitet. An dieser Vorbereitung wird deutlich, welch
Geistes Kind die Bewegung war, die ausserhalb der Tore St.
Gallens Krüsi unterstützte. Es war sicher nicht mehr das Täufertum, das Konrad Grebel vertrat, als er in seinem Brief an
Thomas Müntzer schrieb, man solle das Evangelium und seine
Anhänger oder auch sich selber nicht mit dem Schwert beschirmen; rechte gläubige Christen seien Schafe mitten unter
den Wölfen, Schlachtschafe, die in Angst und Not, Trübsal,
Verfolgung, Leiden und Sterben getauft werden müssten.[44]
Denn wie Krüsi nachher selber gestehen musste, hatten sich
für den Fall, dass man ihn fangen wollte, die Gemeinden Straubenzell, Rotmonten, Bernhardszell, Tablat und noch an die
dreissig weitere verpflichtet, "Leib und Gut für ihn einzusetzen
und ihn zu schirmen."[45] Selbst wenn dies — unter Einwir-
kung der Folter — übertrieben sein sollte (es wäre fast das
ganze Gebiet des Abtes einschliesslich des Toggenburg gemeint),
wird doch durch andere Zeugnisse und vor allem durch die folgenden Ereignisse der Kern dieses Geständnisses bestätigt.

Als Melchior Degen Krüsi gefangengenommen hatte, führte
er ihn zunächst auf das Schloss Oberberg, 7 Kilometer westlich von St. Gallen, Sitz eines äbtischen Vogtes. Auf dem
Weg dahin kam man durch eine kleine Liegenschaft auf der
Grenze zwischen Tablat und Straubenzell, die Watt hiess und
noch zur Kirchgemeinde St. Georgen gehörte. Hier begann
Krüsi — wenn man einem späteren Zeugnis glauben darf —,
laut zu schreien, und rief: "Wo seid ihr jetzt, die ihr mir Hilfe
versprochen habt!?"[46] In Oberberg stellte man ihn daraufhin
hin zur Rede und erfuhr von ihm, "dass ihm viel Schutz und
Schirm zugesagt worden sei, dass er aber wohl sehe, dass ihm
das schwerlich gehalten werden würde."[47] Ähnliches hatte nach
einem Verhör des Siebnergerichts in St. Gallen vom 11. Juli

in diesen Tagen der St.-Galler Michel Haffner beteuert: "Solltet ihr uns unsere Leser fangen wollen, so würden wir euch auch fangen."[48]

Jakob Stapfer, der Hofmeister des Abtes von St. Gallen, meldete die Gefangennahme Krüsis und deren Umstände sofort an die weltlichen Räte des Abtes, die nach Rapperswil gereist waren. Hier fand seit dem 10. Juli ein Rechtstag zwischen dem Abt und seinen Untertanen statt. Stapfer erhielt aus Rapperswil den Bescheid, er solle den Gefangenen sofort nach Luzern bringen lassen, wenn das ohne Sturm und Auflauf möglich sei. Tatsächlich war es nicht sogleich möglich. Die Anhänger Krüsis hatten um das Schloss Wachen aufgestellt, um Krüsi zu befreien, wenn er aus dem Schloss abgeführt werden sollte.[49] So musste Stapfer trotz der ungeduldig drängenden Briefe aus Rapperswil den Vogt von Oberberg mit der Überführung Krüsis warten lassen. Insbesondere fürchtete man, Krüsi durch die Grafschaft Toggenburg führen zu müssen. Denn wenn man ihn durch die Dörfer der Grafschaft führe, könne er anfangen zu schreien — und er sei sehr geneigt zu schreien —, und nachts könne das jeder hören. Bei der Unruhe, in der sich das Toggenburg befände, wage man eine solche Provokation nicht.[50]

Als die weltlichen Räte in Rapperswil trotzdem auf dem sofortigen Abtransport Krüsis bestanden, brachte man ihn am 20. Juli von Oberberg durchs Toggenburg nach Rapperswil und von dort nach Luzern. Luzern fühlte sich unter den vier Schirmorten der Abtei St. Gallen am stärksten verantwortlich für die Erhaltung des Alten Glaubens in der Abtei. Es stellte Krüsi vor das Gericht des vereinigten Kollegiums der Grossen und Kleinen Räte und verurteilte ihn als Ketzer das heiligen christlichen Glaubens zum Feuertod. Am 27. Juli wurde Krüsi "zu Pulver und Asche" verbrannt und die Asche in das Erdreich vergraben.[51] Der Anekdotensammler Rütiner weiss dazu noch eine grausige Geschichte zu erzählen: Krüsi sei auf dem Scheiterhaufen schlecht festgebunden gewesen. Als das Feuer hochschlug, habe er sich losreissen können und sei herausgesprungen. Der Henker aber habe ihn mit einer Heugabel wieder hineingetrieben.[52]

222

Hans Krüsis Büchlein

Wer diese Lebensgeschichte Krüsis kennt, bei dem wird die Nachricht von einem gedruckten Büchlein Krüsis die kühnsten Mutmassungen hervorrufen. Sollten wir in ihm endlich ein Zeugnis für die sonst kaum deutliche Theologie der St.-Galler Täufer gefunden haben? Liegt hier vielleicht gar das täuferische Votum aus der Auseinandersetzung der St.-Galler Täufer mit Vadian vor, das am 6. Juni öffentlich verlesen wurde und auf Grund dessen man das Täufertum verbot? Fällt durch die neue Schrift endlich ein Licht auf das Verhältnis der Täufer zu den Bauernunruhen, in die Krüsi so verflochten war? Haben wir es vielleicht überhaupt mit dem ersten täuferischen Druck zu tun? Welche Auskunft gibt er über seinen Verfasser, dessen Brüder und die Anfänge der Täuferbewegung? Wenn man bedenkt, wieviel wertvolle St.-Galler Dokumente zur Täufergeschichte verschollen sind,[53] dann gewinnt der Fund an Bedeutung.

Ich war deshalb zunächst sehr enttäuscht, als ich das Büchlein in der Hand hielt. Es war keine theologische Abhandlung, auch keine geschichtliche Darstellung oder persönliche Zuschrift an einen Freund oder Feind. Es war lediglich eine Zitatensammlung aus der Bibel. Auf zwölf Blatt waren ausser drei Überschriften ausschliesslich Bibelzitate zusammengestellt. Dazu kamen zwei Holzschnitte, einmal die Auferstehung des Lazarus auf der Rückseite des Titelblattes (Joh. 11), dann die Erweckung des Jünglings von Nain (Luk. 7, 11-17) auf Blatt 8b gegenüber dem Beginn des zweiten Teils. Die erste Überschrift, den Titel des Büchleins, habe ich anfangs wiedergegeben. Die zweite betitelt den ersten Teil: "Von dem glauben Gottes, der allain muss von himel kommen vnd durch den selig werden vnnd nach dem getaufft werden." Die dritte Überschrift gibt den Inhalt des zweiten Teils der Zitatensammlung wieder: "Das war vnd gründtlich Gotts wort von dem Tauff". Eine genaue Überprüfung der Bibelzitate ergibt, dass nur an ganz wenigen Stellen ein eigenes, kommentierendes Wort des Autors eingeflochten ist.

Aber so unscheinbar das Büchlein wirkt — seine Bedeutung übersteigt weit das bescheidene Gewand, in dem es auftritt.

Fehlen auch die originellen theologischen Gedanken und die scharfe kirchliche Auseinandersetzung — im grösseren Rahmen der ersten Täufergeschichte ist die Sammlung ein höchst bemerkenswertes Phänomen.

Zwei theologische Grundvorstellungen sind bei der Bildung der ersten Täufergemeinde von besonders massgebender Bedeutung geworden, ihr Biblizismus und ihre Forderung eines Laienpriestertums. Die Überzeugung, nur aus der Bibel den unverfälschten Willen Gottes erfahren zu können, führte zu einem sehr intensiven Bibelstudium, das Täufer wie Grebel, Mantz oder Hubmaier auf Grund ihrer Sprachkenntnisse mit allen Mitteln der damaligen Wissenschaft betrieben. Auf der andern Seite war die Auslegung der Heiligen Schrift nach dem Glauben der Täufer nicht nur Sache der Gelehrten, sondern die der ganzen Gemeinde. Auch der gemeine Christ musste an die Bibel selber herangeführt werden, um sich in Gemeinschaft mit den Brüdern ein eigenes Urteil bilden zu können. So entstand das, was C. A. Cornelius schon vor über hundert Jahren die "Kirche der radikalen Bibelleser" genannt hat.[54] Gemeint ist mit diesem Begriff nicht nur der unbedingte Gehorsam gegenüber der Bibel, sondern schon rein äusserlich die unermüdliche Beschäftigung der ganzen Gemeinde mit der Schrift. Seinen sichtbarsten Ausdruck fand dieser Zug in den sogenannten Lesungen, Bibelstunden, in denen eine Art kursorische Lektüre getrieben wurde, durch die sich die ganze Gemeinde an der Heiligen Schrift orientieren konnte. Die Folge war eine erstaunliche Belesenheit auch der einfachen Täufer in der Bibel, eine Belesenheit, die durchweg auch den Gegnern der Täufer und den Behörden Eindruck machte.

In diesem Zusammenhang ist nun schon vor etlichen Jahren die Beobachtung gemacht worden, "dass die Bibelkenntnis, die bei den ungelehrten Täufern zu Tage tritt, keine naive, sondern eine systematische ist. Übereinstimmend erscheinen die Bibelstellen für jede dogmatische und ethische Frage herausgesucht und zusammengestellt als Rüstzeug der mündlichen Apologetik und Polemik." Ernst Müller, der diese Worte vor 67 Jahren schrieb,[55] erklärte sich das Phänomen im Anschluss an Ludwig Keller dadurch, dass er eine vorreformatorische Tradition dafür verantwortlich machte: "In den wenigen

Jahren seit dem Erscheinen der Reformationsbibeln gewinnt
der Bauer nicht die Bibelkenntnis, die den gelehrten Prädikan-
ten matt setzt." Wer das Büchlein von Hans Krüsi in der
Hand hält, braucht eine solche Erklärung nicht mehr. Hier
ist dem ungelehrten Bauern der Zugang zur Bibel leicht gemacht. In wenigen Stunden kann er lernen, was für ihn zu
wissen not ist. Den Behörden gegenüber ist er mit den von
Krüsi gesammelten Belegstellen vorbereitet auf die Frage nach
der biblischen Begründung. Krüsis Büchlein bildet so etwas
wie die notwendige Ergänzung zur kursorischen Lektüre der
täuferischen Lesungen und ist ebenfalls eine Frucht der täuferischen Verbindung von Biblizismus und Laienpriestertum.

Hat somit der neugefundene Druck eine einmalige Bedeutung
für die Beleuchtung der frühen Geistesgeschichte des Täufertums, so steht er doch in seiner Art nicht isoliert da, wenn
man die weitere Geschichte des Täufertums berücksichtigt. Unter dem Stichwort "Konkordanz" sind bereits eine ganze Reihe
anderer täuferischer Sammlungen von Belegstellen aus der Bibel
bekannt geworden.[56] Sie sind alle viel späteren Datums und
meist ausgereifter und umfangreicher, dafür aber weniger hand-
lich. Ihre Abzweckung ist von Christian Hege ganz ähnlich be-
schrieben worden: "Für die Verhöre durch weltliche und geist-
liche Gelehrte fanden die Täufer in dem Studium ihrer Kon-
kordanzen ein Rüstzeug, das sie befähigte, die Einwände ihrer
Gegner schlagfertig zu widerlegen. Die aussergewöhnliche Sicher-
heit ihrer biblischen Beweisführung setzte die Theologen viel-
fach in Erstaunen und bereitete ihnen manche Verlegenheit."[57]
Ähnliche Parallelen zur Sammlung Krüsis bieten aus späterer
Zeit auch die Täuferakten. Für einzelne Lehrstücke "colli-
gierte" man Belegstellen, so dass bald schriftliche Sammlungen
davon in Umlauf waren.[58] Als Beispiel solcher Sammlung
kann die "probatio" des hessischen Täuferführers Melchior
Rincks gegen die Kindertaufe (1528) gewertet werden.[59] Aber
auch Bekenntnisse wie das von Schnabel (Marburg 1538) und
Kuchenbecker (Marburg 1578) beruhen auf sorgfältig vorbereiteten Sammlungen von Bibelzitaten.[60] Die Beispiele könn-
ten leicht vermehrt werden. Dass es sich nicht nur um apolo-
getische oder polemische Abzweckung handelt, wird deutlich
aus einer erst kürzlich bekannt gewordenen Trostepistel, "aus

Heiliger Schrift zusammengezogen", die mit ihrer Zitatensammlung Verfolgte und Gefangene trösten will.[61]

Allen diesen Beispielen gegenüber hat das Büchlein von Hans Krüsi den Vorrang zeitlicher Priorität. Das legt die Frage nahe, ob nicht vielleicht auch inhaltliche Abhängigkeiten festzustellen sind.

Krüsis Sammlung gliedert sich in zwei Teile. Der erste enthält 37 Bibelstellen zum Thema "Glauben".[62] Die aus dem Titel ersichtliche Tendenz dieser Zusammenstellung ist, es zu zeigen, dass der Glaube nicht durch äusserliche Zeremonien und Werke, sondern "allein vom Himmel gegeben wird". Die leicht spiritualistische Formulierung erinnert an Zwingli. Krüsi bietet mit diesem ersten Teil ein Kernstück reformatorischer Erkenntnis. Der zweite Teil des Büchleins hat die Taufe zum Thema. Hier wird die täuferische Folgerung aus dem ersten Teil gezogen. Die Reihenfolge der Belegstellen unterliegt einer deutlich erkennbaren Ordnung. Sie beginnt mit einem Zitat zum Beweis der Seligkeit der Kinder. Es folgen die Johannestaufe, Jesu Taufbefehl, die Aussagen Jesu über das Wesen der Taufe und dann die im Neuen Testament berichteten Taufen, beginnend mit der Taufe des dreissigjährigen Jesu und endend mit der Wiedertaufe der Johannesjünger in Ephesus durch Paulus.

Ein Vergleich mit den andern Belegstellensammlungen wird sich wegen des speziell täuferischen Themas auf den zweiten Teil beschränken müssen. Die Beobachtungen, die man dabei macht, sind verblüffend. Wo man hinblickt, findet man das gleiche Schema der Beweisführung. Sowohl die erwähnte probatio Melchior Rincks als auch der Taufparagraph des Bekenntnisses von Kuchenbecker[63] weisen dasselbe Gefälle des Gedankens bei der Anführung der Belegstellen auf. Auch hier beginnt es mit der Johannestaufe und führt über den Taufbefehl Christi zur Taufpraxis der Apostel bis zur Wiedertaufe in Ephesus. Man mag das erklären mit der Reihenfolge der Belegstellen im Neuen Testament. Zweifellos war das massgebend. Aber dass man sich dieser Reihenfolge überall so selbstverständlich anvertraute, ist doch eine auffallende Tatsache. Ich möchte keine direkte Abhängigkeit zwischen dem Büchlein Krüsis und den späteren Sammlungen konstruieren.

Was sich feststellen lässt, ist doch aber zweifellos ein gängiges
Schema der Beweisführung, das allenthalben benutzt wurde und
für das unser Büchlein einen erstaunlich frühen Beleg darstellt.
Ja, dass Krüsis Schrift zu den ersten Täuferdrucken überhaupt
zählt, unterstreicht die Bedeutung des Beweisschemas für die
Täufer.

Ich möchte dafür noch zwei weitere Beispiele anführen. Es
sind nur zwei Beispiele unter vielen andern.[64] Aber sie stammen
aus dem Zürcher Raum und damit ganz aus der Nähe Krüsis.
Das erste ist die Eingabe der Grüninger Täufer an den Zürcher
Landtag von 1527, die wahrscheinlich von den späteren Mär-
tyrern Jakob Falk und Heini Reimann geschrieben wurde.[65]
Natürlich ist die Eingabe keine blosse Sammlung von Bibelstellen, sondern eine zusammenhängende Darstellung der täuferischen Taufanschauung. Aber sehr deutlich spürt man das
bekannte Schema der Beweisführung hindurch, das mit der Taufe
Christi durch Johannes anfängt und dann seinen Gang nimmt.
Das zweite Beispiel ist deshalb besonders wichtig, weil es zeigt,
dass das Schema bereits vor Krüsis Büchlein bekannt war. Es
ist Felix Mantz' Protestation und Schutzschrift an den Rat
von Zürich vom Dezember 1524.[66] Sie beginnt ihre Beweisführung mit einer Darstellung der urchristlichen Taufpraxis:

1. bei Johannes
2. bei Christus (Taufbefehl)
3. bei den Aposteln
   a. Petrus
   b. Paulus

Es fehlt Philippus. Aber sonst entspricht das genau dem, was
wir von Krüsis Buch her kennen. Eine Synopse der besproche-
nen Stücke macht das zusammenfassend deutlich.[67]

Das auf den ersten Blick so unscheinbare Büchlein hat sich
damit als höchst bemerkenswert erwiesen. Sowohl die Tatsache einer solchen Bibelstellensammlung als auch ihr besonderer Inhalt erlauben wichtige Schlüsse, wenn man sie im
grösseren Rahmen der frühen Täufergeschichte betrachtet. Dass
es sich dabei um einen Druck handelt, dazu noch einen so
frühen, gibt der Sammlung gegenüber allen Parallelen ein be-
sonderes Gewicht. Doch beweist die Verwandtschaft der Ge-

dankenführung mit der noch früheren Protestation von Mantz, dass Krüsis Zusammenstellung von Bibelstellen nur ein Glied in einer Kette ist und dass bereits Krüsi jenes Beweisschema übernahm. War vielleicht Felix Mantz der Anfänger in dieser Sache? Die Akten zeigen, dass wir in dieser Frage noch woanders suchen müssen.

Allem Anschein nach war es nämlich Konrad Grebel selber, der den ersten Versuch einer Bibelstellensammlung unternahm. Die Frage ist sogar, ob nicht die unter Krüsis Namen gedruckte Sammlung im Wesentlichen auf Konrad Grebel zurückgeht.

In einem Brief vom 3. September 1524 an seinen Schwager Vadian schreibt Grebel: "Ganz zum Schluss: Ich werde Stellen zusammenschreiben und sammeln, und zwar zu zwei Themen, und damit vor die Öffentlichkeit treten, wenn nicht irgendein anderer [mir] zuvorkommt."[68] Was hier mit den "Stellen, und zwar zu zwei Themen" (locos nempe duos communes) gemeint ist, geht allein aus dem Zusammenhang dieses Briefes noch nicht hervor. "Loci communes" sind im damaligen Sprachgebrauch dogmatische Lehrstellen, Themen. Bender hat hier deshalb mit Recht von "two writings" oder "two booklets" gesprochen, die Grebel schreiben wollte.[69] Sieht man aber genauer hin, dann stand das "locos" zunächst für sich; "nempe duos communes" ist Anhängsel. Für sich genommen aber hat "locos" eine ganz andere Bedeutung. Gerade das vorangestellte Verb "colligere" zeigt, dass "Bibelstellen", "Belegstellen" gemeint sind. Grebel plante also schon so früh eine Belegstellensammlung zu zwei Themen, von denen die Taufe sicher das eine war. Dass er diese Sammlung dann auch anlegte, geht aus einem Brief Grebels an den täuferischen Buchhändler Andreas Castelberger vom Mai 1525 hervor. "Wenn Du etwas Gewisses über Zwinglis Schrift gegen mich und meine unfehlbaren Stellen aus der [Heiligen] Schrift hast", schreibt Grebel, "zeige es mir kurz an."[70] Bender spricht hier treffend von einer "collection of Bible quotations against infant baptism."[71] Schon die Terminologie ("locos") lässt darauf schliessen, dass es sich um dieselbe Sammlung handelt, die er in September 1524 plante. Ich möchte annehmen, dass sie in den letzten Monaten des Jahres 1524 entstand und bereits in der Protestation von Mantz (Dezember 1524) Verwendung fand.

Warum sollte nicht auch Krüsi von ihr Kenntnis gehabt und sie benutzt haben? Die Verwandtschaft zwischen der Art der Beweisführung bei Mantz und der Sammlung von Krüsi legt das nahe. Ausserdem aber gibt es einen noch direkteren Beweis dafür. In dem erwähnten Brief Grebels an Castelberger schreibt Grebel, er habe seine Bibelstellensammlung dem Erasmus Ritter in Schaffhausen gegeben und durch den sei sie ohne Grebels Wissen an Zwingli geschickt worden.[72] Grebel verteilte also Abschriften seiner Sammlung an Personen, bei denen er sich Nutzen davon versprach; sicher nicht nur an Erasmus Ritter. Man rufe sich jetzt ins Gedächtnis, was ich bereits über Krüsis Bekehrung zum Täufertum ausführte: Den entscheidenden Anstoss gab Konrad Grebel Anfang April (unmittelbar nach seinem Schaffhauser Aufenthalt), indem er Krüsi ein Büchlein brachte und es ihm erklärte; das Büchlein sei geschrieben gewesen, nicht gedruckt.[73] Da Grebel um diese Zeit nachweislich noch kein anderes Büchlein geschrieben hatte als seine Bibelzitatensammlung,[74] kann es sich nur um diese gehandelt haben. Krüsis Büchlein steht also mindestens unter dem direkten Einfluss einer ähnlichen Schrift von Konrad Grebel.

Ich möchte aber noch einen Schritt weiter gehen. Was bedeutet "direkter Einfluss" im Falle einer Bibelzitatensammlung zu einem bestimmten Thema? Es bedeutet doch wohl, dass die vom einen gesammelten Belegstellen vom andern übernommen werden. Gewiss kann es dabei Kürzungen, Erweiterungen oder Umstellungen geben. Aber gerade das durchgehend gleiche Schema lässt darauf schliessen, dass Krüsi nur geringe Änderungen vornahm. Dann aber hätten wir im Wesentlichen nicht eine Schrift Krüsis, sondern Grebels vor uns. Ist es nicht auch seltsam, dass man Grebels "locos nempe duos communes" so glatt in Übereinstimmung bringen kann mit den zwei Abschnitten unseres Büchleins? Und muss es nicht jetzt auffallen, dass in dem gründlichen Verhör Krüsis in Luzern nirgends von einer Schrift Krüsis (welch wichtiger Anklagepunkt!), wohl von der Grebels die Rede ist?

Ein letztes Argument bei dieser Beweisführung wird die Frage nach der Drucklegung liefern. Das Büchlein selber nennt lediglich die Jahreszahl 1525, jedoch keinen Druckort oder Drucker. Ich legte deshalb Photokopien des Druckes Herrn

Dr. Josef Benzing, Mainz, vor, der wohl als der beste Kenner
der Typographie des 16. Jahnhunderts gelten darf. Herr Dr.
Benzing schrieb mir daraufhin, der Drucker der Schrift von
Krüsi sei "ganz ohne Zweifel Heinrich Steiner in Augsburg"
gewesen. Die Holzschnitte stammten möglicherweise von Jörg
Breu. Heinrich Steiner war Buchdrucker in Augsburg von
1523 bis 1547. Er druckte Volksbücher, Kalender, Arzneibücher,
Klassiker (Übersetzungen), Luther, Rhegius und Hätzer.[75] Im
Spätherbst 1524 hatte er eine Abendmahlsschrift Karlstadts gedruckt.[76] Wie er an das Manuskript der Schrift von Krüsi gelang-
te, ist unerfindlich. Auffallend ist nur, dass er auf dem Titelblatt
Krüsi irrtümlich als Ledergerber ausgibt. Krüsi lernte nach
Aufgabe seiner Lehrerstelle nachweislich nur das Weberhandwerk.[77] Das Titelblatt wurde also von jemandem aufgesetzt, der
die wahren Verhältnisse nicht genau kannte. Dann war er
wohl auch über die Verfasserschaft gar nicht so genau infor-
miert. Sicher mag das Manuskript aus den Händen Krüsis
stammen. Aber bei der Weitergabe ging das Wissen um den
Einfluss oder gar die entscheidende Autorschaft Grebels verloren, und Krüsi selber, alias Hans Nagel von Klingnau, galt
als Autor.

Man muss deshalb wohl auch als Termin der Drucklegung
die Zeit nach Krüsis Tod annehmen. Bei seiner Gefangennahme im Juli 1525 könnte Krüsi seinen Anhängern das Manuskript der Zitatensammlung hinterlassen haben. Diese sorgten
durch ihre Mittelsmänner für die Drucklegung in Augsburg. An
regen Beziehungen zwischen St. Gallen und Augsburg fehlte es
damals nicht. Man erinnere sich etwa an Hans Denck, der im
Herbst 1525 nach einem Treffen mit den St.-Galler Täufern nach
Augsburg weiterzog.[78] Auf solchen Umwegen konnte sich mancher Irrtum einschleichen.

Mit der uneingeschränkten Annahme der Verfasserschaft von
Hans Krüsi habe ich die Untersuchung des neuen Fundes be-
gonnen. Der Fortgang der Beobachtungen führte zu der Annahme mindestens eines starken unmittelbaren Einflusses, wenn
nicht gar der Verfasserschaft Konrad Grebels. Im Rückblick
enthüllt sich deshalb die Überschrift dieses Aufsatzes als blosser
Arbeitstitel. Von "Hans Krüsis Büchlein" kann man ohne
Einschränkung nicht mehr schreiben. Man könnte den Titel

jetzt sogar von der andern Seite her formulieren: Die Drucklegung der Bibelstellensammlung von Konrad Grebel. Aber
ohne ein Fragezeichen möchte ich auch diese Überschrift nicht
hinsetzen.

Indem ich abschliesse, muss ich betonen, dass die Erörterung
des neuen Büchleins erst eröffnet ist. Als weitere Probleme
seien genannt: Welche Bibelausgaben wurden vom Kom-
pilator der Sammlung benutzt?[79] Welche Bedeutung hat die
Sammlung für das Verständnis des täuferischen Biblizismus?
Drittens: Auch wenn Grebel das Schema einer biblischen Beweisführung für die Glaubenstaufe in Zürich in Gang gebracht
hat, gibt es nicht Vorgänger anderwärts und stösst vielleicht
gerade ihre Berücksichtigung die Forschung auf eine neue Beur-
teilung der Anfänge des Täufertums überhaupt?[80] Und schliesslich: Welches Licht wirft der erste Teil des Büchleins auf das
Verhältnis von Täufertum und Reformation in Zürich? Bei
der Untersuchung dieser Fragen könnte sich noch mancher
wichtige Gesichtspunkt ergeben.

Notes

ABBREVIATIONS

The Complete Writings of Menno Simons c. 1496-1561. Translated from
the Dutch by Leonard Verduin and edited by John C. Wenger (Herald
Press, Scottdale, Pennsylvania, 1956), abbreviated *C.W.*
*Opera Omnia Theologica, of alle de Godtgeleerde Wercken van Menno
Symons* (Amsterdam, 1681), abbreviated *Opera.*
Quotations from the writings of Menno Simons will be referred to by
giving the above two sources in most cases.
Bibliotheca Reformatoria Neerlandica (Hague), abbreviated, *B.R.N.*

Menno Simons' Concept of the Church

CORNELIUS KRAHN

1. *Geschichte des münsterischen Aufruhrs* (Leipzig, 1860), Vol. II, p. 14.
2. W. Köhler, *Gedenkschrift zum 400 jährigen Jubiläum der Mennoniten oder Taufgesinnten* (Ludwigshafen, 1925), p. 53; Emil Egli,
   Aktensammlung zur Geschichte der Züricher Reformation (Zürich,
   1879), p. 299.
3. *C.W.*, p. 312; *Opera.* p. 450a.
4. *C. W.*, p. 310; *Opera*, p. 447a.
5. *Ibid.*
6. *Doopsgezinde Bijdragen* (Leiden, 1884), p. 10; P. Kawerau, *Melchior
   Hoffman als religiöser Denker* (Haarlem, 1954), pp. 39ff.
7. "Münsterite Anabaptists," *Mennonite Encyclopedia*, Vol. III, pp.
   777-783.
8. *B.R.N.*, Vol. X, pp. 17, 472-508.
9. Cornelius Krahn, *Menno Simons (1496-1561). Ein Beitrag zur Geschichte der Taufgesinnten* (Karlsruhe, 1936), pp. 65-67.
10. *C.W.*, p. 603; *Opera*, p. 148b.
11. S. Hoekstra, *Beginselen en leer de oude Doopsgezinden, vergeleken
    met die van de overige Protestanten* (Amsterdam, 1863), pp. 106f.,
    160.
12. *C.W.*, p. 268; *Opera*, p. 421a.

13. *C.W.*, p. 270; *Opera*, p. 523.
14. *C.W.*, p. 790; *Opera*, p. 357a.
15. *C. W.*, pp. 711, 520f., 138, 802f., 514; *Opera*, pp. 281a, 472a, 21b, 364ab, 468b.
16. K. Vos, *Menno Simons (1496-1561)*, Leiden, 1914, pp. 7, 22ff.
17. *C.W.*, p. 294; *Opera*, p. 438b.
18. *Chronica* (Ulm, 1536), III, pp. 181b-182b.
19. *C.W.*, pp. 33ff.; *Opera*, p. 628b.
20. *C.W.*, p. 109; *Opera*, p. 6a.
21. *C.W.*, p. 810; *Opera*, p. 369a.
22. *Ibid.*
23. *C.W.*, p. 81; *Opera*, p. 174b.
24. *C.W.*, p. 205; *Opera*, p. 58b.
25. *Fundament des Christelycken leers,* 1539, O iiij²; P¹.
26. *C.W.*, pp. 1055, 57, 410, 165; *Opera*, pp. 392a, 182a, 632a f., 37a.
27. *Ausgewählte Werke* (München), Vol. VI, p. 375; A. Harnack, *Lehrbuch der Dogmengeschichte* (Freiburg, 1890), Vol. III, p. 705.
28. John Calvin, *Institutes of the Christian Religion,* translated by Henry Beveridge (Grand Rapids, 1957), Vol. II, p. 279.
29. *Ibid.*, p. 283.
30. *The New Schaff-Herzog Encyclopedia of Religious Knowledge* (Grand Rapids, 1950), Vol. III, p. 332; Harnack, *op. cit.*, Vol. I, p. 337; Vol. III, p. 136.
31. Harnack, *op. cit.*, Vol. III, p. 689.
32. O. Scheel, *Evangelium, Kirche und Volk bei Luther* (Leipzig, 1934), p. 15; Karl Holl, *Gesammelte Aufsätze zur Kirchengeschichte. I. Luther.* (Tübingen, 1932), p. 289.
33. Martin Luther, *Werke,* Weimarer Ausgabe, Vol. XIV, p. 75.
34. Emil Händiges, *Die Lehre der Mennoniten in Geschichte und Gegenwart (Ludwigshafen,* 1921), p. 15.
35. O. Schell, *op. cit.,* pp. 20ff. and "Anhang" 1; Karl Holl, *op. cit.*, p. 303; Ernst Troeltsch, *The Social Teachings of the Christian Churches* (London, 1949), Vol. II, p. 694. How strong the *sola fide* approach in Reformation research has remained is evidenced by two doctoral dissertations which were published before World War II. The Lutheran, Fritz Heyer *(Der Kirchenbegriff der Schwärmer,* Leipzig 1939) and the Reformed, Ulrich Bergfried *(Verantwortung als theologisches Problem im Täufertum des 16. Jahrhunderts,* Wuppertal, 1938) view the Anabaptists of the sixteenth century from the vantage point of the reformers as "Schwärmer" (fanatics) and "Heilige" (false saints). They appear never to have read in their Bibles about discipleship and consecration to the cause of the kingdom of God. The former states that the concepts of the church of the Anabaptists and the reformers are irreconcilable (p. 4).
36. *C.W.*, p. 603; *Opera*, p. 148b.
37. John Calvin, *op. cit.*, p. 292.

38. *Doopsgezinde Bijdragen* (Leiden, 1904), pp. 21ff.
39. Alfred Farner, *Die Lehre von Kirche und Staat bei Zwingli* (Tübingen, 1930), pp. 15ff., 111ff.; P. Barth, "Calvins Verständnis der Kirche" in *Zwischen den Zeiten* (Munich, 1930), p. 231; E. Troeltsch, *op. cit., pp.* 590f. and 593-602; A. Hulshof, *Geschiedenis van de Doopsgezinden te Straatsburg van 1525-1557* (Amsterdam, 1905), pp. 61ff., 200f.
40. Hulshof, *op. cit.,* p. 66.
41. Kruske, *J. a Lasco und der Sakramentsstreit* (1901), p. 58; Ulrich Zwingli, *Eine Auswahl aus seinen Schriften,* translated by Finsler, Köhler, and Rüegg (Zürich, 1918), pp. 135, 137, 166f, 226f.
42. *C.W.,* p. 668; *Opera,* p. 256a.
43. *C.W.,* p. 671; *Opera,* p. 257b.
44. *C.W.,* p. 47; *Opera,* 629a.
45. *C.W.,* p. 151f.; *Opera,* p. 29b.
46. *Ibid.*
47. *C.W.,* p. 159; *Opera,* p. 33b.
48. *C.W.,* p. 179; *Opera,* p. 44b.
49. *C.W.,* p. 332; *Opera,* p. 78a.
50. *C.W.,* p. 91; *Opera,* p. 124b.
51. *C.W.,* p. 99f.; *Opera,* p. 129a.
52. J. G. de Hoop Scheffer, *Geschiedenis der Kerkhervorming in Nederland (Amsterdam, 1873),* p. 9ff.; K. Vos, *op. cit.,* p. 15ff.; W. J. Kühler, *Geschiedenis der Nederlandsche Doopsgezinden in de zestiende eeuw* (Haarlem, 1932), p. 33ff.
53. *C.W.,* p. 186; *Opera,* p. 48b.
54. *C.W.,* p. 734; *Opera,* p. 295b.
55. *C.W.,* p. 754; *Opera,* p. 307b.
56. *C.W.,* p. 735; *Opera,* p. 295b.
57. S. Hoekstra, *op. cit.,* pp. 107ff.
58. *C.W.,* p. 312; *Opera,* p. 450a.
59. *C.W.,* p. 713; *Opera,* p. 116a.
60. *C.W.,* p. 397; *Opera,* p. 282a.
61. *C.W.,* p. 667; *Opera,* p. 255b.
62. *C.W.,* p. 234; *Opera,* p. 399.
63. *C.W.,* p. 732; *Opera,* p. 294b.
64. *C.W.,* p. 722; *Opera,* p. 287b.
65. *C.W.,* p. 743; *Opera,* p. 300b.

Menno Simons' View of the Bible as Authority
HENRY POETTCKER

1. *Opera,* fols. 622ff.
2. Ellis Graber, "Menno Simons and the Scriptures" (Hartford Seminary, 1944), lists three hundred such phrases in the first portion of Menno's *Complete Works* (Funk edition).
3. Cornelius Krahn, *Menno Simons, 1496-1561* (Karlsruhe, 1936), p. 104.

4. *C.W.*, p. 1019. Vos reprints the letter in Dutch in his *Menno Simons* (Leiden, 1914), pp. 277-79. A Latin text of the letter is found in Blesdijk-Revius: *Historia Davidis Georgii*, pp. 129f.

5. *Opera*, fols. 445a,b.

6. *Ibid.*, fol. 605b.

7. *Ibid.*, fols. 619f.

8. Martin Micron was a Reformed theologian with whom Menno had several discussions; *vide Opera*, fols. 543-598.

9. *Opera*, fol. 609a.

10. Faber was a minister in Norden and later with a Lasco, the Reformed Superintendent of East Friesland. He also disputed with Menno; *vide Opera*, fols. 274b.

11. "Doorlese de gantsche Schrift/ Moses en die Propheten/ Christum en die Apostelen. . . ." *Opera*, fol. 272b.

12. "Een duytlijcke Letter uyt der gantscher Heylige Schrift," *ibid.*, fol. 274b.

13. "Niet met een eenigh letterken uyt der Schrift," *ibid.*, fol. 310a.

14. "Die gantsche schrift beyde des Ouden en Nieuwen Testaments wijst ons alomme op Christum Jesum/ date wy hem hooren sullen," *ibid.*, fol. 304a.

15. "Alle leeringen beyde des Ouden ende des Nieuwen Testaments recht geleert ende gevaet in den sin oft meyninge Christi/ ende sijner Apostelen/ die sijn goet. . . ." *Ibid.*, fol. 450a. These references may be supplemented with many others: fols. 34a, 597a, 323a, 174b, 150b, 119, 38b, 137b, *et al.*

16. "Wanneermen evenwel de sake op het naeuste met de waege de Heyligen Godtlijcken Woordts uyt wgen sal/ dat 'er eenigheyt in der Schrift blijve, so moetmen aenmercken. . . ." *Ibid.*, fol. 606b.

17. "Recht geleert ende gevaet in den sin oft meyninge Christ/ ende sijner Apostelen. . . ." *Ibid.*, fol. 450a

18. *Ibid.*, fol. 265a.

19. *Ibid.*, fols. 79b, 80a; *C.W.* (1956)), pp. 335f.

20. Otto Piper, *Gottes Wahrheit und die Wahrheit der Kirche* (Tuebingen, 1933), pp. 41f.

21. *Vide, Opera*, fols. 54af., 451a, etc.

22. *Opera*, fol. 627b.

23. F. J. Preuss, *Die Entwicklung des Schriftprinzips bei Luther bis zur Leipziger Disputation* (Leipzig, 1901), p. 10.

24. *Opera*, fol. 474b, 349a.

25. *Idem.*

26. Cf. R. E. Davies *The Problem of Authority in the Continental Reformers* (London, 1946); also J. K. S. Reid, *The Authority of the Scriptures* (London, 1957), pp. 34ff.

27. Preuss, *op. cit.*, pp. 12ff.

28. The *Opera* uses at least four different spellings of *word*—Woordt, Woord, Woort. So also it may be given as *Gods Woordt* or

Godts Woort. There appears to be no consistency in the use of the different spellings.

29. *Opera,* fol. 387b.
30. *Ibid.,* fol. 167a; cf. fol. 163.
31. *Ibid.,* fol. 164.
32. *Ibid.,* fol. 168a.
33. *Ibid.,* fols. 4, 37a.
34. *Ibid.,* fol. 281a.
35. *Ibid.,* fol. 355b.
36. Menno speaks of the church bringing forth children to Christ, from His seed, His holy word, fol. 36bff.; in another context he speaks of the Christian church begotten by the spirit and word of Christ, fol. 297a.
37. *Vide* W. Klassen, "The Hermeneutics of Pilgram Marpeck," Th. D. dissertation (Princeton, 1960), pp. 112ff.
38. *Opera.,* fol. 64b.
39. *Ibid.,* fol. 607a.
40. Preuss, *op. cit.,* pp. 9f.; cf. E. Seeberg, *Luthers Theologie in ihren Grundzügen,* 2nd ed. (Stuttgart, 1950), pp. 140ff.; also E. Harbison, *The Christian Scholar in the Age of the Reformation* (New York, 1956), pp. 129f.
41. S. G. Schultz, *Caspar Schwenckfeld von Ossig* (Norristown, 1947), pp. 27ff.
42. Klassen, *op. cit.,* pp. 48f.
43. Torsten Bergsten, "Pilgram Marbeck und seine Auseinandersetzung mit Caspar Schwenckfeld," *Kyrohistorisk Arsskrift,* 1957 and 1958, pp. 39-135.
44. Walter Klaassen, "Word, Spirit and Scripture in Early Anabaptist Thought," Ph.D. Dissertation (Oxford, 1960), pp. xxxviif.
45. *Opera,* fol. 74bf.
46. *Ibid.,* fols. 113a,b.
47. *Ibid.,* fol. 81a.
48. *Ibid.,* fol. 285a.
49. Reinhold Seeberg, *Textbook on the History of Doctrines,* II (Grand Rapids, 1952), 228f.; 246f.
50. Krebs-Rott, *Conf.,* p. 171; quoted by Klassen, *op. cit.,* pp. 101f.
51. *Opera,* fol. 95a.
52. *Ibid.,* fol. 66b.
53. Luther in his emphasis sought to lift out the fact that the New Testament was gospel, not a code of laws. A poor man in sin must laugh and rejoice if he believes the account as true. "Moses, in his books, drives, compels, threatens, smites and rebukes terribly; for he is a lawgiver and driver . . . [Christ] and the apostles use the words 'I exhort,' 'I entreat,' 'I beg.'" Quoted by Harbison, *op. cit.,* pp. 127f.; cf. Seeberg, *op. cit.,* pp. 130f.
54. Klassen, *op. cit.,* pp. 117ff.

55. Krahn, *op. cit.,* p. 109.
56. *Opera,* fol. 213.
57. *Ibid.,* fol. 189.
58. G. J. Neumann, "'Rechtfertigung' und 'Person Christi' als dogmatische Glaubensfragen bei den Täufern der Reformationszeit," in *Zeitschrift für Kirchengeschichte,* Vierte Folge VIII,LXXX (1959), 62-74.
59. *Opera,* fol. 285b.
60. *Ibid.,* fol. 44a,b.
61. The Anabaptists in general did not go along with Luther and Zwingli in rejecting the Apocrypha as noncanonical. Klaassen, *op. cit.,* p. xxxvi, suggests Wisdom and Ecclesiasticus were most frequently used because of their strong ethical content.
62. Henry Poettcker, "The Hermeneutics of Menno Simons," Th.D. dissertation (Princeton, 1961), p. 152.
63. *Vide* Klassen, *op. cit.,* pp. 93f.
64. *Opera,* fol. 66b.
65. Harbison mentions that both in grammatical and historical matters Luther used theology as the ultimate test. Concerning James, Luther once said: "Let us banish this epistle of James from the university, for it is worthless. It has no syllable about Christ, not even naming him except once in the beginning. I think it was written by some Jew who had heard of the Christians but not joined them." Quoted by Harbison, *op. cit.,* p. 130. Luther did not remove any books from the canon, but he did divide them into three groups, those with "eynige zarte recht heubt Evangelion," those which also promote Christ (Christum treiben), but not so clearly, and then those which did not promote Christ (Hebrews, James, Jude, and Revelation). For a discussion of this division, *vide* W. Koehler, *Dogmengeschichte* (Zürich, 1951), pp. 108ff. Luther "holds the later prophets to build, not only gold and silver on the foundation afforded by Moses and the earlier prophets, but also wood and hay and stubble, that he says the fourth Gospel account of the denial of St. Peter contains many inaccuracies, and that he judges the Epistle of James to be an epistle of straw." Reid, *op. cit.,* p. 24.
66. *Opera,* fol. 78b.
67. Koehler, *op. cit.,* pp. 112ff.
68. *Opera,* fol. 64b.
69. *Ibid.,* fol. 65a; cf. fol. 616b.
70. *Ibid.,* fol. 323a; cf. fols. 277b. 274b, 310a.
71. *Ibid.,* fol. 277; cf. fols. 16b, 19a, 24a, *et al.*
72. Reid has demonstrated that this was also the case with Calvin and Luther, *op. cit.,* pp. 34ff.; cf. Preuss, *op. cit.,* pp. 14, 66; but such extreme statements do not present the total view.
73. *Opera,* fol. 616b.
74. *Ibid.,* fol. 448b. (Italics this writer's.)

75. *Luther's Works, The Sermon on the Mount,* ed. J. Pelikan, XXI (Saint Louis, 1956), 5.
76. *Opera,* fol. 189.
77. *Fondament* (1562 ed.), fol. 381a. Menno would agree with Marpeck, who in his emphasis of this point, indicated his disapproval, both of the spiritualizers who insisted that this referred to any letter, even of the New Testament, and of the group who applied this only to the Old Testament but still sought to retain the law in the Christian church. Marpeck restricted the meaning of Paul's words to the Old Testament. Menno's point here is that citing of the biblical text does not guarantee the correct meaning—one must interpret in the spirit of Christ. Cf. Klassen, *op. cit.,* pp. 105f., for Marpeck.
78. *Luther's Works* (1956), XXI, 254.
79. *Opera,* fol. 448b.
80. *WA,* 20, 350. "Wenn ich predige, predigt er selbst in mir." Quoted by Koehler, *op. cit.,* p. 120.
81. Menno was concerned that an emphasis on the Spirit not kept in check by the bounds set by Scripture would result in another Münster, or more people with tendencies seen in the followers of Joris.
82. In reality Luther had a concern similar to that of Menno, for in his dealings with Müntzer, it was the German reformer's contention that Müntzer relied too much on the Spirit. "Luther's 'Word' was not inflexible, but it was much more fixed and certain than Müntzer's Spirit. Behind Luther's Word stood always the concept of an historical revelation which had been recorded in the Scriptures.[1] Certainly the Word bore the Spirit of God; indeed, it was that Spirit that gave the unlimited power and might of God to the Word whenever and wherever the Word was spoken. But Luther grounded his notion of the Spirit much more firmly in the Bible than did Müntzer." J. Oyer, "The Writings of the Lutheran Reformers Against the Anabaptists" (Ph.D. dissertation, University of Chicago, 1960), pp. 41f.; cf. Koestlin, *Luthers Theologie in ihrer geschichtlichen Entwicklung* (2 vols. 2nd revised ed.; Stuttgart, 1901). II, 220.
83. Calvin readily noticed differences within the New Testament, did not think that Peter wrote the second epistle bearing his name, nor that Paul wrote Hebrews. He inquired about the chronology in the Synoptics and insisted that the Sermon on the Mount was a compilation of detached statements by Jesus. However, he was not as ready with his criticism of a biblical book as was Luther. Cf. P. T. Fuhrmann, "Calvin, the Expositor of Scripture," in *Interpretation,* IV (April 1952), 193ff.

BIBLIOGRAPHY

Bergsten, Torsten. "Pilgram Marbeck und seine Auseinandersetztung mit Caspar Schwenckfeld," *Kyrohistorisk Arrskrift,* 1957 and 1958.

Davies, R. E. *The Problem of Authority in the Continental Reformers.* London, 1957.

Fuhrmann, P. T. "Calvin, the Expositor of Scripture." *Interpretation,* IV, April 1952.

Graber, E. "Menno Simons and the Scriptures." Paper at Hartford Seminary, 1944.

Harbison, E. *The Christian Scholar.* New York, 1956.

Klaassen, Walter. "Word, Spirit and Scripture in Early Anabaptist Thought." Ph.D. dissertation, Oxford, 1960.

Klassen, William. "The Hermeneutics of Pilgram Marpeck." Th.D. dissertation, Princeton Seminary, 1960.

Koehler, W. *Dogmengeschichte.* Zürich, 1951.

Koestlin, J. *Luthers Theologie in ihrer geschichtlichen Entwicklung.* 2 vols.; 2nd revised edition, Stuttgart, 1901.

Krahn, Cornelius. *Menno Simons, 1496-1561.* Karlsruhe, 1936.

Luther, Martin. *Luther's Works, The Sermon on the Mount.* Ed. J. Pelikan; XXI. Saint Louis, 1956.

Neumann, G. J. "'Rechtfertigung' und 'Person Christi' als dogmatische Glaubensfragen bei den Täufern der Reformationszeit." *Zeitschrift für Kirchengeschichte,* Vierte Folge VIII, LXXX, 1959.

Piper, Otto. *Gottes Wahrheit und die Wahrheit der Kirche.* Tübingen, 1933.

Poettcker, Henry. "The Hermeneutics of Menno Simons." Th.D. dissertation, Princeton Seminary, 1961.

Preuss, J. *Die Entwicklung des Schriftprinzips bei Luther bis zur Leipziger Disputation.* Leipzig, 1901.

Reid, J. K. S. *The Authority of the Scripture.* London, 1957.

Schultz, S. G. *Caspar Schwenckfeld von Ossig.* Norristown, 1947.

Seeberg, E. *Luthers Theologie in ihren Grundzügen.* 2nd ed., Stuttgart, 1950.

Seeberg, R. *Textbook on the History of Doctrines.* II, Grand Rapids, 1952.

Simons, Menno. *Fondament.* 1562.

Simons, Menno. *Opera Omnia Theologica.* Amsterdam, 1681.

————— *The Complete Writings of Menno Simons.* Translated by L. Verduin, ed. J. C. Wenger, Scottdale, 1956.

The Incarnation, A Central Theological Concept

WILLIAM KEENEY

1. Abraham Hulshof, *Geschiedenis van de Doopsgezinden te Straatsburg van 1525 tot 1557* (Amsterdam: J. Clausen, 1905), pp. 218ff.
2. *Ibid.,* pp. 220f.
3. For a detailed explanation of the significance of the prepositions and proof that Menno and Dirk considered them of crucial importance, see William Keeney, "The Development of Dutch Anabaptist Thought and Practice from 1539-1564" (unpublished Ph.D. thesis,

Hartford Theological Seminary, 1959), pp. 135ff. and Appendix II, pp. 333-351. See also the article "Incarnation of Christ," *Mennonite Encyclopedia,* Vol. III, pp. 18-20 (Scottdale, Pa.).

4. See the *Bibliotheca Reformatoria Neerlandica,* V, (ed.) Samuel Cramer. (The Hague: Martinus Nijhoff, 1909), p. 311. Also W. I. Leendertz, *Melchior Hoffman* (Haarlem: De Erven F. Bohn, 1883), p. 205f.

5. Dirk Philips, *Enchiridion* or *Handbook of the Christian Doctrine and Religion.* Translated by Abram B. Kolb (Elkhart, 1910), p. 150. The original appears in reprint in *BRN,* X (1910), p. 111. In further citations the English translation is referred to as HB. See also Menno Simons, *Opera Omnia Theologica* (Amsterdam: Joannes van Veen, 1681), p. 368a; or in English translation, *The Complete Writings of Menno Simons, c. 1496-1561;* translated by Leonard Verduin, edited by John C. Wenger (Scottdale: Herald Press, 1956), p. 870. Henceforth cited as *Opera* and *CW* respectively.

6. *Opera,* p. 563b, *CW,* p. 863.

7. See George Sarton, *Introduction to the History of Science,* "Science and Learning in the Fourteenth Century," Vol. III (Baltimore: The Williams and Wilkens Co., 1948), p. 1229. Cf: Thomas Aquinas, *Summa Theologica.* Q. 92, art. 1, and Q. 92, reply objection 1, and the citation to Aristotle, *De gener, Anim.,* IV, 2, and Q. 81, art. 4-5).

8. See *Opera,* pp. 363b, 376a. *CW* pp. 801, 822. Cf: John Calvin, *Institutes of the Christian Religion,* II:XIV:1,2.

9. *Opera,* p. 366b. *CW,* p. 350.

10. *BRN* X, p. 316. *HB,* p. 296. Cf: *Opera,* p. 461a, *CW,* p. 503.

11. *Opera,* p. 461a, *CW,* p. 504. *BRN* X, p. 331; *HB,* p. 313. Cf: *Opera,* pp. 373bff., 583b; *CW,* pp. 876, 893. *BRN* X, 165. *HB,* p. 129.

12. Cf: *Opera,* pp. 26b, 27b, 29a, 469a, 194a, 632b. *CW,* pp. 146, 148, 151, 515, 967f., 410. *BRN* X, pp. 78, 118, 123, 153, 231, 258, 346. *HB,* pp. 29, 75, 80, 115, 201, 234, 329.

13. *BRN* X, pp. 148-149.

14. Cf: *Opera,* pp. 180a, 368b. *CW,* pp. 54, 164, 809.

15. See *BRN* X, pp. 96f., 109, 208f., 283f., 342, 449. *HB,* pp. 49f., 64, 176, 258ff., 325, 448. *Opera,* pp. 627a, 15a, 24bf., 31b. *CW,* pp. 42, 125, 143, 155, 1063.

16. *Opera,* pp. 406b, 416b, 266, 272b. *CW,* pp. 245, 261, 685. *BRN* X, pp. 81, 100, 103, 396f. *HB,* pp. 32, 54, 57, 386f.

17. Note their frequent qualification that regeneration and baptism applied only to people who have reached the "age of understanding," *den verstandigen.* Cf: *Opera,* pp. 124a ff., 404, 264, 277a. *CW,* pp. 90ff., 241, 682f., 704. *BRN* X, pp. 94, 97, 321. *HB,* pp. 47, 51, 302.

18. *BRN* X, p. 114.

19. *CW*, p. 145f. *Opera*, p. 26a. See also *CW*, p. 721. *Opera*, pp. 287f. *BRN* X, p. 122f. *HB*, p. 79f.
20. John Calvin, *Institutes*, IV:I:13; Guy de Bres, *La Racine Source et Fondement des Anabaptistes ou Rebaptisez de nostre Temps* (n. p. Abel Clemence, 1565), p. 122. J. H. Wessel *De leerstellige Strijd tusschen de Nederlandsche Gereformeerden en Doopsgezinden in de zestiende Eeuw*. (Assen: Van Gorcum & Comp., 1945), p. 215.

Grace in Dutch Mennonite Theology

J. A. OOSTERBAAN

1. Cf: Thomas Aquinas, *Summa Theologica* 1:2 Q 110, A 1 and 2.
2. *Ibid.*, 1:2 Q 110, A 4.
3. *Ibid.*, 1:2 Q 112, A 1.
4. *Ibid.*, 1:2 Q 95, A 1.
5. *Ibid.*, 1:2 Q 93, A 3.
6. *Ibid.*, 1:2 Q 100, A 1.
7. *Ibid.*, 1:2 Q 82, A 4.
8. *Ibid.*, 1:2 Q 85, A 1.
9. *Ibid.*, 1:2 Q 110, A 1 and 2.
10. *Ibid.*, 1:2 Q 113, A 1.
11. *Ibid.*, 1:2 article 2.
12. *Concilii Tridentini*, session VI, canon 10, 11. Cf: Henricus Denzinger, *Enchiridion Symbolorum* (1955), pp. 820-21.
13. Aquinas, 3 Q 62, A 1.
14. *Ibid.*
15. *Ibid.*, 1:2 Q 112, A 5.
16. *Ibid.*, 3, Q 65, A 3.
17. Philip Melanchthon, *Corpus Reformatorum*, I (Halle, 1834), p. 35.
18. *Ibid.*
19. *Ibid.*, p. 751.
20. *Ibid.*, p. 752.
21. *Ibid.*
22. John Calvin, *Institutes of the Christian Religion*, II, 17.
23. Denzinger, p. 810.
24. Hans Denck, *Schriften*, II (1956), pp. 57-58. Cf: Menno Simons, *Opera Omnia Theologcia* (1681), p. 463.
25. See my article "The Theology of Menno Simons" *Mennonite Quarterly Review*, XXXV (July 1961), pp. 187-196.
26. Menno Simons, p. 463.
27. *Ibid.*, pp. 82b, 83a.
28. *Ibid.*, pp. 88b, 89a.
29. *Ibid.*, pp. 463.
30. *Ibid.*, pp. 14b, 17b, 18, 32, 266b, 276, etc.
31. *Ibid.*, pp. 18b, 266a.
32. *Ibid.*, pp. 296b, 320a.
33. *Ibid.*, p. 538.

Sinners and Saints
Cornelius J. Dyck

1. Alvin J. Beachy, "The Concept of Grace in the Radical Reformation" (unpublished Ph.D. dissertation, Divinity School, Harvard University, 1960). John C. Wenger, "Grace and Discipleship in Anabaptism," *MQR,* XXXV (January 1961), 50-69.

2. See Robert Friedmann, "The Doctrine of Original Sin as Held by the Anabaptists of the Sixteenth Century," *MQR,* XXXIII (July 1959), 206-14. Also N. van der Zijpp, "Original Sin," *Mennonite Encyclopedia,* IV (1959), 82-83.

3. Sebastian Franck, *Chronica, Zeitbuch und Geschichtbibel* (Strasbourg, 1531), pp. 317ff.

4. Hans de Ries was born in Antwerp and died in Alkmaar. From 1575 on he played a prominent role in the Waterlander congregations, being their primary spokesman for most of this period until his death in 1638. This chapter is based on my research, carried on under Jaroslav J. Pelikan, entitled, "Hans de Ries: Theologian and Churchman. A study in Second Generation Dutch Anabaptism" (unpublished Ph.D. dissertation, Divinity School, The University of Chicago, 1962).

5. Hans de Ries to Hendrik van Berg, October 31, 1576 (*Archief* No. 469).

6. *Ibid.,* p. 3.

7. *Ibid.,* pp. 9f.

8. *Ibid.,* p. 7.

9. Hans de Ries, *Ontdeckinge der dwalingen* (Hoorn: J. J. van Rijn, 1627), p. 257.

10. de Ries to van Berg, p. 8.

11. *Ibid.,* pp. 9, 16.

12. Cornelius J. Dyck, "The First Waterlandian Confession of Faith," *MQR,* XXXVI (January 1962), article XI.

13. Thomas Aquinas, *Summa Theologica* (New York: Benziger Brothers, Inc., 1947), 2:2 Question 163-165; 2:3 Question 62.

14. Hans de Ries, Tegen het leerstuk van de erfzonde an 's menschen verdorvenheid. November 1583. (*Archief* No. 649.)

15. *Ibid.,* p. 3.

16. Dyck, *MQR,* XXXVI (January 1962), article XI.

17. Hans de Ries to Laurens Jacobs, n.d. (*Archief* No. 657).

18. Hans de Ries, Rekenschap van gevoelens afgelegd voor de overheid te Middelburg. April 7, 1578, p. 4. (*Archief* No. 425).

19. Dyck, *MQR,* XXXVI (January 1962), article XI.

20. Hans de Ries, *Korte Belijdenisse des Geloofs,* 1609 (Amsterdam: Joannes van Veen, 1686), article XIX. Translated as appendix III in my "Hans de Ries: Theologian and Churchman." The confes-

sion is sometimes listed jointly under de Ries and Lubbert Gerrits, his colleague. It is clear, however, that it is primarily the work of the former. The dating is not precise, with 1609 being the most likely date. It could also have been written late in 1608 or early in 1610.

21. de Ries, *Ontdeckinge der dwalingen,* p. 257.
22. de Ries, Rekenschap van gevoelen . . . p. 3.
23. de Ries, Tegen het leerstuk van de erfzonde, p. 5.
24. *Ibid.,* pp. 2-3.
25. *Ibid.,* p. 4.
26. *Ibid.,* p. 5.
27. *Ibid.,* p. 10.
28. de Ries, *Korte Belijdenisse,* article XXII.
29. de Ries, Tegen het leerstuk van de erfzonde, p. 12. Italics mine.
30. Hans de Ries to Reynier Wybrandts, n.d. (*Archief* No. 1345).
31. de Ries, *Korte Belijdenisse,* Article V.
32. Emil Brunner, *Man in Revolt* (London: Lutterworth Press, 1947), p. 79.
33. de Ries, *Korte Belijdenisse,* Article VII.
34. *Ibid.,* Article XXIII.
35. *Ibid.,* Article VI.
36. *Ibid.,* Article XXXX.
37. de Ries, Rekenschap van gevoelen, p. 3.
38. de Ries, *Korte Belijdenisse,* Article I. Italics mine.
39. *Ibid.,* Article XVII.
40. *Ibid.,* Article XVIII.
41. *Ibid.,* Article XI.
42. *Ibid.,* Article VII.
43. *Ibid.,* Article XX.
44. Dirck V. Coornhert, "Wt-Roedinge van der Verderfs plantinghe, draghende die verderffelijcke Vrucht," *Wercken,* III, p. 304f.
45. Hans de Ries to Simon Jacobs. n.d. (1583?) (*Archief* No. 652).
46. Hans de Ries, "Dat de Almogende Godt niet onemogelycx den gelovigen heeft geboden." November 1583. (*Archief* No. 651).
47. de Ries to Simon Jacobs, p. 1.
48. *Ibid.,* p. 3 .
49. Augustine, "A Treatise on the Grace of Christ, and on Original Sin," *Nicene and Post-Nicene Fathers,* V (New York: Christian Literature Co., 1887), pp. 217ff.
50. de Ries, Dat de Almogende Godt, Articles 2 and 3.
51. de Ries to Simon Jacobs, p. 4.
52. *Ibid.,* p. 5.
53. *Ibid.,* p. 7.
54. *Ibid.,* p. 4.
55. William R. Cannon, "John Wesley's Doctrine of Sanctification and Perfection," *MQR,* XXXV (April 1961), p. 94.

56. de Ries to Simon Jacobs, p. 15.
57. Harold Lindström, *Wesley and Sanctification* (London: Epworth Press, 1950), p. 132. The author here describes a Kempis and William Law as mystics in relation to the thought of Wesley. Cf: R. Newton Flew, *The Idea of Perfection in Christian Theology* (London: Humphrey Milford, 1934), pp. 293ff.
58. William Law, *A Serious Call to a Devout and Holy Life* (London: Methuen & Co., 1950), p. 30. "For the question is not," says Law, "whether Gospel Perfection can be fully attain'd, but whether you come as near it as a sincere intention and careful diligence can carry you."
59. de Ries to Simon Jacobs, pp. 11, 12.
60. *Ibid.,* p. 13.
61. Hans Mattijs of Leeuwarden to Hans de Ries of Emden. December 14, 1596. (*Archief* No. 493).

Dutch Anabaptist Hymnody of the Sixteenth Century

ROSELLA R. DUERKSEN

1. Martin Luther, *Sämmtliche Schriften* edited by Dr. J. G. Walch (St. Louis: Concordia Publishing House, 1880), Vol. XIV: 429-430.
2. F. C. Wieder, *De Schriftuurlijke liedekens* ('s-Gravenhage: Martinus-Nijhoff, 1900), pp. 134-36.
3. *Ibid.,* p. 155, No. 71.
4. *Ibid.,* pp. 145-46. These dates of publication are taken from the preface of the second major Anabaptist publication, *Een nieu Liedenboeck* of 1562, in which the printer, Biestkens, indicates that the hymns of this second book were prepared while the first went through two printings in 1560 and 1562 respectively; he adds the hope that the second book may experience a popularity similar to that of the first.
5. K. Vos, *Menno Simons* (Leiden: E. J. Brill, 1914), pp. 150-56.

Dutch Painters in the Time of Vondel and Rembrandt

HENDRICK W. MEIHUIZEN

1. W. Martin, *De Hollandsche schilderkunst in de zeventiende eeuw,* I (Amsterdam: n.d.), p. 52.
2. See my *Menno Simons, ijveraar voor het herstel van de Nieuwtestamentische gemeente* (Haarlem, 1961), pp. 62, 169ff.
3. W. J. Kühler, *Geschiedenis der Nederlandsche Doopsgezinden in de zestiende eeuw* (Haarlem, 1932), pp. 449ff, 459ff.
4. H. F. Wijnman, "Nieuwe gegevens omtrent den schilder Lambert Jacobsz," I, *Oud Holland,* 47. jaargang (Amsterdam, 1938), p. 146.
5. Gerardus Maatschoen, *Aanhangzel, dienende tot een vervolg of derde deel van de geschiedenisse der Mennoniten, weleer in 't latijn beschreven door den Heere Hermannus Schijn* (Amsterdam, 1745), p. 24.

6. Kühler, *Geschiedenis,* pp. 432, 458.
7. It seems to me, for example, that this cannot be said of Carel van Mander, who joined the Old Flemish at Haarlem. A study of his Mennonite convictions and activities within that brotherhood is highly desirable. The information shared by his biographer in the well-known *Schilderboek,* particularly of his early years, gives no justification for the assumption that van Mander eagerly desired the rigorous ethic of the Mennonites already in his youth. One of his experiences is included in P. H. van Moerkerken's novel about the Münsterite movement, his *Het Nieuwe Jeruzalem.* See also *The Mennonite Encyclopedia,* III (1957), p. 453. Kühler, *Geschiedenis der Doopsgezinden in Nederland, tweede deel, 1600-1735* (Haarlem, 1940), p. 124. A. F. Mirande and G. S. Overdiep (Editors), *Het leven der doorluchtighe Nederlantsche en Hooghduytsche schilders* (Amsterdam, 1948), p. 17. P. H. van Moerkerken, *De gedachte der tijden.* I (Amsterdam, n.d.), pp. 136-138.
8. Wijnman, *Oud Holland,* 47. jaargang, p. 150. 51. jaargang, p. 251.
9. Maatschoen, *Aanhangsel,* p. 161.
10. Arnold Houbraken, *De groote Schouburgh der Nederlantsche Konstschilders en schilderessen* (Amsterdam, 1718), p. 126.
11. See my *Galenus Abrahamsz, strijder voor onbeperkte verdraagzaamheid en verdediger van het Doperse spiritualisme* (Haarlem, 1954), pp. 44-53.
12. L. A. Rademaker, *Didericus Camphuysen* (Gouda 1898), pp. 111, 279.
13. Lubbert Gerrits, *Sommighe Christelijcke Sendtbrieven,* referred to in Kühler, *Geschiedenis der Nederlandsche Doopsgezinden in de zestiende eeuw,* p. 460.
14. J. Six, "Bevestigde Overlevering," *Oud Holland,* 37. jaargang (Amsterdam, 1919), p. 82.
15. Ulrich Thieme and Felix Backer, *Allgemeines Künstlerlexikon der bildenden Künstler von der Antike bis zur Gegenwart,* XVIII (Leipzig, 1925), p. 259.
16. Six, *Oud Holland,* 37. Jaargang, p. 82.
17. A reproduction included in the article by S. H. N. Gorter, *Doopsgezind Jaarboekje* (Assen, 1936), pp. 67-72.
18. Thieme and Backer, *Künstlerlexikon,* Vol. 32 (Leipzig, 1938), p. 514.
19. Karl Rembert, "Cleve," *The Mennonite Encyclopedia,* I, pp. 623f.
20. Houbraken, *De groote Schouburgh,* II (Amsterdam, 1719), pp. 19ff.
21. Wijnman, *Oud Holland,* 47. jaargang, p. 150.
22. J. van Lennep (editor) *De Werken van J. van den Vondel.* Revised edition by J. W. H. Unger (Leiden, n.d.), dl. 1654-1655, p. 166.
23. *Ibid.,* dl. 1648-1651, pp. 103ff.
24. Houbraken, *De groote Schouburgh,* II, p. 25.
25. Wijnman, *Oud Holland,* 47. jaargang, p. 252.
26. *Ibid.,* p. 155.

27. N. van der Zijpp, "Hooghsaet," *The Mennonite Encyclopedia*, II, (1956), 805.
28. J. van Lennep, *Vondel*, dl. 1630-1636, pp. 27, 35, 343, 345.
29. K. O. Meinsma, *Spinoza en zijn kring* (The Hague, 1896), p. 211.
30. Houbraken, *De groote Schouburgh*, II, p. 23.
31. Martin, *De Hollandsche schilderkunst*, II (Amsterdam, 1936), p. 116.
32. *Ibid.*, p. 116.
33. *Ibid.*, p. 118.
34. Houbraken, *De groote Schouburgh*, II, p. 21.
35. S. H. N. Gorter, "Tweemaal Jakob," *Doopsgezind Jaarboekje voor 1940* (Assen, 1939), pp. 64-69.
36. J. van Lennep, *Vondel*, dl. 1656-1657, pp. 206ff.
37. *Ibid.*, dl. 1652-1653, p. 214.
38. Thieme and Backer, *Künstlerlexikon*, Vol. 12 (Leipzig, 1916), pp. 97-99.
39. H. F. W. Jeltes, "Flinck," *The Mennonite Encyclopedia*, III (1957), p. 133. Cf: Maatschoen, *Aanhangsel*, p. 41.
40. J. van Lennep, *Vondel*, dl. 1621-1625, pp. 49-50.
41. Martin, *De Hollandsche schilderkunst*, I, p. 305.
42. H. F. W. Jeltes, "Mierevelt," *The Mennonite Encyclopedia*, III (1957), p. 133.
43. Carel van Mander, *Schilderboek*, p. 483.
44. The event took place about 1646. See J. C. van Slee, *De Rijnsburger Collegianten* (Haarlem, 1895), p. 135.
45. See my *Galenus Abrahamsz, 1622-1706.* (Haarlem, 1954), p. 45.
46. J. van Lennep, *Vondel*, dl. *1667-1671*, p. 72.
47. A. Bredius, "Michiel Jansz van Mierevelt, eene nalezing," *Oud Holland*, 26 jaargang (Amsterdam, 1908), p. 15.
48. Martin, *De Hollandsche schilderkunst*, I, p. 306.
49. *Ibid.*, II, p. 32.
50. Carel van Mander, *Schilderboek*, pp. 481, 482.
51. Martin, *De Hollandsche schilderkunst*, I p. 302.
52. H. F. Wijnman, "Het leven der Ruysdaels," *Oud Holland*, 49. jaargang (Amsterdam, 1932), p. 173.
53. Wolfgang Stechow, *Salomon van Ruysdael* (Berlin, 1838), p. 24.
54. A. van der Willigen Pzn, *Geschiedkundige aanteekeningen over Haarlemsche schilders en andere beoefenaren van de beeldened kunsten* (Haarlem, 1866), p. 183. Willigen, *Les artistes de Haarlem, notices historiques sur la Gilde de St. Luc* (Hoorlem, 1870), p. 255.
55. Meihuizen, *Galenus Abrahamsz*, pp. 108-111.
56. Willigen, *Geschiedkundige aanteekeningen*, pp. 183, 255.
57. Martin, *De Hollandsche schilderkunst*, II, pp. 280, 282.
58. D. M. van der Woude, "Menniste namen," *Doopsgezind Jaarboekje voor 1942* (Assen, 1941), p. 45.
59. Van Lutterveld, R., *De buitenplaatsen aan de Vecht*, Lochem 1948, bl. 19-22.

60. Stechow, *Salomon van Ruysdael,* p. 36.

The Dutch Aid the Swiss Mennonites
NANNE VAN DER ZIJPP

1. See Ernst Müller, *Geschichte der Bernischen Täufer* (Frauenfeld, 1895); Johannes Huizinga, in his preface to *Stamboek . . . van Samuel Peter (Meihuizen) en Barbara Frey* (Groningen, 1890); Samuel Geiser, *Die Taufgesinnten Gemeinden* (Karlsruhe, n.d.); Delbert Gratz, *Bernese Anabaptists* (Scottdale, 1953); and others.
2. Dutch edition, 1685, II, pp. 827-830.
3. *Inventaris der Archiefstukken,* edited by J. G. de Hoop Scheffer (Amsterdam, 1883-84), 2 vols., No. 1248.
4. *Ibid.*
5. *Archief* No. A 1250.
6. Müller, *Geschichte der Bernischen Täufer,* on page 193 incorrectly gives 1681 as the date.
7. *Archief* Nos. A 1062-64, 1127-37, 1143-49, 1422-26.
8. *Archief* Nos. A 1749, 1755.
9. Müller, pp. 45-58.
10. *Archief* Nos. A 1254 a and b.
11. *Archief* No. A 1255 a.
12. *Archief* No. A 1009.
13. *Archief* No. A 1392.
14. *Archief* No. A 1779.
15. *Archief* No. A 1371.
16. *Archief* Nos. A 1375-85.
17. In the *Rotterdam Yearbook* of 1959 I have written about "Mennonite Emigrants who traveled via Rotterdam." Also found in *Mennonitischer Gemeinde-Kalender,* 1962.

The Discordant Voice of Jan de Liefde
FRITS KUIPER

1. Justus Hiddes Halbertsma, 1789-1869, *De Doopsgezinden en hunne herkomst* (Deventer, 1843). Samuel Muller, 1785-1875, *Beoordeeling van eenige Kerkredenen van J. H. H.* (Amsterdam, 1844). Jan Boeke, 1805-1854, and A. M. Cramer, *Twee brieven ter toelichting en toetsing der schets van J. H. Halbertsma over de herkomst der Doopsgezinden* (Amsterdam, 1844).
2. Wopco Cnoop Knoopmans, 1800-1849, was Muller's younger colleague as professor at the Mennonite seminary in Amsterdam after 1827. He never published his many theological writings and even ordered them to be destroyed after his death. Thus, besides his inauguration lecture, only some notes from his dictated lectures, made by students, remain of the work of this outstanding Mennonite theologian of the first half of the nineteenth century.
3. Hermann Friedrich Kohlbrügge, 1803-1875, was born in Amster-

dam as the son of a German Lutheran family, but after 1830 he wished to be a Calvinist. His influence in our days on Karl Barth has been important, although not decisive. See Karl Barth, *Die protestantische Theologie im 19. Jahrhundert* (Zollikon-Zürich, 1947), pp. 579-587. Willem de Clercq, 1795-1844, was especially disturbed with the doctrine of predestination, *in malam partem*, whereby it was taught that many people were doomed from before creation to be sinners that could never be redeemed.

4. Nevertheless, in 1901, F. J. Holl published a long article on Jan de Liefde's ideas in *Doopsgezinde Bijdragen* (Leiden, 1901), pp. 133-195.

The Mennonites of Russia and the Great Commission
GERHARD LOHRENZ

1. Horst Penner, *Weltweite Bruderschaft* (Karlsruhe: Heinrich Schneider Verlag, 1955), p. 71.
2. Adolf Ehrt, *Das Mennonitentum in Russland* (Berlin: Julius Beltz, 1932), p. 23.
3. P. M. Friesen, *Die Alt-Evangelische Mennonitische Brüderschaft in Russland, 1789-1910* (Halbstadt: Raduga Press, 1911).
4. Ehrt, p. 32.
5. P. B. Kamensky, *Vopros ili Nedorazumeniye* (Moscow, 1895), p. 91.
6. Cornelius Krahn, "Some Social Attitudes of the Mennonites of Russia," *Mennonite Quarterly Review,* IX (October 1935), pp. 165ff.
7. Heinrich Goerz, *Die Molotschna Ansiedlung* (Winnipeg: Echo Verlag, 1951), p. 70.
8. Friesen, p. 669.
9. Karl Lindemann, *Von den deutschen Kolonisten in Russland* (Stuttgart, 1924), p. 9.
10. D. H. Epp, *Die Chortitza Mennoniten* (Odessa: Schultz Verlag, 1889).
11. Waldemar Lütsche, *Die Westliche Quellen des Russischen Stundismus* (Kassel, 1956), p. 78f.
12. Robert Kreider, "The Anabaptist Conception of the Church in the Russian Mennonite Environment, 1789-1879'" *MQR,* XXV (January 1951), p. 22.
13. Lindemann, p. 37.
14. Kreider, *MQR,* XXV, p. 17.
15. Friesen, p. 83.
16. *Ibid.,* p. 78.
17. Goerz, p. 64f.
18. Friesen, p. 79.
19. C. D. Bondar, *Sekta Mennonitov v Rossiyi* (Petrograd, 1916), p. 102.
20. *Ibid.*
21. Kamensky, pp. 27ff. Cf: Friesen, pp. 490-92.

22. *Ibid.,* p. 29.
23. Heinrich Dirks (ed.) *Mennonitisches Jahrbuch, 1910,* p. 102
24. Friesen, p. 492.
25. Heinrich Ediger (ed.), *Beschlüsse der von den geistlichen und anderen Vertretern der Mennonitengemeinden Russlands abgehaltenen Konferenzen 1879-1913* (Berdyansk, 1914), p. 8.
26. *Ibid.,* p. 12.
27. *Ibid.,* p. 39.
28. *Ibid.,* p. 35.
29. Ehrt, pp. 60ff.
30. Bondar, p. 156.
31. Gutsche, p. 73. Cf. Cornelius Krahn, "Stundism," *Mennonite Encyclopedio,* IV (1959) p. 649.
32. *Ibid.,* p. 78.
33. Bondar, pp. 157ff.
34. *Ibid.,* p. 165.
35. *Ibid.,* p. 165.
36. *Ibid.,* p. 182.
37. *Ibid.,* p. 183.
38. *Ibid.,* p. 184.
39. Dirks, p. 8.
40. Adolf Ehrt, *Russische Blätter,* II, p. 76.
41. Lindemann, p. 60.
42. N. J. Salloff-Astakhoff, *Christianity in Russia* (Loizeaux, 1941), p. 72.
43. *The Canadian Mennonite,* June 1, 1956, p. 1. Another illustration of this spirit is found in the work of John Peters and his wife. Upon graduating from the Berlin Bible School shortly before World War I they returned to Russia. Beginning in 1918 Peters, his wife, sister Helen, and a relative Johann Kehler, traveled by boat, train, and other means into the region 300 miles north of Tomsk. In this area, from Kolpashevo to the Arctic 2000 miles beyond, an area untouched by civilization, lived the pagan Ostjakes and Tunguse. Here these four, without help from any congregation, began their work. The hardships endured are indescribable. I met him in Moscow in 1925 when he came to address a conference. Perhaps they are still working there.
44. Ehrt, *Das Mennonitentum* p. 61.
45. *Ibid.*
46. E. G. Kaufman, *The Development of the Missionary and Philanthropic Interest Among the Mennonites of North American* (Berne, Indiana: The Mennonite Book Concern, 1931), p. 98.
47. Friesen, p. 118-119.
48. *Ibid.,* p. 113.
49. Dirks (1903), pp. 84, 86; (1909), p. 59; (1910), p. 24.
50. Cornelius Krahn, "Dirks, Heinrich," *Mennonite Encyclopedia,* II (1956), p. 67.

51. The names of missionaries sent to the East Indies before 1910 were as follows (from Friesen, p. 559, and other reports):

Name	Home Church	Date of Departure	Place
Heinrich Dirks and wife	Gnadenfeld	1869	Sumatra
Gerhard Nickel	Rudnerweide		Sumatra
Nickolaus Wiebe			Sumatra
Nickolas Wiebe		1890	
Johann Fast	Orloff	1891	Java
Johann Hiebert and wife	Lichtenau	1893	Java
Johannes Klassen and wife		1899	
Nikolaus Thiessen and wife	Schönsee	1904	Java
Johann Siemens and wife	Chortitza	1904	Java
Peter Loewen	Halbstadt	1910	Sumatra
Peter Nachtigal	Gnadenfeld	1912	
Helene Goosen	Nickolaifeld (Zagradovka)	1911	Java (nurse)
Susie Richert	Nickolaifeld (Zagradovka)	1911	Java (nurse)
Johann Thiessen and wife	Einlage		Sumatra
David Dirks	Gnadenfeld	1908	Sumatra
Peter Nachtigal and wife	Ladekopp		Java
Johann Klassen and wife	Ladekopp		Java
Jacob Thiessen and wife			Java
Dietrich Janzen	Gnadenfeld	1911	
Maria Reimer	Orloff		Egypt

52. Dirks (1903), p. 79.
53. Kaufman, p. 102.
54. The following missionaries went out from the Mennonite Brethren Church (from Friesen, p. 568, and other reports, yearbooks, etc.):

Name	Home Church	Date of Departure	Place
Abraham Friesen and wife	Einlage	1890	India
Heinrich Unruh and wife		1899	India
Abraham Huebert and wife		1898	India
Johann Wiens and wife		1904	India
Katharine Reimer		1904	India
Kornelius Unruh		1904	India
Franz Wiens and wife		1909	India
Anna Peters	Ladekopp	1909	India
Heinrich Reimer	Tiege (Zagradovka)		SW Africa (Baptist)
Johann Wiebe			East Africa

Agnes Neufeld   India
Anna Epp (Later Bergthold)   India
Johann Penner and wife   India
Johann Pankratz (candidate)

55. Dirks (1903), p. 84.
56. Waldemar Janzen, "Interest in Foreign Missions Among the Mennonites in Russia" (unpublished paper), p. 17.
57. Friesen, p. 145.
58. *Unser Blatt*, No. 6, March 1928, p. 143.
59. Dirks (1903), p. 85.
60. D. H. Epp, *Johann Cornies* (North Kildonan: Echo Verlag, 1946).
61. Krahn, *MQR*, IX, pp. 171ff.
62. C. H. Wedel, *Abriss der Geschichte der Mennoniten* (Newton: Schulverlag von Bethel College, 1901), p. 164.
63. Bondar, p. 87.
64. The trade schools had a four-year program, the business school an eight-year program. Students in both of these institutions had to take three languages: Russian, German, and French or English. An eight-year finishing school for girls (*Gymnasium*) was operated in Halbstadt with an enrollment of approximately 150. See Peter Braun, "Education Among the Mennonites in Russia," *Mennonite Encyclopedia* II (1956), p. 157.
65. Abram A. Toews, *Mennonitische Märtyrer,* I (Selbstverlag, 1949), p. 370.
66. Paul Schäfer, *Woher, Wohin, Mennoniten,* III (Altona: D. W. Friesen, 1946), p. 46.

Die Danziger Mennoniten: der Stand der Herkunftsfragen

HORST QUIRING

1. *Mennonitische Geschichtsblätter,* 1937, S. 32.
2. Johan S. Postma, *Das niederländische Erbe der preussisch-russländischen Mennoniten* (Leeuwarden, 1959).
3. Gustav E. Reimer, *Die Familiennamen der westpreussischen Mennoniten.* Schriftenreihe des Mennonitischen Geschichtsvereins, Nr. 3 (Karlsruhe, 1940).
4. *Ibid.,* S. 99.
5. Jules Lambotte, "La disparition des mennonites belges" in *Histoire du Protestantisme en Belgique,* Robert Collinet (editor), (Brussels, 1959), S. 214.
6. Benjamin H. Unruh, *Die niederländisch-niederdeutschen Hintergründe der mennonitischen Ostwanderungen* (Karlsruhe, 1955), S. 142.
7. Lambotte, S. 234.
8. *Ibid.*

9. *Mennonitische Geschichtsblätter,* 1961, S. 16.
10. Unruh, S. 111.
11. *Mennonitische Geschichtsblätter,* 1961.
12. Postma, S. 102.
13. *Ibid.*
14. *Mennonitische Geschichtsblätter,* 1939, S. 39.

Das älteste rheinische Täuferbekenntnis

J. F. G. GOETERS

1. Der Verfasser, J. F. G. Goeters, hat die Anmerkungen in Klammern hinzugefügt.
2. *Menno Simons (1496-1561). Ein Beitrag zur Geschichte und Theologie der Taufgesinnten* (Karlsruhe, 1936), S. 62-64.
3. *Op. cit.,* S. 64.

Hans Krüsis Büchlein über Glauben und Taufe

HEINOLD FAST

1. Johannes Kessler, *Sabbata,* hg. v. E. Egli u. R. Schoch, St. Gallen, 1902, S. 147, 18.
2. *Historisch-biographisches Lexikon der Schweiz* VI (1931), 622f.
3. Rütiners Tagebuch (Stadtbibliothek St. Gallen): "Avus illius praefectus S. Georgen fuit a matre" (II 158 Nr. 347; Original 191). Für diese 1538 geschriebene Notiz nennt Rütiner seinen Freund Johannes Kessler und den Pfarrer Matthäus Alther als Zeugen.
4. Freundliche Auskunft von Herrn Stiftsarchivar Dr. P. Staerkle.
5. Stiftsarchiv St. Gallen LA 38 (Register!).
6. Verdächtig ist vor allem der "Hannss Krüsy, den man nempt priester- oder pfaffenkrüsy", der 1521 einen Teil des Hofes Otten empfängt (LA 38,360). Schon 1492 hatte hier ein Hans Krüsi gesessen (ebd. S. 36).
7. Stadtarchiv St. Gallen, Ratsprotokoll vom 17. Juni 1525.
8. Zweimal wird er in den Akten so genannt. Erstens im St.-Galler Ratsprotokoll vom 1. Juni 1525 (ebd.); zweitens im Luzerner Geständnis vom 27. Juli 1525. Dies Geständnis ist dreimal gedruckt worden: 1. Theodor von Liebenau, Ein Wiedertäufer aus Klingnau (Argovia, Jahreszeitschrift der Historischen Gesellschaft des Kantons Aargau, 6, 1871, 472-477); beste, leider in Vergessenheit geratene Darstellung des Lebens von Krüsi. 2. Willy Brändly, Täuferprozesse in Luzern im XVI. Jahrhundert (Zwingliana VIII 67ff.). 3. Joseph Schacher, Luzerner Akten zur Geschichte der Täufer (*Zeitschrift für Schweizerische Kirchengeschichte* 51, 1957, 1ff.).
9. "Joannes Krüssy ludimagistri Klingnow filius" (Rütiner; vgl. Anmerkung 3).
10. Hermann J. Welti, Die Stadtschreiber von Klingnau, Klingnau 1937, S. 8f. Weltis Zeugnis, dass der Vorname des Vaters "Mathias" war,

ist jedoch recht zweifelhaft, weil seine Belege damit nicht übereinstimmen, es sei denn "die Notizen von Lehrer Bilger sel.", auf die er sich beruft, hätten darüber etwas enthalten. Übrigens gab es nach dem Tablater Lehenbuch (Anm. 5) einen Hans Nagel auch in Tablat, der seit 1515 als in Rüti bei St. Georgen wohnhaft, aufgeführt wird. Doch lebte er weit über 1525 hinaus.

11. St.-Galler Ratsprotokoll vom 17. Juni 1525 (Emil Egli, *Die St.-Galler Täufer,* Zürich 1887, 36f.).

12. Ein Hans Kern von Tablat ist im Lehenbuch von Tablat (Anm. 5) von 1493 bis 1527 als Besitzer oder Pächter verschiedener Güter aufgeführt. Doch kann weder er noch sein gleichnamiger Sohn unser Krüsi sein. Erstens liegen die Güter (Schäfatshorn und Grubenmansgut) nicht in St. Georgen, zweitens wird er nach 1527 noch samt Sohn als lebend bezeichnet. Das St.-Galler Bussenbuch nennt 1523 zweimal einen "Kern von St. Jörgen" (Stadtarchiv St. Gallen, Bd. 175, 8. 10). Doch ist auch dieser Beleg zu vieldeutig.

13. "Und anfengklich sye er zu Wyll gsyn provoser" (Bekenntnis; vgl. Anm. 8). Die Lesung "provoser" ist eindeutig. Es wird aber "proviser" gemeint sein, d.h. Schulgehilfe, Unterlehrer (*Schweizerisches Idiotikon,* V 506). Dass Krüsi Mönch gewesen sei (P. Peachey, Die soziale Herkunft der Schweizer Täufer, Karlsruhe 1954, 109) trifft nicht zu.

14. P. Staerkle, *Beiträge zur spätmittelalterlichen Bildungsgeschichte St. Gallens,* St. Gallen 1939, 53 ff.

15. Ehrat, *Chronik der Stadt Wil,* S. 191.

16. "Persuasus heresi catabaptismi ab Joanne Ramsower, M. Bomgarter et allis" (vgl. Anm. 3).

17. Kessler, a. a. O., 107, 20f.

18. Egli, a.a.O., 55. Weitere Einzelheiten in den "Quellen zur Geschichte der Täufer in der Schweiz II: Ostschweiz", die von Leonhard von Muralt und mir ediert werden.

19. Der schwer zu übersetzende Satz des Geständnisses (vgl. Anm. 8) lautet: "Item der jung Grebell habe zum ersten anzöggt und im ein büchly bracht und anzöggt; das selb büchly sye geschrieben gsin und nit trückt."

20. In Wil "da wärend sine gselln: Petter Koich, Rüggimann, Felix Gerwer" (ebd.).

21. Fortsetzung des Zitats in Anm. 20: "und der schulmeister von Clingnow." Das war zu dieser Zeit nicht mehr Krüsis Vater, sondern Michael Wüst, der Vetter und Studienfreund Heinrich Bullingers. Wüst wurde 1526 Täufer. Das wurde hier wohl vorbereitet (vgl. *Zwingliana* I 447; Z VIII 561f.; H. Fast, *Heinrich Bullinger und die Täufer,* Weierhof/Pfalz, 1959, 23).

22. Ebd.: "Ouch sye Hans Nüsch im Schneggen Püntt sin gsell gewesen; derselb habe ouch gepredigt, und sy bed habend einandern gelertt."

23. Ebd.: "Ouch sye er ettwa by dem schulmeister zu Sant Gallen gsin und inn ouch ettwas gefragtt, da er habe wöllen predigen."
24. Egli, a.a.O., 15.
25. Geständnis (vgl. Anm. 8): "Item wan er allso gelesen und gelert habe, so habend im die lüt ettwas geschenckt und zu essen geben, im und siner frown; namlich haben im Hensly Studer uss der statt Sent Gallen ein gülden geschenckt und der Spicherman 1 ticken pfenig und ettlich 3 baczen und ettlich minder, darum das er das weberhantwerck lernen möchte."
26. Vgl. Egli, a. a. O., 32ff.; Theodor Müller, *Die St.-Gallische Glaubensbewegung zur Zeit der Fürstäbte Franz und Kilian (1520-1530)*, St. Gallen 1910, S. 28f.; Werner Näf, *Vadian* II, St. Gallen 1957, S. 220ff.
27. *Die Tagebücher Rudolf Sailers,* hg. v. Joseph Müller, St. Gallen 1910, S. 409, Anm. 1 (mit weiteren Literaturangaben).
28. Dies und das Folgende im Bericht Degens, Eidgenössische Abschiede IV, 1a, S. 672 (Regest und teilweiser Abdruck).
29. Man vgl. aus dem Geständnis auch folgenden Satz: "Item er rett, was den lyb antreff, da sölle einer ein schaden erlyden, aber was die sel antreff, solle sich niemand lassen abwysen."
30. Vgl. H. Fast, Die Sonderstellung der Täufer in St. Gallen und Appenzell (*Zwingliana,* Band XI, Heft 4, 1960, Nr. 2), S. 230f.
31. Nach dem Bericht Degens (Anm. 28).
32. Geständnis (Anm. 8).
33. Vgl. dazu Punkt 4 der Voruntersuchung durch Jakob Stapfer vom 20. Juli 1525 (von Liebenau [Anm. 8], S. 474f.; Regest bei Joh. Strickler, *Actensammlung zur Schweizerischen Reformationsgesschichte* II, S. 399).
34. Ebd. Punkt 1.
35. Geständnis (Anm. 8).
36. Kessler, Sabbata, S. 147, 11ff.
37. So z. B. Chr. Neff im *Mennonitischen Lexikon* II 579f. und in der *Mennonite Encyclopedia* III 250f., wo unter dem Stichwort "Krüsi" gleich auch die Täufergeschichte von Teufen abgehandelt wird.
38. Verhör des Siebnergerichts am 26. Juni 1525 (Stadtarchiv St. Gallen Bd. 79, 49). Inhaltsangabe bei H. Fast, Sonderstellung (vgl. Anm. 30), S. 229f., Anm. 20.
39. Ratsprotokoll vom 16. Juni 1525 (Stadtarchiv St. Gallen f. 113af.).
40. "A Joanne Ahenarius iterum in viam aeductus quia intime conquestus ei ins tantiam illorum" (Fortsetzung des Zitates von Anm. 16).
41. Geständnis (vgl. Anm. 8).
42. An Appenzell: Eidgenössische Abschiede IV, 1a, S. 692, und Appenzeller Urkundenbuch II, S. 50. — An St. Gallen: Stadtarchiv St. Gallen, Missiven 1501-1525.
43. Kessler, *Sabbata*, S. 147, 18ff.

44. *Quellen zur Geschichte der Täufer in der Schweiz* I, hg. v. Leonhard von Muralt und Walter Schmidt, Zürich 1952, S. 17.
45. Geständnis (vgl. Anm. 8).
46. "Vi abductus, per Watt ductus, clamavit: 'Ubi iam estis qui mihi promisistis adiutorium!'?" (Rütiner; vgl. Anm. 3).
47. Punkt vier der Voruntersuchung (vgl. Anm. 33).
48. Stadtarchiv St. Gallen Bd. 797,50.
49. "Aber so man also umb das Schloss gewachet hant, och ich vor mir ghört, wemman inn hinweg füren, welten sy lib und leben daran seczen und inn by recht schüczen und handthaben, und mit vyl mer ungeschickter worten" (Brief Stapfers an den Tag in Rapperswil am 20. Juli 1525; Regest: Eidgen. Absch. IV, 1a, S. 705f.; Original: Staatsarchiv Luzern A 1,224. Vgl. auch den Brief vom 17. Juli: Eidgen. Absch. IV, 1a, S. 734).
50. Brief Stapfers vom 17. Juli (s. vorige Anm.).
51. Geständnis (Vgl. Anm. 8).
52. "Super Oberberg ductus inde Lucernam, ubi misere cruciatus, quia ex igne male ligatus evasit, executor furca iterum intrusit" (Fortsetzung von Anm. 46).
53. C. Bonorand, Joachim Vadian und die Täufer (*Schweizer Beiträge zur Allgemeinen Geschichte* II. 1953, 43-72), zählt auf S. 51f. die verschollenen Schriften auf.
54. *Geschichte des Münsterischen Aufruhrs* II, 1855, S. 14.
55. E. Müller, *Geschichte der Bernischen Täufer*, Frauenfeld 1895, S. 54.
56. *Mennonitisches Lexikon* II 541f. (Hege); *Mennonite Encyclopedia* I 665 ff. (Friedmann).
57. *Mennonitisches Lexikon* II 542.
58. Vgl. die Anfrage Jorg Schnabels an seinen Glaubensbruder Peter Tesch (1538), ob dieser nicht etwas "colligiert" habe. Tesch antwortet: "Ja, ich habe wol vil und nutzliches, aber diesmal neit bei mir" (*Urkundliche Quellen zur hessischen Reformationsgeschichte, IV: Wiedertäuferakten* 1527-1626, hg.v. Günther Franz, Marburg 1951, S. 158).
59. Ebd. Nr. 5 E.
60. Ebd. Nr. 63 und 187.
61. Kunstbuch Nr. 39 (Vgl. H. Fast, Pilgram Marbeck und das oberdeutsche Täufertum, *Archiv für Reformationsgeschichte* 47, 1956, S. 222).
62. Der ganze Text wird mit den St.-Galler Täuferakten veröffentlicht werden (vgl. Anm. 18).
63. *Hessische Wiedertäuferakten* (vgl. Anm. 58) S. 425.
64. Vgl. z.B. auch: *Glaubenszeugnisse oberdeutscher Taufgesinnter* I, hg. von Lydia Müller, Leipzig 1938, S. 91 ff.; 111 ff.; 193 ff.; 238 ff.
65. *Quellen* I (vgl. Anm. 44) S. 234-238.
66. Ebd. S. 23-28; vor allem S. 24, 19 ff.
67. Siehe Synopse auf der nächsten Seite.

67. In der folgenden Synopse sind links die Bibelstellen bei Krüsi der Reihe nach angeführt. Rechts deutet ein Gleichheitszeichen (=) die genaue Entsprechung an. Steht das Zeichen in Klammern, dann steht dasselbe Wort in anderer Reihenfolge. Entspricht das Zitat nicht genau dem von Krüsi, dann ist der abweichende Vers, sofern er doch annähernd dem Krüsis entspricht, angeführt. Zusätzliche Zitate sind auf der rechten Seite weggelassen.

K r ü s i		Mantz	Grüningen	Rinck	Kuchenbecker
Deut. 1,39	Verheissung an Kinder		Vgl. hierzu Quellen I 18, 9f.		
Matth. 3, 11. 13-15	Johannes der Täufer	Matth. 3, 10		Matth. 3, 1. 2.5.6	=
Matth. 28, 18-20	Missionsbefehl		=		=
Mark. 16, 15.16	Missionsbefehl		=	=	=
Luk. 7, 29.30	Johannestaufe scheidet Bussfertige u. Pharisäer		(=)		
Matth. 20, 20-23a	Tauf(=Kreuz-)verheissung für die Zebedäussöhne				
Luk. 12, 49.50	Jesu Leidensankündigung: Kreuz als Taufe	(=)			
Luk. 3, 21-23a	Taufe Jesu mit 30 Jahren	Luk. 3,9	(=)		
Joh. 3, 22	Jesus tauft				
Apg. 2, 38	Jesus ruft zur Busse und Taufe		=	=	=
/Ohne Anführung des Textes werden hier genannt: 1. Kor. 10; Kol. 4: Röm. 6; Apg. 21; Röm. 1/					
Apg. 8, 35-37a	Taufe des Kämmerers durch Philippus	(Röm. 6)	(Eph. 4, 5; Röm. 6, 2.4)	(Röm. 6, 3)	
Joh. 3, 5	Wiedergeburt nötig		=		
Apg. 9, 17b-19a	Taufe von Paulus	Apg. 22, 14 bis 16		=	
Apg. 10, 34f. 44-48	Taufe von Cornelius	=		=	=
Apg. 16, 27-34	Taufe des Kerkermeisters			=	=

68. "Postremo omnium est, quod conscribam et culligam locos . . . nempe duos communes, nisi alius quispiam praeveniat, in publicum deturbaturus" (*Quellen* I S. 12; vgl. Anm. 44).

69. H. S. Bender, *Conrad Grebel*, Goshen, Ind., 1950, S. 164 und 271 Anm. 1.

70. "Si quid certi habes de Zinlii scriptione adversus me meosque infallibiles locos e scriptura . . ., paucis ostende" (*Quellen* I S. 71; vgl. Anm. 44).

71. Bender, a.a.O., S. 140.

72. "Locos quos habere aiunt Zinlium eos esse indicant quos Scaphusiae cuidam dederim. Si ita est, Erasmo dedi nesciens num . . . Zinlio miserit" (*Quellen* I. S. 72; vgl. Anm. 44).

73. Vgl. Anm. 19.

74. Noch am 30. Mai 1525 stellt Grebel sein schon lange geplantes Büchlein gegen die Kindertaufe nur in Aussicht (*Quellen* I, S. 79; vgl. 18; 89; 90). Tatsächlich schrieb er diese Schrift erst etwa im Frühling 1526 (vgl. Bender, a.a.O., S. 164 und 186 ff.).

75. Josef Benzing, *Buchdruckerlexikon*.

76. J. F. Gerhard Goeters, Ludwig Hätzer, Gütersloh 1957, S. 63.

77. Vgl. o. Anmt. 25.

78. Der Aufenthalt Dencks in St. Gallen ist jetzt auf Anfang September 1525 zu datieren. Er traf dort mit Täufern zusammen, die merkwürdigerweise aus der Nähe gerade von Krüsi bekannt sind: Hans Ramsauer, Spichermann, Beda Miles, Nikolaus Guldin, Martin Baumgarter und Lorentz Hochrütiner (Stadtarchiv St. Gallen Bd. 797,51).

79. Diese Frage habe ich bereits untersucht und werde das Ergebnis bei der Veröffentlichung des Textes (vgl. Anm. 62) vorlegen.

80. Man vgl. z.B. die Begründung seiner Taufanschauung durch Clemens Ziegler in Strassburg 1524: *Quellen zur Geschichte der Täufer* VII: *Elsass*, I. Teil: *Stadt Strassburg 1522-1532, Gütersloh* 1959, S. 12 ff.

Index

Aken, Gillis van, 19
Aken, Jan van (Andriesz, Johan), 144
Ammann, Hans, 150
Ancken, Hans, 153
Anklam, Joachim van, 140
Anslo, Cornelisz Claesz, 125
Aquinas, Thomas, 57, 71-75, 89
Augustine, 32, 73, 87, 93, 162, 243
Backer, Jacob Adriansz, 124-125
Barth, Karl, 11, 85, 248
Baumgarter, Martin, 215-216, 220
Beachy, Alvin J., 87, 242
Becker, Johannes, 142
Beets, Cornelis, 140
Bekker, Benjamin, 179, 180
Bender, Harold S., 13, 228, 257
Benzing, Josef, 230, 257
Berg, Hendrik van, 88, 242
Bergman, Herman A., 176
Bergsten, Torsten, 42, 236, 238
Biestkens, Nicolasen, 105, 108
Boeke, Jan, 160-162, 166, 247
Bondar, C. D., 176, 178, 183, 248
Bonhoeffer, Dietrich, 11
Bontemps, Petrus (Pierre), 138
Braght, T. J. van, 138, 142
Breitinger, Jacobus, 137
Brunner, Emil, 94, 243
Bucer, Martin, 25-26, 32
Calvin, John, 23-27, 32, 34, 36, 54, 81, 93, 104, 162, 233, 237-238
Camphuysen, Dirck Raphaelszn, 122
Capito, Wolfgang, 25-26
Castelberger, Andreas, 228
Castellio, Sebastian, 21
Catherine II, 10
Centen, Gosen, 125
Clercq, Willem de, 165, 248
Coornhert, Dirck V., 93, 96, 98, 243
Cornelius, C. A., 18, 224
Cornies, Johann, 188, 251
Cramer, Steven Abrahams, 153
Dathenus, Peter, 110, 112
Degen, Melchior, 217, 221
Delff, Willem Jacobsz, 122, 127

Denck, Hans, 19, 80, 230, 241, 257
Derks, Alle, 152-153, 155
Deunk, Machiel, 116
Dircusoen, Gisbert, 116
Dirks, Heinrich, 182, 184-186, 249
Doornkaat-Koolman, J. ten, 196
Duerksen, Rosella Reimer, 5, 103-118, 244
Dyck, Cornelius J., 6, 9-14, 87-102
Ehrt, Adolf, 171-172, 178, 182-183
Everling, Jacob, 142, 144
Faber, Gellius, 33, 44, 136, 235
Fagel, 147-149
Falk, Jakob, 227
Fast, Bernhard, 175-176, 184
Fast, Heinold, 5, 213-231, 252
Flinck, Govert, 124-128, 133-135
Floh, Jan, 142
Folkema, J., 122
Franck, Sebastian, 19, 21, 53, 88
Frederick I, 149
Frerichs, Jan, 145
Fries, Abraham, 140
Friesen, Abraham, 185, 250
Friesen, Nikolas, 177
Friesen, P. M., 172, 175, 181, 248
Froese, Peter, 179
Froschauer, Christopher, 21
Gansfort, Johan Wessel, 104
Gerrits, Lubbert, 120, 122, 127, 243
Gerrits, Thijs, 121
Giger, Gabriel, 215
Goerz, Heinrich, 176, 248
Goeters, J. F. G., 5, 197-212, 252
Goyer, Pieter de, 133
Grebel, Conrad, 215-216, 221, 224, 228, 230-231, 256, 257
Guldin, Nikolaus, 215, 217
Haan, Galenus Abrahamsz de, 133
Haes, Gottfried von, 197, 199
Haetzer, Ludwig, 5
Halbertsma, Justus Hiddes, 160, 166, 247
Hardenberg, Albert, 199
Hattavier, Izak, 137-138
Hauser, Josephus, 196

Heese, Peter, 176
Hege, Christian, 225, 255
Heidanus, Abraham, 141
Hendricks, Joost, 138
Hershberger, Guy F., 12
Hoffman, Melchior, 18-19, 21, 55-56, 136, 232
Honnoré, Jan, 151
Hooghsaet, Catharina, 125
Hooghsaet, Jan Cornelisz, 125
Horst, Irvin B., 13-14
Hottonus, Godefridus, 137
Hubmaier, Balthasar, 213, 224
Huebert, Henry, 179
Huebner, Martin, 180
Jacobsz, Lambert, 121-125, 133, 135, 244
Jacops (Jacapssoen), Joest, 116
Joris, David, 18-19, 32
Kalff, Cornelis Michielsz, 149
Kamensky, N. B., 176
Kant, Immanuel, 98
Kauenhoven, Kurt, 193, 196
Kaufman, Edmund G., 185, 249-250
Keeney, William, 5, 14, 55-68, 239
Keller, Ludwig, 224
Kempis, Thomas a, 99, 244
Kessler, Johannes, 214-215, 219
Keyser, Leonart, 137
Klassen, John, 179-180
Klassen, Maria, 188
Klingnau, Hans Nagel (Hans Kern) von, 213, 215, 230
Klock, Lenaert, 109-110
Knoopmans, Wopco Cnoop, 162, 165, 247
Koehler, W. (see Köhler)
Kohlbrügge, Hermann Friedrich, 166, 250
Köhler, Walther, 232, 237-238
Krahn, Cornelius, 5-6, 9-14, 17-30, 172, 211, 232, 234, 237, 239, 248
Krahn, Hilda Wiebe, 11
Krahn, Kornelius, 10
Krahn, Maria (Penner), 10
Kroeker, J. F., 185
Krüsi, Hans (Johannes), 213-231
Kuchenbecker, 225-226
Kuiper, Frits, 5, 159-168, 247
Lambotte, Jules, 193, 251
Lasco, J. a, 20, 25, 38, 210, 234-235
Law, William, 99, 244

Leendertz, W. I., 240
Leiden, Jan van, 18-19, 22
Lepp, Aaron, 180
Leyden, Jan van, 32, 35
Liefde, Jan de, 159-168, 247
Liesveldt, Jacob van, 21
Lievens, Antonette, 116
Lindemann, Karl, 173, 182, 248-249
Lohrenz, Gerhard, 5, 171-191, 248
Luthard, Christoph, 141
Luther, Martin, 18, 21, 23-25, 32-36, 41-42, 45-46, 49-50, 52-54, 81, 87, 97, 104, 116, 230, 233, 236
Maatschoen, Gerard, 122, 244-246
Maihuser, Samuel Peter, 156
Mander, Carel van, 127-128, 133
Mangold, Jeremias, 138
Mantz, Felix, 137, 224, 227-228
Marpeck, Pilgram, 39, 42, 45-46, 48-49, 236-238, 255
Maurik, Wilhelm van, 140, 146
Meihuizen, Hendrik W., 6, 119-135, 157, 244, 246
Melanchthon, 71, 76-78, 241
Menno Simons, 9, 11-12, 17-60, 62-68, 71, 80-83, 85, 91, 96, 105, 136-137, 192, 210-212, 234, 237
Meulen, (Jacob) Peter van der, 166
Micron, Martin, 25, 33, 51-53, 235
Mierevelt, Jan van, 128
Mierevelt, Michiel Jansz van, 127-128, 133-134, 246
Mierevelt, Pieter van, 128
Miles, Beda, 215, 220, 257
Morosowa, Evrosina, 179
Müller, Ernst, 138, 224, 247, 255
Muller, Samuel, 160-162, 165-168
Müntzer, Thomas, 221
Neufeld, Henry, 179-180
Obbesz, Nittert, 101
Oosterbaan, J. A., 6, 69-85, 241
Ottius, J. H., 138
Oudaen, Joachim, 128
Pedacenko, Andrew, 179
Pelagius, 87, 94
Penner, Horst, 193, 248
Penner, P. A., 185
Pennypacker, S. W., 158
Philips, Dirk, 19, 55-68, 85, 121, 137, 195, 239, 242
Piper, Reynard (Reinhard), 198, 199, 212

Poettcker, Henry, 6, 14, 31-54, 234
Postma, Johan S., 193, 196, 251
Quins, Hans, 196
Quiring, Horst, 6, 192-196, 251
Raboshapka, Ivan, 180
Ramsauer, Johannes (Hans), 215-216, 220, 257
Reimann, Heini, 227
Reimer, Gustav E., 193-194, 251
Reimer, Jacob, 179, 181
Reimer, Maria, 185, 250
Rembrandt, 122, 125-126, 135, 244
Rennenberg, Wilhelm von, 197, 199
Reyst (Reist), Hans, 150
Rhegius, Urban, 230
Ricken, Daniel, 153
Ries, Hans de, 88-102, 109, 120, 127, 137, 195, 242-244
Rincks, Melchior, 225-226
Ring, Yeme Jacobsz de, 122
Ritter, Georg, 146-148, 150
Roggenacher, Antoni, 215
Rooleeuw, Anthony, 144
Rooleeuw, Henry Jacobsz, 125
Ruebsam, Tewes, 198, 212
Ruisdael, Isaac, 133
Ruisdael, Jacob, 133
Runckel, Johann Ludwig, 146, 149-151, 154
Rütiner, Johannes, 215, 220, 222
Ruysdael, Salomon van, 133-135
Salloff-Astakhoff, N. J., 182, 249
Sarany, Jacob, 179
Sasserath, Thönis von, 198
Sattler, Michael, 137
Scheffer, J. G. de Hoop, 13, 234
Schiemer (Schoener), Leonhard, 137
Schijn, Herman, 122, 140, 145-146, 152, 244
Schlatter, David, 173, 184
Schmidt, John F., 14
Schmidt, Peter, 185
Schnabel, Jorg, 225, 255
Schneider, Gottlob, 184
Schwenckfeld, Caspar, 36, 41-42, 53, 55, 93, 96, 236, 238-239
Serbulenko, Mathvey, 179
Seylemaker, Dirck, 124-125
Smith, C. Henry, 12

St. Saphorin, Sir, 147-148
Stapfer, Jakob, 222, 254
Suderman, Jan, 140
Tauler, Johann, 97
Tempel, Abraham Jacobsz van den, 124
Theunisz, Jacob, 121
Tiene, Marri, 116
Toren, Henrik, 140, 148
Townshend, Lord, 148
Troeltsch, Ernst, 26, 233
Uliman, Wolfgang, 215, 219
Unger, Abram, 179-180
Unger, Gerhard, 180
Unger, Johann, 180
Uylenburgh, Hendrick (Henry) van, 122, 125
Vadian, Joachim, 217, 223, 228, 255
Velius, Theodorus, 124-125
Vermeulen, Quirin, 195
Vlaming, Hans, 139, 141, 143
Volboet, Abraham Davidsz, 138
Vollebier, Dietrich, 197
Vondel, Joost van den, 121, 124-125, 127-128, 135, 244-246
Vorsterman, Jacob, 140, 148, 151
Vos, Karel, 21, 233-234, 244
Voth, Tobias, 175, 183-184
Vreede, Adolf de, 141
Warkentin, Abraham, 11
Wedel, Peter, 176
Wedel, C. H., 11
Weller, E., 213-214
Wenger, John C., 87, 239-240, 242
Wesley, John, 99, 243
Wied, Herman von, 197, 211
Wieder, F. C., 104-105, 244
Wieler, Gerhard, 178-180
Wieler, John, 181
Wiens, Agnes, 185
Wiens, P. J., 185
Wilhelm, Johann, 145
William III of Orange, 145
Willink, Jan, 140
Zahlen, Melcher, 153
Zell, Heinrich, 198, 211
Zijpp, Nanne van der, 6, 136-158, 193, 242, 246-247
Zwingli, Ulrich, 24-26, 104, 215, 217, 226, 228, 234, 237